On This Day

Published by
Ambassador Emerald International
427 Wade Hampton Blvd.
Greenville, SC 29609 USA

and

Ambassador Productions Ltd.
Providence House
Ardenlee Street
Belfast BT6 8QJ, Northern Ireland

www.emeraldhouse.com

cover design and page layout by Sam Laterza

This book is lovingly dedicated to the memory of

WILMA GREENE

Whose devotional life and love for God's
Word was like none I have ever known.

My mother-in-law
Whom I miss very much

Many, many, many thanks to

DOT ROSSER for the many hours she spent correcting my many mistakes. I will forever be in debt to her for her selflessness, willingness, and sacrifice to help in this project.

I am especially grateful for the greatest earthly love of my life, my wife **SHERRY**, without whose support and encouragement I may have never got done.

"I thank my God upon every remembrance of you."
(Philippians 1:3)

Foreword

My collection and search for "dates" began with a daily radio broadcast that I called *A Thought About Your Day.* In those two-minute broadcasts I took something that had happened on each day and used it as a daily devotional. Although several years have passed since those daily broadcasts, I still meet people who mention those daily devotionals.

It is my prayer that these daily devotionals will be both interesting and inspirational. It has been my goal to write this book in such a way that it can be used in your daily devotions, giving you a verse to meditate on each day, a historical story intended to make your reading interesting, and closing with a thought to help you in your Christian life. I have also tried to write it in such a form that it could serve as a source of illustrations for speakers.

I have tried very hard to verify each date, but occasionally I found there were disagreements as to the date certain things happened. I have also tried to verify the facts associated with the stories I have shared. Even then I found there are disagreements. Yet, to the best of my ability, researching countless sources, I have sought to present to you actual happenings, events, and stories. If, in your opinion, you find a mistake, please forgive me.

Someone has said that history is in reality "His-Story." I hope that you will find these stories of history a pleasure to read, but most of all, they will help you to love the God of history even more.

Ken D. Trivette

January 1

Psalm 89:15, "Blessed is the people that know the joyful sound: they shall walk, O Lord, in the light of thy countenance."

ON THIS DAY in 1953, Country and Western singer Hank Williams Sr. died en route to a concert date in Canton, Ohio. Eli Waldron in the "*Life and Death of a Country Singer*," described the 29 year old as a painfully thin figure, tortured by sleeplessness, driving himself with alcohol and drugs. A few weeks prior to his death Williams had appeared in Los Angeles with Minnie Pearl. In an effort to keep him away from the bottle, the Grand Ole Opry comedian had driven him around the city the afternoon of the show. "Well let's sing!" said Williams trying to co-operate. They began to sing, "I Saw the Light," a gospel song that was popular with Williams. As they sang, Williams buried his face in his hands and cried out, "But there ain't no light! There ain't no light!"

As we stand at the threshold of a new year, it is beyond our ability to predict what the days ahead may bring. For some it may bring rich blessings, while for others it may bring much trial and sorrow. Yet, the believer does not have to face the future saying, "There ain't no light." We can walk daily in the light of the Heavenly Father's countenance knowing that He is aware of the future and has appointed the future. We may not know what tomorrow holds, but we know who holds tomorrow. We have the assurance, "*But the path of the just is as the shining light, that shineth more and more unto the perfect day*" (Prov. 4:18). We can say, "There is light! There is light!" Today, thank God for the light of the Father's countenance.

Psalm 40:8, "I delight to do thy will, O my God: yea, thy law is within my heart."

ON THIS DAY in 1870, the construction of the Brooklyn Bridge began. During the construction the engineer of the bridge was injured. For many long months he was unable to visit the construction site so his wife carried his plans to the workmen. When the great bridge was completed the invalid architect asked to see it. He was placed upon a cot and carried to the bridge. He was placed where he could see the magnificent structure in all its beauty. His eyes scanned the great cables, massive piers, and mighty girders. He noted every detail carried out just as he had seen it in his dreams and plans. As the joy of achievement filled his soul, he cried out, "It's just like the plan; it's just like the plan."

At the beginning of a New Year we often make our resolutions and set goals for the months ahead. Our greatest achievement in the year to come would be to *"prove what is that good, and acceptable, and perfect, will of God"* (Rom. 12:2). As George W. Truett said, "To know the will of God is the greatest knowledge. To find the will of God is the greatest discovery. To do the will of God is the greatest achievement." The greatest resolution we can make or the greatest goal we can set for the year before us is to do the will of God. Our desire ought to be that when we stand before our Lord we will hear Him say concerning our life, "It's just like the plan; it's just like the plan." Today, bow your head and pray, *"I delight to do thy will O my God."*

1 Peter 4:12-13, "Beloved, think it not strange concerning the fiery trial which is to try you, as though some strange thing happened unto you: But rejoice, inasmuch as ye are partakers of Christ's sufferings; that, when his glory shall be revealed, ye may be glad also with exceeding joy."

On This Day in 1959, Alaska became the 49th state. When Secretary of State William H. Seward negotiated the purchase of Alaska from Russia in 1867, many called it "Seward's Ice Box." Many felt that it was a foolish purchase. However the Klondike Gold Rush changed all that. Between 1897 and 1900, prospectors mined more than 50 million dollars in gold. What was thought to be a foolish purchase turned out to be a land that most believe to hold just about every mineral needed for modern industry and possesses most of the undiscovered oil and natural gas in the U.S. More than one-fifth of all the petroleum produced in the U.S. comes from Alaska. It possesses more coal and hydroelectric potential than any other state and is the richest fishing grounds in the U.S.

There are times when we question the benefit of the things we go through. Have we not all at one time or another asked God why He let something happen? Many times the trials of life seem to be without reason or rhyme. Yet the storm clouds that gather over our heads are often the means of bringing us the greatest showers of blessings. What may appear to be without benefit or value may be the very thing that brings the greatest blessings into our life. Today, give thanks that what we now dread may be that which in the days to come will bring "*exceeding joy.*"

January 4

Rev. 21:1, "And I saw a new heaven and a new earth: for the first heaven and the first earth were passed away; and there was no more sea."

ON THIS DAY in 1965, President Lyndon Johnson delivered his "Great Society" State of the Union Address. In 1964 Johnson was elected to a full term and launched a program of social and economic welfare programs to create what he called a "Great Society." His vision included aid to education, attack on disease, urban renewal, beautification, conservation and development of depressed area's, wide scale fight against poverty, as well as control and prevention of crime. He had put together 14 tasks forces to study nearly all-major aspects of the U.S. society. Johnson encouraged the nation "to build a great society, a place where the meaning of man's life matches the marvels of man's labor."

Man may dream of a society in which such things as disease and crime no longer exist, but history has proven time and time again, that man can never achieve such a society. The Bible does tell us of a place in which such things no longer exist. John saw a new heaven and earth in which "*the former things are passed away*" and he described a society in which there will "*be no more death, neither sorrow, nor crying, neither shall there be anymore pain*" (Rev. 21.4). The new heaven and earth will be a society in which all the things that plague our world will be absent. D.L. Moody used to speak of heaven as a prepared place for a prepared people. What a joy to face a New Year knowing that we are prepared people awaiting a prepared place. Today, give thanks that you are part of a new society, which is the real "Great Society."

January 5

Daniel 3:25, "He answered and said, Lo, I see four men loose, walking in the midst of the fire, and they have no hurt; and the form of the fourth is like the Son of God."

ON *THIS* DAY in 1922, Sir Ernest Henry Shackleton died. In 1907 Shackleton attempted to be the first to reach the South Pole overland. He came within 111 miles. In 1915, commanding an expedition, after his ship Endurance was crushed in the ice; he led his men to Elephant Island and orchestrated their rescue. Later he wrote about his march for help, "I have no doubt that Providence guided us, not only across the snowfields, but across the storm-white sea that separated Elephant Island from our landing place on South-Georgia. I know that during that long and racking march of thirty-six hours over the unnamed mountains and glaciers of South-Georgia it seemed to me often that we were four, not three."

When the three Hebrew children were cast into the fiery furnace they found with them a fourth one in the fire. They found that in the trials of life the Lord would not abandon them. What strength it brings to our hearts to know that we are not alone when we pass through the fire. The Lord promised, "*I will never leave thee, nor forsake thee*" (Heb. 13:5). The Psalmist declared that the Lord was "*a very present help in the time of trouble*" (Psa. 46:1). The Bible speaks of the three Hebrew's deliverance from the fiery furnace, but says nothing about the "fourth" leaving the furnace. Why? When we find ourselves in the "fire" He will be with us. Today rejoice that there is "Someone" with us.

January 6

Psalm 103:2, "Bless the Lord, O my soul, and forget not all his been

ON THIS DAY in 1850, Charles Haddon Spurgeon was saved. Spurgeon wrote of the day of his conversion, "It is not everyone who can remember the very day and hour of his deliverance; but, as Richard Knill said, 'At such a time of the day, clang went every harp in heaven, for Richard Knill was born again,' it was e'en so with me. The clock of mercy struck in heaven the hour and moment of my emancipation, for the time had come. Between half-past ten o'clock, when I entered that chapel, and half-past twelve o'clock when I was back home, what a change had taken place in me! I had past from darkness into marvelous light, from death to life."

The day of salvation is a red-letter day. It is a day never to be forgotten. As Spurgeon wrote, "It mattered not to me whether the day itself was gloomy or bright, I had found Christ; that was enough for me." To reflect on the day of our salvation leaves the heart singing, "Oh happy day, oh happy day, when Jesus washed my sin away." It does our heart and souls good to stroll down memory lane and often recall the day of our conversion. It will keep us from losing the wonder of the many benefits of God's grace. It is a good antidote for a cold heart. As Spurgeon said, "There I once found conversion, and there I shall ever find refreshing and renewal." With the Psalmist may we never *"forget all His benefits"* especially the day of our salvation. Today, *"bless the Lord"* for the day of your salvation. It is indeed a red-letter day on the calendar of our heart. It is the day of all days for it is the day that marks our spiritual birthday!

January 7

Ephesians 6:11, "Put on the whole armour of God, that ye may be able to stand against the wiles of the devil."

On *This* Day in 1945, Major Thomas McGuire, America's second highest scoring ace, crashed to his death. McGuire was a member of the 475th Fighter Group based at Dobodura, New Guinea. Thirty-eight victory flags graced his P-38, nicknamed Pudgy after his wife. McGuire was leading a mission when a lone Japanese plane, piloted by Japanese ace Akira Sugimoto, attacked his squadron. McGuire was attempting to shoot Sugimoto off his wingman's tail when he stalled his plane and crashed to his death. McGuire was just three victories short of setting a new record as a fighter pilot—two victories behind Major Richard I. Bong.

Paul tells believers they are engaged in a spiritual warfare. Our enemy is an ace in spiritual warfare and he is decked with many victory flags. Many "aces" in spiritual warfare have ended up as another score for Satan. Peter warned, *"Be sober, be vigilant; because your adversary the devil, as a roaring lion, walketh about, seeking whom he may devour"* (I Pet. 5:8). When General Douglas Macarthur spoke to the graduating class at West Point, he quoted Plato to the effect, "that only the dead have seen the end of war." The spiritual warfare of the believer is a daily conflict and will continue until we are home with the Lord. No matter how many victories we have won in the past, there is always the danger of falling. How tragic it would be to become a casualty when we are so near the ultimate victory. Today ask God to help you to be a victor and not a victim and never forget the enemy is always looking for the opportunity to shoot us down.

January 8

John 14:27, "Peace I leave with you, my peace I give unto you: not as the world giveth, give I unto you. Let not your heart be troubled, neither let it be afraid."

ON *THIS* DAY in 1918, President Woodrow Wilson outlined his "Fourteen Points" of peace after World War I. In a joint meeting of Congress, Wilson presented his peace proposal which called for peace in Europe and a post war League of Nations. In 1919, Wilson was awarded the Nobel Peace Prize for his efforts.

Jesus spoke of a peace which cannot be achieved by this world, and neither finds its source in this world. It is a peace that is internal rather than external. This peace does not depend on treaties or the absence of troubling times.

In a competition for artists, the contestants were to paint a picture representing peace. Among the paintings were those showing quiet rural scenes such as meadows with sheep and cattle, fields with waving grain, birds and butterflies flying through the air. All were charming pictures of peace. But the one that won the prize was altogether different. This painting showed a wild and rocky shore against which angry billows burst in towering clouds of spray. But far above the rocky crag, hidden in the cleft of the rock and sheltered from the wind, sat a bird, safe and secure in her nest, looking out with a serene and untroubled eye at the turmoil below. Many a believer has found that in the troubling times of life there is a peace "*which passeth all understanding*" (Phil. 4:7). It is a peace that comes not from "fourteen points" but a John chapter fourteen promise. Today let the peace of God fill your heart with a peace that is beyond one's ability to describe. It is a peace that only Jesus can give.

January 9

1 Thessalonians 4:17, "Then we which are alive and remain shall be caught up together with them in the clouds, to meet the Lord in the air: and so shall we ever be with the Lord."

ON THIS DAY in 1969, the first trial flight of the Concorde took place in Bristol, England. Engineers in Britain and France were convinced they could design an aircraft that could travel at supersonic speeds (faster than the speed of sound). The British Aircraft Corporation and Areospatiale of France teamed to develop the Concorde, which introduced the age of the supersonic airplane. The Concorde could travel at a maximum speed of 1,450 mph or twice the speed of sound. The Concorde routinely flies between London and Paris to New York and Washington in an average of three hours, less than half the time taken by conventional airliners.

The Bible speaks of a marvelous change that will take place for every believer. Paul declared, "*Behold, I shew you a mystery; We shall not all sleep, but we shall all be changed, In a moment, in the twinkling of an eye, at the last trump: for the trumpet shall sound, and the dead shall be raised incorruptible, and we shall be changed*" (1 Cor. 15:51-52). Scientists have computed that it takes one-fiftieth of a second to blink an eye. One glorious day "*the Lord Himself shall descend from heaven with a shout*" (1 Thess. 4:16). One minute the believer is on earth and in the twinkling of an eye will be in heaven. On that day we will pass through the heavens at a speed which makes the Concorde look slow. Today look up and rejoice that He could return this day!

January 10

Luke 24:2-3, "And they found the stone rolled away from the sepulcher. And they entered in, and found not the body of the Lord Jesus."

ON THIS DAY in 1917, William F. "Buffalo Bill" Cody died. At the young age of eleven, Cody left his Leavenworth, Kansas home, and the life he would live would be told in newspaper accounts, dime novels and would be etched into American history. His life offered the stuff from whence legends are made. He got the nickname Buffalo Bill for his skill in supplying buffalo meat for railroad workers. He died in his sister's home in Denver and was buried, as he requested, atop Lookout Mountain overlooking Denver. The Buffalo Bill Memorial Museum and his grave have been visited by millions since his death and is one of the top visitor attractions in Denver, Colorado.

The grave of the Lord Jesus has been visited by millions and is one of the top attractions in Israel. Yet, thousands do not visit His grave each year because it holds His body, rather, because it is empty. In 1885, General Gordon discovered the Garden Tomb in Jerusalem which is believed to be the tomb in which Jesus was laid. It had been hidden for centuries and covered with rubbish twenty feet deep. When the spot was cleared, with great caution all the dust and debris was gathered and sent to the Scientific Association of Great Britain. Every part was analyzed, but there was not found any trace of human remains. If indeed, the tomb is the one in which Jesus was laid, one would not expect anything less. If Christ's human remains had been found we would have no cause to celebrate. Today rejoice that we serve a risen Saviour! He is alive forevermore!

January 11

I Corinthians 9:24, "Know ye not that they which run in a race run all, but one receiveth the prize? So run, that ye may obtain."

ON *THIS* DAY in 1991, Canadian sprinter Ben Johnson ran his first race after being stripped of his Olympic Gold Medal for steroid use. The 1988 men's 100-meter final at Seoul was hyped as one of the greatest showdowns ever in the Olympics. American Carl Lewis and Johnson, the world's two fastest human beings, would run against each other. Johnson defeated Lewis shattering the world record. Soon after the event, Johnson tested positive for steroid use. He was stripped of his gold medal and world record. After his return in 1991, he once again took possession of the world record only later to be banned for life in 1993, after testing positive after a meet in Montreal.

One of Paul's great fears was that he would do something that would disqualify him as a runner in the race of life. He knew that sin in his life or a stain on his character could render him a "castaway" (1 Cor. 9:27). The word "castaway" describes someone who was "disapproved or disqualified." Paul did not want to be disqualified and stripped of his reward. Those who run the race well are promised an incorruptible crown. We are to run for the prize and see that we do nothing which would cause us to forfeit that prize. We must guard our lives lest we become disqualified. Losing an eternal reward is not worth an earthly moment of pleasure. Today ask God to help you run a race that will be honored with a heavenly reward. As it has been said, "We are too near the crown to lay down the cross."

January 12

2 Timothy 2:3, "Thou therefore endure hardness, as a good soldier of Jesus Christ."

ON THIS DAY in 1967, a Louisville draft board refused exemption for boxer Cassius Clay (who later adopted the name Muhammad Ali). Ali's strategy to "float like a butterfly, sting like a bee" made him the first boxer to win the world heavyweight boxing championship title three different times. Yet he was suspended as heavyweight champion in 1967 when he refused induction into the U.S. armed forces on religious grounds. Ali declared, "I ain't got no quarrel with them Viet Cong." In 1971 the U.S. Supreme Court upheld his draft appeal.

Paul speaks of the believer as being a "soldier" in God's army. The Lord Jesus Christ is our heavenly commander, the Bible our sword in battle, and the world, the flesh, and the devil are our enemies. Enlisted into His army we are to be "good soldiers" for Jesus Christ. Every believer was "drafted" into God's army when they were born into the family of God. In 2 Timothy 2:3 Paul tells us that we have been "chosen" to be a soldier. The word "chosen" speaks of being enlisted or drafted into His army. We may protest our enlistment or be spiritually AWOL (absent while on duty), yet regardless of the grounds on which one may protest, the Supreme Court of Heaven will never overturn our induction.

There was a time when D.L. Moody did not want his song leader Ira D. Sankey to use the hymn *Onward Christian Soldiers*. Moody thought that the Church did not look or act as an army of Christian soldiers. Today ask God to help you be a good soldier of Jesus Christ. Let's be the kind of soldier, that if Moody were alive, he would think differently about the Church.

January 13

Galatians 5:7, "Ye did run well; who did hinder you that you should not obey the truth?"

On This Day in 1864, Stephen Foster died in Bellevue Hospital in New York City. Most of us grew up with the songs of Foster: "Camptown Races," "Oh! Susanna!" "Jeanie with the Light Brown Hair," "My Old Kentucky Home," just to name a few. His music has touched the world. Yet, when Foster died, he was an unknown beggar from the Bowery. He had been found lying naked bleeding from a deep gash in his throat. He was dumped in a paddy wagon and dropped off at Bellevue Hospital where he died three days later. When he died, the man whose music made the world sing, was just another beggar living on the street. His health was gone and he was starving. Like so many others, he lived only to drink. He was only thirty-eight but looked twice his age. A friend seeking him was directed to the local morgue. His only possessions were thirty-eight cents found in the pocket of his shabby coat and a scrap of paper with the words, "Dear friends and gentle hearts" in the other pocket.

To start well is one thing, but to end well is another matter. Paul said to the Galatians, "Ye did run well." Paul was able to say when he came to end of his life, "*I have fought a good fight, I have finished my course, I have kept the faith*" (2 Tim. 4:7). He started well and ended well. It is not enough to run well for many years only to finish poorly. By God's help, may we "*run with patience the race that is set before us*" (Heb. 12:2), and finish our course. Today ask God to help you to both run well and finish well! We have had a glorious start; let's see to it that we have a glorious finish.

January 14

Romans 10:13, "For whosoever shall call upon the name of the Lord shall be saved."

On This Day in 1963 George Wallace was sworn in as governor of Alabama. He would be elected governor of Alabama in 1970, '74, and '82. In 1963, he received the largest vote ever for a gubernatorial candidate in the state. In his address as newly elected governor he stated: "Segregation now; segregation tomorrow; segregation forever." Wallace promised to defy Federal orders to integrate, and in June blocked the path of two black students attempting to enter the University of Alabama. Years later, Wallace would express regret for his former stance, and his election in '82 was with the support of the African Americans of Alabama.

The Lord's offer of salvation jumps all racial barriers and includes all peoples of all nations. The offer of salvation is extended to "whosoever." As the little children's song declares, "Jesus loves the little children; All the children of the world. Red and yellow, black and white, they are all precious in His sight. Jesus loves the little children of the world." No one is ever turned away because of race or skin color.

The story is told that when Abraham Lincoln joined a church in Washington, a poor man came forward to join as well. The pastor said, "It is good to have President Lincoln coming to unite with our church." Lincoln stopped him and said, "Start with the other fellow. The ground is level at the foot of the cross." God's offer of salvation is extended to everyone, and no one is ever turned away. Today, thank God that salvation is for "whosoever." No matter who or what a person has done, all can come. That's why I am God's child.

January 15

Revelation 21:16, "And the city lieth foursquare, and the length of is as large as the breadth: and he measured the city with the reed, twelve thousand furlongs. The length and the breadth and the height of it are equal."

On This Day in 1943, the world's largest office building, the Pentagon, was completed. The Pentagon houses the U.S. Department of Defense. It is a five-sided building covering twenty-nine acres. It stands over seventy-seven feet high and the length of each outer wall is 921 feet. There are a total of seventeen and a half miles of corridors with a gross floor area of 6,636,360 square feet. 5.5 million cubic yards of earth and 41,492 concrete piles contributed to its foundation. 680,000 tons of sand and gravel were processed into 435,000 cubic yards of concrete and used for the Pentagon form. The building was built at an approximate cost of $83 million.

John saw an even greater building. He saw a new heaven and earth and a city that measured 12,000 furlongs in its length, breadth, and height surrounded by walls measuring 144 cubits. A cubit is eighteen inches, which means the walls surrounding the city are 216 feet high. A furlong is 582 feet that means the city is 1,342 miles in its length, height, and breadth. It has been calculated that the total base area of the city would be 1,750,329 square miles. The base of this city would reach from Maine to Florida, and from the Atlantic Ocean to Pike's Peak in Colorado. The splendor of this city is beyond description, and the size gives one the idea that there is plenty of room for everyone in this new city. Today, rejoice that in that marvelous city there is a mansion with your name on it, prepared just for you, and waiting for your arrival.

January 16

Matthew 24:42, "Watch therefore: for ye know not what hour your Lord doth come."

On This Day in 1941, U.S. Vice Admiral Patrick Nieson Lynch Bellinger warned of an assault on Pearl Harbor. Just before 8:00 am on the "day that will live in infamy" bombs and torpedoes began to be dropped on the Battleship Arizona. 1,103 of the ship's crew of 1,400 were killed. A total of eighteen ships were destroyed, 188 planes destroyed, 162 damaged, and 2,400 people killed. Months before the bombing, several, including Bellinger, had warned of an attack by Japan. Bellinger was the senior officer present during the Japanese attack, and he sent out the first radio alert, "Air raid, Pearl Harbor. This is no drill."

Jesus warned of being unprepared for His return. In the case of His return, there have been hundred of years of warnings. Yet, many ignore His warning and go on as if there were no cause for alarm. Week after week the warning continues to go out, but in many cases the warning goes unheeded.

The Milwaukee Journal once told of Ladbrokes, a London bookmaker, who had lowered the odds against a visit from outer space to 33-to-1 from 100-to-1. Because of a rash of bets from all over the United States, the odds had been lowered. The firm said it now stands to lose nearly $500,000 if somebody does drop in. I would recommend the odds be dropped much lower if not altogether completely, for one of these days this earth will have a visitor from outer space. The Lord Jesus promised He would return; if you are not ready don't ignore His warning. His return is sure! Today, if you are ready, look up. This may be the day Jesus returns. I would not recommend betting against it.

John 3:3, "Jesus answered and said unto him, Verily, verily, I say into thee, Except a man be born again, he cannot see the kingdom of God."

On This Day in 1806, the first child was born in the White House. Martha Randolph, one of President Jefferson's two daughters, gave birth to her eighth child—a son. The child, James Madison Randolph, was named after James Madison, Jefferson's Secretary of State and close friend. The first child of a president to be born in the White House was Esther, the daughter of Grover Cleveland in 1893.

In the conversation Jesus had with Nicodemus, He spoke of a special birth. The value of this birth is not due to where it occurred, but because of its nature. Jesus told Nicodemus that he needed a second birth. In order for him to enter the kingdom of God, Jesus told him that he must be born again. Nicodemus needed more than a physical birth. He needed a spiritual birth.

The new birth is a special birth. God becomes our heavenly Father, and we are given eternal life. We may not have had the privilege of being born in the White House, but we have had a special birth. Our physical birth may not make the history books, but our spiritual birth has been recorded in the Lamb's Book of Life. The place of our physical birth may not have been the Executive Mansion, but our spiritual birth has made us heirs of a heavenly mansion. We may not be able to claim that a President is our ancestor, but we can claim that we have a family relationship with the King of Kings and Lord of Lords. We have been born again and that is a special birth. Today give thanks that you have been born again.

January 18

Galatians 6:9, "And let us not be weary in well doing: for in due season we shall reap, if we faint not."

On This Day in 1983, the International Olympic Committee restored to the children of Jim Thorpe the gold medals he had won in the 1912 games. Thorpe has often been called the greatest American athlete. A Native American, he starred in college and pro football and played major league baseball. In the 1912 games at Stockholm, Thorpe won the decathlon and pentathlon. He was later stripped of his medals and his name removed from the Olympic record book because he had been paid $25 in semi-pro baseball. In 1982 his name was restored to the Olympic record book and seventy years after the fact, his gold medals were returned to his children.

Oftentimes in the work of God we get discouraged and feel that we are getting nothing done. We sow, but it seems that the harvest never comes. Maybe a pastor feels that his ministry is going nowhere, or a Sunday school teacher feels as if they are bearing little fruit and having little impact on their students. Maybe you as a parent feel as if your prayers are not availing. Our hearts ache for spiritual fruit and reward, but it seems that no matter how much we pray, give, and labor, there is no reaping to be enjoyed. We are assured that if we faint not, "in due season we shall reap" our spiritual harvest and reward. God's "due season" may be just around the corner for many a weary heart. For others it may be months and years down the road. In either case, don't give up, for there is a harvest to be reaped. Today let your heart be encouraged by God's promise. God's promises are always true.

January 19

Nehemiah 9:17, "...but thou art a God ready to pardon, gracious and merciful, slow to anger, and of great kindness..."

On This Day in 1977, President Ford pardoned Iva Toguri D'Aquino, better known as Tokyo Rose. During World War II, Tokyo Radio attempted to make American troops in the Pacific homesick by broadcasting dance music and nostalgic reminiscences about everyday American life. D'Aquino, an American citizen of Japanese descent, was the favorite of U.S. troops who fondly referred to her as "Tokyo Rose." After the Japanese surrender, officials arrested D'Aquino and charged her with treason. She was fined $10,000 and sentenced to ten years in prison. She served six years, and after her release she spent the next two decades trying to clear her name. She had maintained that she was visiting a sick aunt in Japan and had not been able to return to the United States after Japan bombed Pearl Harbor. She claimed she had been forced to work for Tokyo Radio. She finally received a pardon from President Ford on the last day of his administration.

Isaiah declared that the Lord "*will abundantly pardon*" (Isa. 55:7). The Lord has granted untold numbers of pardons to sinners guilty of many crimes. No one who has ever requested a pardon has ever been rejected. In 1830 George Wilson was convicted and sentenced to be hanged. President Andrew Jackson issued a pardon for Wilson, but he refused to accept it and was hanged. It's hard to understand why anyone would turn down a pardon, but God's offer of a pardon is turned down every day. God is "ready to pardon." Today, rejoice that one day God offered you a pardon. Aren't you glad you accepted the pardon He offered?

January 20

John 1:14, "And the Word was made flesh, and dwelt among us, (and we beheld his glory, the glory as of the only begotten of the Father,) full of grace and truth."

ON THIS DAY in 1948, the famed Indian leader Mahatma Gandhi was assassinated. Sometimes called the "father of modern India," Gandhi became the political and spiritual leader of India, leading his people to independence from Great Britain in 1947. On one occasion he led thousands on a 200-mile march to call attention to his message of tolerance. A Hindu extremist, who objected to Gandhi's tolerance for the Muslims, fatally shot Gandhi while he was on one of his prayer vigil's in New Delhi. Albert Einstein said of Gandhi, "Generations to come, it may be, will scarce believe that such a one as this ever in flesh and blood walked upon this earth."

There was a day when God robed Himself in human flesh and became one of us. The angel had announced that He would be called "Emmanuel" (Mt. 1:23), which means, "God with us." The marvel of the ages is that God would love us enough to clothe Himself with flesh and blood and walk upon this earth.

One hundred years after the birth of Robert Stevenson, the famous Scottish engineer and grandfather of the well-known writer, Robert Louis Stevenson, a great demonstration was held honoring the distinguished engineer. In the procession was a group of peasants who carried a small banner on which were written the words: "He was one of us." God dwelt among men in flesh and blood and walked upon this earth. He was one of us, one with us, and one for us. Today, meditate on the glorious truth that God became flesh—became flesh to be our Saviour! It is hard to understand that He would love us that much.

January 21

Ephesians 4:31, "Let all bitterness, and wrath, and anger, and clamour, and evil speaking, be put away from you with all malice."

On This Day in 1990, tennis player John McEnroe was expelled from the Australian Open for throwing a tantrum and swearing at an official. McEnroe can claim many accomplishments as a professional tennis player: No.1 player in the world four times, four time U.S. Open Champion, three time Wimbledon champ, and he finished his career with seventy-seven singles championships, just to name a few. Added to his long list of accomplishments is that he was the first to be expelled from the Australian Open. Dubbed "Superbrat" by the English tennis press, McEnroe's tirades have become a part of his legacy.

Someone has said, "Control yourself! Anger is only one letter short of danger." Will Rogers was correct when he said, "People who fly into a rage always make a bad landing." Oftentimes we are like buttons. We pop off at the wrong time. Alan Redpath wrote: "There are many queer ideas about cross bearing. I recall a man once saying to me, "I have a fierce temper, but I suppose that is my cross!" "My friend," I said to him (lovingly, I hope!), "That is not your cross, but it is your sin!"

Often times in a moment of anger we say things and do things that we later regret. When a man's temper gets the best of him, it brings out the worst in him. We must never forget that a "hot head" will lead to a spiritually "cold heart." It is true that the more you grow up, the less you blow up. Anger is to be "put away." It is to be confessed and conquered. Today, if you have a problem with anger, ask God to forgive you and give you sufficient grace.

January 22

2 Corinthians 5:17, "Therefore if any man be in Christ, he is a new creature: old things are passed away; behold, all things are become new."

On This Day in 1973 the Supreme Court handed down its "Roe verses Wade" decision which legalized abortion in the U.S. The "Jane Roe" of the case was Norma McCorvey. In the years that followed, McCorvey was working in a women's health clinic in Dallas. The national headquarters for Operation Rescue moved next door to this women's clinic. It was there that McCorvey met Philip Benham, head of the pro-life organization. Benham showed her love and compassion, and the two became friends. McCorvey began to visit the offices of Operation Rescue, even offering to do odd jobs. The seven-year-old daughter of the office manager invited McCorvey to church. McCorvey accepted, and that very night received Jesus Christ as her Saviour. She now is an outspoken opponent of the cause for which her name will always be associated–"Roe verses Wade."

An old song says, "What a wonderful change in my life has been wrought, Since Jesus came into my heart." When a person is saved, a marvelous change occurs in the heart and life. Old things pass away, and all things become new. Moody, speaking of when he got saved, said, "I went outdoors and fell in love with everything. I never loved the bright sunshine as much as I did that day. When I heard the birds sing, I fell in love with the birds. Everything was different." Many can say, "Thanks to Calvary I am not what I used to be." Since Jesus came into our heart, everything is different. Today, give thanks for the change Jesus made in your life.

January 23

Malachi 4:2, "But unto you that fear my name shall the Sun of righteousness arise with healing in his wings..."

ON THIS DAY in 1849, Elizabeth Blackwell became the first woman physician in the U.S. Born in Bristol, England, she came to the United States in her youth. She attended Geneva College (now Hobart College) and graduated with the highest grades in her class and was granted an M.D. In 1857, she along with her sister, Emily, also a doctor, founded the New York Infirmary for Women and Children. The institution was later expanded to include a women's college for the training of nurses and doctors. In 1875 she returned to England where she became professor at the London School of Medicine for Women.

We are grateful for the skilled doctors who help with our physical infirmities, but we are extremely grateful for the greatest Physician of them all. Earthly doctors may mend a damaged heart, but Jesus is able to heal a broken heart. He has but to speak the word, and our hurting hearts are cheered.

Max I. Reich told of passing a repair shop and seeing a sign in the window that read, "We mend everything except broken hearts." Brother Reich entered the store, and when a young lady came forward he asked, "I saw your sign, and want to ask what you do with people who have broken hearts." "Oh!" she said, "We send them to the hospital."

Jesus is a physician to whom we can bring our broken hearts. He specializes in heart trouble. As our great Physician He will *"arise with healing in his wings."* Today, if needed, make a trip to THE Doctor's office. He is a specialist in healing broken hearts.

January 24

John 19:30, "When Jesus therefore had received the vinegar, he said, It is finished: and he bowed his head, and gave up the ghost."

ON THIS DAY in 1972, Shoichi Yokoi was discovered after hiding for twenty-eight years in the jungles of Guam. Yokoi, a Japanese sergeant had been unaware that World War II had ended. When the U.S. forces took back Guam in 1944, Yokoi, left behind by retreating Japanese forces, had gone into hiding. For the next three decades he survived in the jungle waiting for the return of the Japanese. Local farmers discovered Yokoi and informed him the war was over. He was sent home to Japan, discharged, and hailed as a national hero. He later married and returned to Guam for his honeymoon.

The cry of Jesus from the cross was a shout of victory. He did not say, "I am finished," but "It is finished." Jesus was declaring that the battle had been fought, and the victory had been won. Jesus was announcing that the work He had come to do was finished. Salvation's plan was now complete.

A man once approached Alexander Wooten and said to him sarcastically, "What must I do to be saved?" Wooten knowing that the man was not serious replied, "It's too late." The man, alarmed by the answer then said, "No, no, what must I do to be saved?" "It's too late!" answered Wooten, "It's already been done!" As believers, our salvation rests in the finished work of Christ. Salvation is not what we "do" but what Jesus has "done." How tragic that many do not realize, "It is finished." Today, rejoice in the victorious work of Christ and that salvation is not what we DO but what Christ has DONE!

January 25

Matthew 24:24, "For there shall arise false Christ's, and false prophets, and shall shew great signs and wonders; insomuch that, if it were possible, they shall deceive the very elect."

ON *THIS* DAY in 1971, cult leader Charles Manson was convicted of the murder of actress Sharon Tate and six others. Manson had attracted a following and had convinced them that to murder celebrities would attract attention to the cult and his cause. On August 7, 1967, Manson's followers murdered Leno and Rosemary LaBianca and the next night at Manson's orders, four of his followers broke into Tate's home, murdering a pregnant Tate and four others in the home. Manson's cult was based on his distorted ideal that out of a racial war in America there would emerge five ruling angels; himself, taking on the role of Jesus Christ. The four members of the Beatles would take the other roles. Manson was given the death sentence, but in 1972, the California Supreme Court abolished the death penalty and his sentenced was reduced to life in prison.

Jesus warned of those who would claim they were the Christ. It has been estimated that there have been over 1,100 religious leaders in the last fifty years who have claimed to be Christ and the Savior of the world. The American Banking Association once sponsored a training program to help tellers detect counterfeit money. During the training the tellers never looked at a counterfeit bill. All they did was handle the real thing until they were so familiar with the true they could readily detect the false. It is easy to spot a false prophet when you know the real Christ. Today, let's get better acquainted with the real Christ. He is a wonderful person to know.

January 26

John 1:45, "Philip findeth Nathanael, and saith unto him, We have found him, of whom Moses in the law, and the prophets, did write, Jesus of Nazareth, the son of Joseph."

ON THIS DAY in 1905, the world's largest diamond, the 3,106-carat Cullinan diamond, was found in South Africa. It was discovered in the Premier Mine during a routine inspection by the mine's superintendent. Joseph Asscher, head of the Asscher Diamond Company of Amsterdam, later cut the diamond. He examined the diamond six months before cutting. On the first day, fearful of how his heart might react to a blunder, a doctor stood by his side as he hit the first blow. Asscher successfully divided the diamond and with the second blow fainted. The diamond was cut into 106 polished diamonds valued at tens of millions of dollars. The largest cut called the Star of Africa, 530.2 carats, was presented to King Edward VII and can be found among the crown jewels in the Tower of London.

Philip made a wonderful discovery. It was such a wonderful discovery that he wanted others to know about it. He found Nathanael and said, "*We have found Him.*" Philip had found One whose value was far greater than all the diamonds of the world. Before asking God for anything, J. Wilbur Chapman would give thanks for God's gifts to him. One day as he meditated upon God's gifts, the Lord seemed to say, "Son, what do you want?" Chapman replied, "Lord, I have what I want now. I have you." Have you made this wonderful discovery? If you have, then you know that you have found the greatest treasure that man could ever find. Today enjoy the riches you have in Jesus!

January 27

John 8:36, "If the Son therefore shall make you free, ye shall be free indeed."

On This Day in 1979, a group of Muslim militants in Teheran, Iran, took sixty-six U.S. citizens hostages. Thirteen were soon released, but negotiations and a U.S. commando operation failed to secure the release of the remaining fifty-three. The failure to get the hostages released led to the defeat of President Carter's reelection. They were released the day he left office. The hostages were held for 444 days at the U.S. Embassy in Iran. The goal was to pressure the U.S. to deport Shah Mohammed Reza Pah lavi who had fled in exile.

Many are held hostage to sin and Satan. All around us we see those who are bound by the chains of sin. We see and know those who are enslaved by everything from alcohol and drugs to personal habits. The chains of sin are humanly difficult if not impossible to break. The greatest escape artists of the world have often found their match in their own personal enslavements.

There is only One who can set us free from the chains and bondage of sin. Jesus promises that all who come to Him, He will set them free. Exactly two years from the day of their capture, President Ronald Reagan greeted the fifty-three former American hostages, telling them during a visit to the White House, "Welcome home." For many of us who know what it is like to be held hostage by sin and Satan, how we bless the day we heard our Saviour say, "You are free!" As Paul says in Romans 8:2, *"For the law of the Spirit of life in Christ Jesus hath made me free from the law of sin and death."* Today live as a free person!

January 28

Proverbs 4:23, "Keep thy heart with all diligence; for out of it are the issues of life."

ON THIS DAY in 1986, the space shuttle *Challenger* exploded seventy-three seconds after lift-off from Cape Canaveral. It was the worst disaster in the history of the American Space Program. All eight astronauts were killed. The cause was a rubber O-ring in the solid rocket boosters (SRB's) strapped on the outside of the shuttle. The O-ring was supposed to prevent the rocket fuel from burning through the SRB's. On the morning of the Challenger watch, the temperature was below freezing, the rubber O-rings were hard and did not flex during the lift-off. Ordinarily, the boosters would fire for two minutes and then be discharged. Before the shuttle reached the point where the boosters would let go, one of the rockets burned through its O-ring. The flames shot out and caused the shuttle to explode. Investigators found that on previous flights, flame damage had occurred to the O-rings. This was a warning sign that a serious problem could occur, but the problem had been ignored.

As believers there must be a daily inspection of our life. Is there some sin that needs to be confessed and cleansed? Is there some weakness or temptation that needs to be faced and conquered? Is there anything in our heart that could potentially lead to serious problems in our Christian life? Many a spiritual disaster could have been prevented if certain thoughts, feelings, desires, and temptations had not been ignored. Daily, we need to guard our heart from anything that could lead to greater problems. Have you checked the "O-rings" of your heart today? Today, an inspection of your heart is recommended!

January 29

Hebrews 11:13, "These all died in faith, not having received the promises, but having seen them afar off, and were persuaded of them, and embraced them, and confessed that they were strangers and pilgrims on the earth."

ON THIS DAY in 1936, the first players were selected to the Baseball Hall of Fame. Selected were, Ty Cobb, Babe Ruth, Honus Wagner, Christy Mathewson, and Walter Johnson. The baseball Hall of Fame was established in 1935 to commemorate the 100th anniversary of baseball. It is housed in Cooperstown, N.Y., where the game of baseball was invented. Nominated players must have played at least part of ten seasons in the major leagues and have been retired at least five but no more than twenty years. The Baseball Writers Association of America elects the inductees. Players not elected by the writers can become eligible via the Veteran's Committee twenty-three years after retirement.

In Hebrews 11 we have God's Hall of Fame. The inductees include names that are very familiar and some that are not so well known. Some of the inductees are not even named. The one qualification of their placement in the chapter was their faith in God. These inductees remind us that God does not reward ability but availability. His honors are not bestowed on His people for being great speakers, great singers, or because they possess extraordinary talents and skills. He honors those who honor Him (See I Samuel 2:30). You may never hit sixty home runs like Babe Ruth or have a .362 lifetime batting average like Ty Cobb, but if you honor God with your life, He will honor you. Today, ask God to help you to honor Him in all that you do.

January 30

1 Corinthians. 3:3, "For ye are yet carnal: for whereas there is among you envying, and strife, and divisions, are ye not carnal, and walk as men?"

ON THIS DAY in 1798, Vermont State Representative Matthew Lyon spat in the face of Connecticut Representative Roger Griswold in the House of Representatives. Lyon, a republican, became angry when Griswold accused him of carrying a wooden sword during the Revolution. His expression was the same as calling him a coward. Lyon got up, walked over and spit tobacco juice in Griswold's eye. The fight didn't end there. On February 15, Griswold, still seething, walked over to Lyon and began beating him with a cane, while the House cheered.

Sadly, it is not unusual to hear of such behavior in the House of God. One said that some churches have split so much they have become splinters. Paul tells us that such behavior is a mark of spiritual immaturity and carnality. We are often like the two porcupines which were trying to huddle together to stay warm. They needed each other but kept needling each other. Paul tells us that we should endeavor *"to keep the unity of the Spirit in the bond of peace"* (Eph. 4:3). It is not a matter of uniformity where everyone looks and thinks alike. Neither is it a matter of unanimity where there is complete agreement across the board. There will be times when we disagree. It is a matter of unity where there is a oneness of heart and a common purpose. Let Christ, His Word and work serve as a point of unity. Today, pray for your enemies and pray for spiritual growth. It is amazing how spiritual maturity solves much strife and division.

January 31

Ezekiel 18:31, "Cast away from you all your transgressions, whereby ye have transgressed; and make you a new heart and a new spirit: for why will ye die, O house of Israel?"

ON THIS DAY in 1986, Mary Lund became the first female recipient of an artificial heart. Lund, a nursing-home worker in Minnesota received a pump, a mini-Jarvik 7, which was receiving its first trial. The pump was replaced six weeks later with a human heart. Shortly thereafter, Lund, plagued by kidney problems and breathing difficulty, succumbed to multiple organ failure. She was forty.

The Bible tells us that we all have a heart problem. The prophet tells us, "*The heart is deceitful above all things, and desperately wicked: who can know it*" (Jeremiah 17:9)? There are many signs that we have a heart problem. Jesus said, "*For out of the heart proceeds evil thoughts, murders, adulteries, fornications, thefts, false witness, blasphemies*" (Matthew 15:19). This heart problem is called sin, and our sins manifest our problem. You could say that the heart of the problem is the problem of the heart. Like much heart disease, it is hereditary. It has passed from the first man to all men. It is a problem so severe that more is needed than a bypass or new valve. We need a transplant. We need a new heart! That is what salvation does for us. It gives us a new heart. God's promise through the prophet Ezekiel is that He will make us "a new heart." We never have to fear that this new heart will fail. All who have received this new heart have lived forever. Today, give thanks that one day God gave you a new heart.

February 1

Psalm 50:6, "And the heavens shall declare his righteousness: for God is judge himself. Selah."

On This Day in 1790 the U.S. Supreme Court convened for the first time. The first meeting was held at the Royal Exchange Building in New York City. Chief Justice John Jay presided. George Washington appointed six judges, John Jay of New York, John Rutledge of South Carolina, William Cushing of Massachusetts, John Blair of Virginia, Robert Harrison of Maryland, and James Wilson of Pennsylvania. The Constitution granted the Supreme Court ultimate jurisdiction over all the law.

Often in the Psalms we find the word "Selah." It is uncertain what the word actually means. Some have suggested that it was a signal for the congregation to sing or recite or the choir to sing in a louder or higher pitch. It has even been suggested that it was a signal to fall prostrate on the ground. It is largely held that the word indicates a pause. It would seem to suggest that when the word is found, that one is not to rush on in their reading but pause and give serious thought to what has just been said.

The Psalmist declares, "God is judge Himself." This is a truth that should not be quickly read and dismissed. God is the ultimate Judge and His law is the ultimate law. His law is a righteous law and has ultimate jurisdiction over all men of every nation. One day each of us will have to stand before God. The laws of God cannot be broken without facing the righteous judgment of the righteous Judge. Today, live as if this were the day when you will be called to stand before the Judge of judges.

February 2

Joshua 23:14, "And, behold, this day I am going the way of all the earth: and ye know in all your hearts and in all your souls, that not one thing hath failed of all the good things which the Lord your God spake concerning you; all are come to pass unto you, and not one thing hath failed thereof."

ON THIS DAY in 1870, the Cardiff Giant, supposed to be a petrified human, was proven to be false. In Cardiff, N.Y., a farmer named Newell complained that his well was running dry. While he and his neighbors were digging a new well, they came upon what appeared to be the fossilized remains of a man twelve feet tall. Before the day was out, Newell had erected a tent and was charging a dollar for a glimpse of the giant and three dollars for a longer look. Throngs descended upon Cardiff and the find drew worldwide attention. However, it was not long before scientists determined the giant had been carved from a block of gypsum. It had all been a hoax.

There is one thing that is absolutely true and that is the Word of God. Every word in God's Word is reliable and dependable. Every promise God made will come to pass. Not one word of God's holy book has ever failed. An article in *Time* said: "Archeological digging in Israel continues to turn up new evidence that the Bible is surprisingly accurate in historical particulars, more so than earlier generations of scholars ever suspected." While I rejoice at the evidence that continues to surface that the Bible is reliable, if we never had one single piece of evidence, we could rest assured that it is true. Why? God Himself said so, and that is all we need. Today, give thanks for the Bible, God's Word, that is a book we can always believe.

February 3

Romans 6:23, "For the wages of sin is death; but the gift of God is eternal life through Jesus Christ our Lord."

ON *THIS* DAY in 1998, Texas executed Karla Faye Tucker. Tucker was the first woman to be executed in Texas since the Civil War. She was pronounced dead at 6:45 pm, eight minutes after receiving an injection at the State Prison in Huntsville. She had been convicted of killing Jerry Dean (and Deborah Thornton, an overnight guest) during a burglary at his Houston apartment with a three-foot-long pickax. Tucker's execution drew nationwide attention even from Christian leaders. After being convicted, Tucker was led to Christ during a prison service.

The question may be asked, can someone go to heaven who is guilty of committing such a brutal crime as Karla Faye Tucker? I remind you that the "*blood of Jesus Christ His Son cleanseth us from all sin*" (I John 1:7). God will forgive all sin, even murder. There is no sin that God will not forgive. When Karla Faye Tucker received Jesus Christ as her Saviour, God forgave her sin and promised her a home in heaven. Yet, even though her sins were forgiven, there were still consequences to be paid for what she had done. Her death reminds us that sin has consequences. We must never forget that God will forgive sin, but oftentimes there are consequences to reap. Tucker's final words were, "I love you all very much. I will see you all when you get there. I will wait for you." I expect to see Karla Faye Tucker in heaven, but she reminds us all that sin can have a heavy price to pay. Today, in light of the consequences of some sins, ask God to give you a love for righteousness and a hatred for sin.

February 4

1 Corinthians 1:18, "For the preaching of the cross is to them that perish foolishness; but unto us which are saved it is the power of God."

ON THIS DAY in 1873, George Bennard was born. Bennard was a devoted minister of the Methodist Episcopal Church busily involved in conducting revival services throughout the states of Michigan and New York. He is best known as the author of the great hymn, *The Old Rugged Cross*. During a trying experience in his life, he began to think seriously about the cross and what it meant to the believer. He saw the cross not as a beautiful religious symbol but rather an old rugged cross that stands at the very heart of the gospel.

Christians cherish the symbol of the cross. It is the "emblem of suffering and shame" endured and experienced by the Lord Jesus for every sinner. Yet, the cross is more than a symbol. It is as Bennard discovered, the very heart of the gospel. By the cross we have been reconciled unto God (see Eph.2:16). It was a cross "stained with blood so divine," a cross on which "Jesus suffered and died to pardon and sanctify" all who would come to the Lord Jesus. The world looks upon the message of the cross as foolishness. But to those who have knelt at the cross it has a "wondrous attraction." It is a cross cherished by all who believe for they have found it to be the power of God unto salvation. It is the place where "the dear Lamb of God left His glory above" to die that the lost might be saved. Today may we say with Bennard, "To the old rugged cross I will ever be true, its shame and reproach gladly bear." As believers, the cross of the Lord Jesus should always be cherished.

February 5

1 Corinthians 15:26, "The last enemy that shall be destroyed is death."

ON THIS DAY in 1973, funeral services were held for Army Lt. Colonel William B. Nolde. During the Vietnam War more than 54,000 American soldiers were killed and 150,000 seriously wounded. There were 8.5 million veterans of the Vietnam era (1965 to 1973). A total of 2.8 million served in Southeast Asia and of those, 1 million saw combat. Nolde was one among many that gave their life in Vietnam. What makes his death significant is that he is listed as the last U.S. soldier killed before the Vietnam ceasefire. He was buried in the Arlington National Cemetery.

In the early chapters of Genesis death was introduced to this world. Since then the cemetery has become a part of the earth's landscape. A funeral home can be found in every town. The largest cemetery in the world is the Ohlsdorf Cemetery in Hamburg, Germany. It covers 990 acres, with 972,020 burials and 408,471 cremations as of December 31, 1995. It has been in use since 1877. Yet, it is but one of many that testifies to the reality of death. Death is no respecter of age. But one of these days Death will claim its last victim. The Bible tells us that the enemy death will be destroyed. One of the great promises concerning heaven is that "there shall be no more death" (Rev. 21:4). What a blessed day it will be when death will no longer take from us those that we love. One day the last funeral will be held and the last victim of death will be claimed. Today, give thanks that even though death may take our loved ones, we will see them again.

February 6

Proverbs 24:16, "For a just man falleth seven times, and riseth up again: but the wicked shall fall into mischief."

ON THIS DAY in 1935 the board game "Monopoly" went on sale for the first time. Monopoly became the best selling board game board in the world, licensed or sold in eighty countries and produced in twenty-six languages. More than 200 million have been sold worldwide, and it is estimated that more than 500 million have played the game. More than 5 billion of the little green houses have been made. During the height of the Depression, Charles D. Barrow of Germantown, Pa., showed his idea for the game to the executives at Parker Brothers. They rejected it due to "fifty-two design errors." Undaunted, Barrow had the game manufactured on his own and sold 5,000 handmade sets to a Philadelphia department store. It was an instant hit and Barrow could not keep up with the demand for the game. Barrow went back to Parker Brothers, and as they say, the rest is history.

Solomon describes a person who perseveres and refuses to give up. Regardless of how many times they get knocked down they always get back up and go at it again. The person who refuses to quit praying when it seems no answer is coming and who refuses to quit believing when it seems impossible is the person who will ultimately succeed. Are you praying for someone? Don't quit. Keep praying. Are you believing God for something? Don't quit, keep believing. God honors the person who refuses to give up, give out, or give in. As Charles Spurgeon said, "By perseverance the snail reached the Ark." Today, ask God to help you never to give up. If you get knocked down, get back up and keep going.

February 7

Proverbs 12:5, "The thoughts of the righteous are right: but the counsels of the wicked are deceit."

ON THIS DAY in 1839, Henry Clay declared in the Senate, "I would rather be right than president." Henry Clay exercised a leadership in American politics that has seldom been equaled. He served as a senator and representative from Kentucky and as Secretary of State under Quincy Adams. He served as Speaker of the House longer than any other during the 19th century. He was called the "Great Compromiser" for his ability to get differing sides to come together on a matter. He ran for president on three different occasions but without success. Many of his quotes have become a part of his historical record but none as famous as his remark, "I would rather be right than be president."

Right is never for sale, no matter what the wrong offers. It has been well said that wrong is wrong if everybody is for it and right is right if everybody is against it. J. C. Penney's first venture as a retail proprietor, a butcher shop in Longmont, Colorado opened in 1899 and failed almost immediately, after he refused to bribe an important local hotel chef with a weekly bottle of bourbon. "I lost everything I had," said Penney, "but I learned never to compromise." Right should never be for sale no matter where you are, whom you are with, or what you are doing. The line must be drawn in the sand. At times it will require courage to do what is right. Oftentimes you will find yourself in the minority, yet the cost of doing wrong is far more expensive than doing what is right. Today, make right the standard of your day and ask God to help you to always do what is right. Remember it is never right to do what is wrong and never wrong to do what is right.

February 8

John 19:17-18, "And he bearing his cross went forth into a place called the place of a skull, which is called in the Hebrew Golgotha: Where they crucified him, and two others with him, on either side one, and Jesus in the midst."

ON *THIS* DAY in 1924 the first execution by lethal gas was performed in the United States. The execution was performed in Carson City, Nevada and the victim was Tong Lee, a member of a Chinese gang who was convicted of murdering a rival gang member. In 1921 the state of Nevada adopted lethal gas as a more humane method of execution as opposed to the traditional methods of hanging, firing squad, and electrocution.

The angry crowd cried, "Crucify him!" They would settle for nothing less than an execution. The victim was led away to the place of execution and nailed to a cross between two condemned criminals. While the majority of the American public has consistently backed the death penalty, it has not been without its critics. However, this execution was necessary for if Jesus had not died, we could not live. Regardless of how one may feel about capital punishment, the death of Jesus was one execution that should cause us to bow before God and give thanks that it occurred. Death by crucifixion was one of the most inhumane ways for one to be executed, yet Jesus, *"being found in fashion as a man, he humbled himself, and became obedient unto death, even the death of the cross"* (Phil.2:8). Jesus was the innocent dying for the guilty. Today, gives thanks that Jesus paid the price for your sins by dying on the cross.

February 9

Proverbs 18:8, "The words of a talebearer are as wounds, and they go down into the innermost parts of the belly."

ON THIS DAY in 1950, Senator Joseph Raymond McCarthy accused the State Department of having been infiltrated by Communists. McCarthy announced during a speech in Wheeling, West Virginia that he had in his hand a list of 205 Communists who had infiltrated the U.S. State Department. These shocking accusations prompted the Senate to form a special committee to investigate the charges. McCarthy never produced documentation for a single one of his charges although the reputations of hundreds of innocent citizens and officials were marred or destroyed. Eventually the Senate voted to condemn him for his misconduct.

They were a happy little family, living in a small town in North Dakota. Then one day a village gossip started a story, saying that the husband was being unfaithful to his wife, a story entirely without foundation. But it eventually came to the ears of the young wife, and it was more than she could bear. That night when her husband came home there was no one to meet him at the gate, no laughter in the house, no fragrant aroma coming from the kitchen only coldness and something that chilled his heart with fear. Down in the basement he found the three of them hanging from a beam. Sick and in despair, the young mother had first taken the lives of her two children, and then her own. Later the rumor was proven untrue. Many a life has been scarred and reputation destroyed by the tongue of another. Today, ask God to help you to speak only well of others. If we can't say anything good let's not say anything.

February 10

1 Corinthians 12:21-22, "And the eye cannot say unto the hand, I have no need of thee: nor again the head to the feet, I have no need of you. Nay, much more those members of the body, which seem to be more feeble, are necessary."

On This Day in 1969, Pete Maravich scored sixty-nine points in a basketball game despite losing to Tulane 101-94. Shaggy hair, floppy gray socks, and a pregame warm-up that included spinning the basketball on his index finger, then off his head and into the basket, "Pistol Pete" was the talk of college basketball. During his college career he had the best scoring average for one season (44.5), highest career scoring average (44.2), most points scored (3,667), six times scored more than fifty or more points in a game, and all done in three seasons without the three point shot. During his senior year at LSU he was touted with the ballad: "Love to fake, Love to score, Love to hear the people roar, Just a boy of twenty-two, You made a name of LSU." Yet, in spite of scoring sixty-nine points in the loss to Tulane, "Pistol Pete" was but one player. He could not do it alone.

There are no unimportant members in the family of God. The family of God is like a team and every member is vital to fulfilling the task that has been assigned to them by God. Each member has different roles and the work of God depends on every member of the body fulfilling their role and function in the body. You may not be the high scorer but you have a role. Your role is very important and vital to the ministry of the Body. Today, give thanks for your place in the Body and realize how important you are to God's work. You may not hear others chant your name, but you are as important as anyone else.

February 11

Colossians 3:9, "Lie not one to another, seeing that ye have put off the old man with his deeds."

ON THIS DAY in 1847, Thomas A. Edison was born. Edison was one of the most productive inventors of his time. In spite of schooling that was limited to three months, at his death he held 1,300 U.S. and foreign patents. Among his major inventions were the phonograph, electric light bulb, microphone, fluoroscope and the telephone transmitter. Thomas Edison invented the phonograph at age thirty, yet he was almost totally deaf from childhood. He could only hear the loud noises and shouts. This kind of delighted him, for he said, "A man who has to shout can never tell a lie!"

A little boy was asked what a lie was and he replied, "A very present help in the time of trouble." We often excuse lies as an exaggeration of truth but in Proverbs we find that lying is one of the things God hates (Prov.6:16-19). With God there are no little white lies. They are all dark and hated by Him. Lying can take many forms. The exaggeration of who you are or what you have done is nothing more than a lie. Adding to a story and making it more than what it was is a lie. Mark Twain, who was not the most reverent man in the world, used to say that there are a hundred different ways of lying, but that the only kind of lying that is flatly forbidden in the Bible is bearing false witness against our neighbor. Yet, God's Word forbids lying in any form. A Christian is to put away lying. If there is any person whose word should be reliable it is the Christian. Today, ask God to give you a hatred for lying in any form. Ask God to search your heart for any lies you may have told. Oh, by the way, be honest with yourself.

February 12

Daniel 12:3, "And they that be wise shall shine as the brightness of the firmament; and they that turn many to righteousness, as the stars for ever and ever."

ON *THIS* DAY in 1915, the cornerstone for the Lincoln Memorial in Washington, D.C., was laid. The memorial was erected in honor of the 16th president of the United States, Abraham Lincoln and the nation he sought to preserve during the Civil War. Architect Henry Bacon modeled his design for the building after the Greek Parthenon. The thirty-six exterior Doric columns represented the thirty-six states in the Union at the time of Lincoln's death. Those states are listed on the frieze above the columns. Above those states are listed the forty-eight states in the Union when the memorial was built. The exterior is made of Colorado Yule marble with a walkway made of Massachusetts's granite and Potomac River stones. The nineteen foot Lincoln statue inside was designed and created by Daniel Chester French made of Georgia White marble.

D.L. Moody once said that the only monument he wanted when he was gone was one walking on two feet. The greatest monuments one can leave behind are those they have led to Christ. It is a memorial of far greater value than one of expensive marble and eloquent design. Nothing should thrill the heart anymore than to know that someone will live in heaven because of your life and witness. You may accomplish many things in life; yet the greatest accomplishment in life is being humanly responsible for the salvation of another person. Today, ask God to give you a burden for souls and to allow you the privilege to win someone to Christ. What a great monument to leave behind.

February 13

Proverbs 10:1, "The proverbs of Solomon. A wise son maketh a glad father: but a foolish son is the heaviness of his mother."

ON THIS DAY in 1866 Jesse James held up his first bank. He took $15,000 from a bank in Liberty, Missouri. Jesse James is by far the most infamous and best-known outlaw in American history. To some he was a hero and to others a villain. He committed dozens of robberies and killed at least half a dozen men or more. On top of all that he was a preachers kid. His father, Robert, was pastor of the Kearney Baptist Church in Kearney, Missouri. His mother Zee took care of the manual chores around the house while Robert spent his time preparing his fiery Sunday sermons.

Many parents have had their hearts crushed by a child that forsook their religious upbringing. They know the heaviness that is felt when a child turns their back on God and abandons their religious upbringing. But God is able to reach a son or daughter that has gone astray. If you taught them right and brought them up in a godly home, there has been deposited in their heart blessed truths that they will never be able to escape. The godly home you provided for them can become a hook in the hands of the Holy Spirit to bring them back. We must put them in the hands of God, love them, encourage them to come back to God and pray for them daily. They may not listen to you anymore but there is One that knows how to get their attention. Today, maybe your heart is broken over a child that is away from God. Call their name out to God in prayer. He loves them as much as you do. He wants them to be saved and serve Him as much as you do.

February 14

2 Corinthians 11:14, "And no marvel; for Satan himself is transformed into an angel of light."

On This Day in 1929 seven gangsters were killed in Chicago in what is known as the St. Valentines Day Massacre. Gunmen in the employment of Al Capone murdered seven members of the "Bugs" Moran gang. Moran contested Capone's control of organized crime in Chicago, therefore Capone ordered the elimination of Moran and his gang. Capone's men lured the Moran gang to a garage on North Clark Street with an offer of buying some high quality whiskey at a low price. After the Moran gang arrived, the assassins opened fire killing six of the men instantly and fatally wounding the seventh. Capone's men were dressed as policemen. Moran arrived late and saw the so-called policemen entering the building and he was able to escape.

Satan is a master of disguise. He is a pro at hiding his hideous self and evil purposes. In the Middle Ages, the people were frequently amused by the miracle plays. These were a sort of religious pageant in which religious stories were acted out on the stage. The audience learned to look for one character on the stage who was always dressed in red, wore horns on his head, and had a tail dangling out behind him. His hoofs were cloven, and he had a pitchfork in his hand. Contrary to this popular image, Satan often appears as an angel of light. He is a master deceiver and the ultimate destroyer. Because Satan is a master deceiver we are told, "*to be sober, be vigilant*" (I Pet.5:8). Today, ask God to make you wise to Satan's disguises lest you become another victim. He may come as an angel, but he is always an adversary.

February 15

Numbers 32:23, "But if ye will not do so, behold, ye have sinned against the Lord: and be sure your sin will find you out."

On This Day in 1978, serial killer Ted Bundy was recaptured in Pensacola, Florida. Bundy allegedly murdered at least thirty-six victims and many more who were unaccounted for. The real number Bundy carried to his grave. Bundy managed to escape twice after being caught. The first time he jumped from an open window at the Aspen courthouse but was recaptured six days later. Seven months later he crawled into the ceiling of the Garfield County Jail and made his way to another part of the building and simply walked out the door. His escape went unnoticed until the following afternoon, some fifteen hours after his escape. Bundy was later recaptured and executed in 1989.

Someone has said that when we break the laws of God, the laws of God will eventually break us. A certain law of heaven is that somewhere and at sometime we can be sure that our sin will find us out. A person may escape the penalty of earthly law, but the law of heaven cannot be broken without a payday. It is folly to think that you can sin and get by with it. Somewhere sin will catch up with you. That's a promise! God tells us that if we confess our sins He is faithful and just to forgive us of our sin (I John 1:9). Putting our sin under the blood of the Lord Jesus is the only way to escape the punishment of sin. You can run if you want to, but you will not escape. You can be sure your sin will find you out. Today, spend time with God dealing with any sin in your life. It is better for you to ask forgiveness than to wait for God's chastening.

February 16

Romans 6:13, "Neither yield ye your members as instruments of unrighteousness unto sin: but yield yourselves unto God, as those that are alive from the dead, and your members as instruments of righteousness unto God."

On This Day in 1862, General Ulysses S. Grant earned the nickname "Unconditional Surrender Grant." Grant's forces had surrounded the Confederates at Fort Donelson, Tennessee. Realizing that their situation was hopeless the Confederate leaders surrendered. Brig. General Simon B. Buckner, an old friend of Grant, asked on what terms he would accept his surrender. "No terms," was the reply, "except an unconditional and immediate surrender." Since Grant's initials were U.S., from that time on he was known as "Unconditional Surrender Grant."

The only terms that God accepts are unconditional and immediate surrender to His will. We cannot come to God on our terms and expect Him to accept it. God accepts nothing but total surrender. These are His terms. It is like taking a blank sheet of paper and signing your name at the bottom. The signing of your name is an act of saying, "Lord, I surrender my life to you. I have left the page blank so you can fill in whatever you want. I will do whatever you want, with no reservations or conditions." The kind of surrender God seeks is a surrender that is unconditional. It is saying, "Yes," to His will regardless of what He would ask. Today, surrender to God unconditionally and immediately. He accepts nothing less. Why not be known as an "Unconditional Surrender" Christian. That's a good name to have.

February 17

Proverbs 14:34, "Righteousness exalteth a nation: but sin is a reproach to any people."

On This Day in 1776, the first volume of Edward Gibbon's *Decline and Fall of the Roman Empire* was published. Gibbon, an English historian, had very little formal education but was an avid reader. It was on a visit to Rome that he conceived the idea of his panoramic history of the Roman Empire. Eventually he wrote 6 volumes that covered more than 1,300 years of history. His work has become one of the most read historical works of modern times. Not without its critics, who speak of his bias that placed moral judgment on the material decline of the Roman Empire, it remains one of the most respected works on the history of the Roman Empire.

The decline and fall of a nation is not without a cause. The secret to a nation's strength is not a strong economy, military, or even its form of government. Such things are often the fruit of a greater cause. The real strength of a nation is righteousness. Nations may rise to power without righteousness over time but eventually they will crumble. If righteousness exalts a nation, then unrighteousness is the cause for the decline and fall of a nation. The hope of America, or any other nation, is not in politics but in revival. Government cannot, and in most cases will not, legislate righteousness. Only revival can produce a national morality and righteousness. It is not new laws we need but the Lord. Today, pray for revival. Pray that God will once again visit our nation. Revival is critical. The greatness of our nation depends on it.

February 18

Ecclesiastes 12:14, "For God shall bring every work into judgment, with every secret thing, whether it be good, or whether it be evil."

ON THIS DAY in 1856 the "Know-Nothing Party" convened in Philadelphia to nominate its first presidential candidate. The movement consisted of several secret societies to resist foreign influences in America, especially Roman Catholic immigrants from Ireland and Italy. The Know-Nothings sought for legislation to prevent immigrants from holding public office. Whenever members of these societies were questioned by the press they would often reply they knew nothing, hence the name "Know-Nothing Party." In 1855 they adopted the name American Party and dropped much of their secrecy. They met in 1856 to nominate their first presidential candidate and formally abolish the secret character of their organization.

There are no secrets with God. There is nothing that He does not know. We can't hide anything from Him. We read in Luke 8:17, *"For nothing is secret, that shall not be made manifest; neither any thing hid, that shall not be known and come abroad."* The thought of such knowledge can be either a disturbing or delightful thought. It is a great comfort to know that nothing touches our life that escapes the eye of God. Yet, it is deeply troubling when we realize that God is aware of every secret sin (Psalm 90:8). Today, give thanks that God knows what you are going through and that He cares. At the same time don't forget that He knows the bad as well as the good. That's right. He knows everything, and I mean everything.

February 19

1 Corinthians 9:24, "Know ye not that they which run in a race run all, but one receiveth the prize? So run, that ye may obtain."

ON THIS DAY in 1913, the first prize was put into the Cracker Jack boxes. Frederick William Rueckheim, a German immigrant, went to Chicago to help clean up after the Great Fire. To make a living he started selling popcorn from a one-popper stand on a street corner. His business grew until in 1893, Rueckheim introduced a unique confection of popcorn, peanuts, and molasses at the World's Columbian Exposition, Chicago's first World Fair. Louis Rueckheim, F.W.'s brother and partner, discovered the process for keeping the molasses-covered popcorn from sticking together, a secret formula that is still in use. He gave the treat to a salesman who exclaimed, "That's a Cracker Jack!" "So it is," said Rueckheim, who had the words trademarked. Since the first prize was inserted, there have been more than 17 billion toys found inside boxes of Cracker Jacks.

Paul spoke of a prize he coveted when he declared, *"I press toward the mark for the prize of the high calling of God in Christ Jesus"* (Phil. 3:14). The prize that he sought was a heavenly reward. One which he encouraged others to obtain. As a believer the prize of all prizes is to live a life that will be honored with a heavenly reward. All believers are runners in the race of life and all who run well will receive this heavenly prize. Today, ask God to help you run your race well. When all is said and done you will be glad you did. There is a prize waiting. It is a prize out of this world!

February 20

Proverbs 25:25, "As cold waters to a thirsty soul, so is good news from a far country."

ON THIS DAY in 1792 the U.S. Postal Service was created. President George Washington appointed Samuel Osgood of Massachusetts as the first Postmaster General of the U.S. When Osgood took office there were seventy-six post offices. It was initially called the Post Office Department until 1971, when it was changed to the U.S. Postal Service. Now it is the largest postal service in the world handling about half of the total volume of the world's mail. In the late 1980's, there were 780,000 employees of more than 40,000 post offices and postal substations in the United States. Their motto: "Neither snow, nor rain, nor heat, nor gloom of night stay these couriers from the swift completion of their appointed rounds."

The greatest news that has ever been delivered is the Gospel. The word "gospel" means "good news." The gospel is the message that Jesus died for our sins, was buried, and rose again the third day (1 Cor. 15:1-3). No greater message has ever been delivered for it is the message by which we are saved. How we ought to thank God for those who delivered this wonderful message to us. We will forever be indebted to that heavenly postal carrier that delivered us this good news. Today, ask God to let you share with someone the greatest news that has ever been delivered. It is good news that everyone needs to hear. It is such good news, why would we want to keep it to ourselves. Rain, snow, sleet, nor gloom of night should stop us from delivering this good news. You don't even need a stamp to deliver this good news.

February 21

Nehemiah 6:3, "And I sent messengers unto them, saying, I am doing a great work, so that I cannot come down: why should the work cease, whilst I leave it, and come down to you?"

ON *THIS* DAY in 1885, the Washington Monument was dedicated. The Continental Congress first considered the idea for a monument to honor George Washington in 1783, but it was not until 1833 that the Washington National Monument Society was organized and undertook the building of a "great National Monument to the memory of Washington at the seat of Federal Government." On July 4, 1848 the cornerstone was laid with elaborate Masonic ceremonies. Work progressed favorably until 1854, when the building of the monument became involved in a political quarrel. For almost twenty-five years the monument stood incomplete. Finally on August 2, 1876, President Grant approved an act that gave authority to the federal government to complete the erection of the monument. It was dedicated on this day in 1885 and opened to the public on October 9, 1888.

As Nehemiah worked to rebuild the walls of Jerusalem, he was not without adversaries who tried to discourage him and stop his work. Yet, he declared that he was involved in "a great work" and refused to let anything or anyone stop him. As believers we are involved in the greatest work in the world and that is telling others about the Lord Jesus and doing God's will in the world. There will always be things and even people, who can discourage us and even get us to cease our work, but it is a great work and we cannot and must not let anything or anyone stop us. Today, keep working for the Lord. It is indeed a great work.

February 22

Psalm 109:22, "For I am poor and needy, and my heart is wounded within me."

ON *THIS* DAY in 1932, the Purple Heart Award was re-instituted. The ORDER of the PURPLE HEART for MILITARY MERIT, commonly called "The Purple Heart" is the oldest military decoration in the world still in use and the first award made available to the common soldier. Intrinsically, the Purple Heart is the world's costliest military decoration. There are nineteen separate operations involved in its making, from the heart stamped from bronze to the finished medal, plated with gold and enameled in various colors, suspended from a purple and white ribbon. The award is given to members of the armed forces of the U.S. who are wounded by an instrument of war in the hands of the enemy. Created by General George Washington, it was originally called the Badge of Military Merit. After the Revolutionary War, no American soldier was given the award until the War Department announced they had changed its name and the new award was called the Purple Heart.

The wounded heart is not uncommon in God's work. God has His order for the wounded heart. We read, *"He healeth the broken in heart, and bindeth up their wounds"* (Psalm 147:3). If you have been wounded in the battle of life, God is aware of your hurt and He rewards you with His grace, strength, and comfort. He that was wounded in the house of His friends (Zech. 13:6), God knows how you feel. Today, if you have been wounded, remember that God can heal those broken in heart. Today you can become a member of God's Order of the Wounded Heart. There is a reward for all soldiers that have been wounded.

February 23

Job 26:7, "He stretcheth out the north over the empty place, and hangeth the earth upon nothing."

On This Day in 1997, scientists in Scotland announced they had succeeded in cloning an adult mammal, producing a lamb named "Dolly." Although born in July 1996, the news of her arrival and the cloning technique was not published until February 1997. Scientists at the Roslin Institute produced Dolly by taking the nucleus out of a cell from the mammary gland of an adult animal, and fusing it, using an electric current, into another sheep egg cell from which the nucleus had been removed. In 1998 it was announced that a calf had been cloned; "Mr. Jefferson" was a healthy ninety-eight pound Holstein breed, born in Virginia on Presidents Day in the U.S.

Almost every day we are amazed at the advancement of science and the expanding ability and achievements of man. The cloning of a sheep and calf only makes one wonder what man will be able to achieve in the years to come. Is the cloning of a human being next? As amazing as it may be, the achievements of man all pale in significance to God's act of creation. All that God brought to pass started with nothing. What man has done is take what God created and expand his knowledge of that creation and his ability to work with that creation. God took nothing and He created a world out of it. Today, give thanks that the God of creation is your heavenly Father. If He can take nothing and create this world in which we live, then I know He can take care of you.

February 24

Psalm 31:15, "My times are in thy hand: deliver me from the hand of mine enemies, and from them that persecute me."

ON *THIS* DAY in 1582 Pope Gregory XIII announced a new style calendar. The Gregorian calendar or New Style (N.S.), replaced the former Julian calendar (named after Julius Caesar). It is the calendar most freqently used today. First adopted by Roman Catholic countries, it was not until 1752 that the new calendar was adopted in England, 1912 in China, and 1918 in Russia. The Gregorian calendar was the first to mark January 1 as the beginning of the New Year. Previous calendars began the year on December 25 (England, March 25). It also extended the cycle of the year to three hundred sixty-five days and a leap year of three hundred sixty-six days in every four years.

It is encouraging to know that regardless of the day, week, or month, our times are in God's hand. *"The Lord knoweth the days of the upright: and their inheritance shall be forever"* (Psalm 37:18). Furthermore, we are told that the Lord determines our days. We read in Job 14:5, *"Seeing his days are determined, the number of his months are with thee, thou hast appointed his bounds that he cannot pass."* The events of our days and the end of our days are all in His hands. There are no accidents in our days, only appointments. God keeps His own calendar. The commencement of life, the conclusion of life, and all that happens in between are in His hands. Today, give thanks that your times (days, weeks, months, years) are in His hands. This is the day the Lord hath made. Rejoice and be glad in it.

February 25

Matthew 22:21, "They say unto him, Caesar's. Then saith he unto them, Render therefore unto Caesar the things which are Caesar's; and unto God the things that are God's."

ON THIS DAY in 1913 the sixteenth amendment to the Constitution was ratified authorizing income tax. The U.S. had few taxes in its early history from 1791 to 1802. The U.S. was supported by internal taxes on distilled spirits, carriages, refined sugar, tobacco, property sold at auctions, corporate bonds and slaves. In 1817 the U.S. did away with all internal taxes, relying on tariffs on imported goods. In 1862, in order to support the Civil War, Congress enacted the nations first income tax law, a forerunner of the present law in that it was based on the principles of graduated taxation and of withholding income at the source. With the 16th amendment, the income tax law became a permanent fixture, giving Congress legal authority to tax income of both corporations and individuals. The withholding tax on wages was introduced in 1943.

When Jesus was questioned about paying taxes, He encouraged obedience to the tax laws of the land. In the same breath, He demanded obedience to the laws of God. The failure to pay our taxes may result in various penalties and even imprisonment, but the failure to obey God carries far greater consequences. There is the loss of blessings and eternal reward. What we render to the government is important, but what we render to God is more important. Today, don't leave God out of your plans and activities. If you buy anything today you will for sure render to Caesar what is Caesar's. Why not render to God what is God's.

February 26

Colossians 1:20, "And, having made peace through the blood of his cross, by him to reconcile all things unto himself; by him, I say, whether they be things in earth, or things in heaven."

ON THIS DAY in 1933, groundbreaking ceremonies were held for the Golden Gate Bridge. Heralded as one of the top ten construction achievements of the 20th century, at the time of its completion it was the longest suspension bridge in the world. It spans 4,200 feet, with a total length of 9,266 feet. It features two main towers 746 feet tall (tallest in the world) supporting two main cables capable of supporting 200 million tons each. The deepest foundation is 110 feet. Upon its completion someone wrote:

"At last the mighty task is done;
Resplendent in the western sun.
The bridge looms mountain high;
Its piers grip ocean floor,
Its great steel arms linking shore to shore,
Its towers pierce the sky."

The songwriter wrote, "Oh the mighty gulf that God did span at Calvary." Man was separated from God by sin and the gulf was so wide that it was impossible for man to span that gulf. Yet at Calvary the cross became the bridge that spanned that mighty gulf thereby becoming the only way to God. Its length reaches from heaven to earth. The arms of the cross, link shore-to-shore, nation-to-nation. Its foundations reach to the lowest in sin and its towers pierce the ages as a testimony that the mighty gulf of sin has been spanned. There is no toll for its crossing is free, paid for by the blood of the Lord Jesus. Today give thanks that the Lord Jesus, through His blood, provided a bridge that spanned a gulf we could not span.

February 27

Deuteronomy 6:12, "Then beware lest thou forget the Lord, which brought thee forth out of the land of Egypt, from the house of bondage."

ON THIS DAY in 1864, the infamous Confederate prisoner of war camp, Camp Sumter, opened near Andersonville, Georgia. The largest of all Confederate POW camps, it initially covered sixteen and one-half acres and was later expanded to twenty-six and one-half acres to handle the number of prisoners. During the fourteen months of its existence 49,485 Union soldiers were imprisoned there and nearly 13,000 died from disease, impure water, malnutrition, and exposure to the elements. Hundreds died daily. The "dead house" outside the prison was filled beyond capacity and bodies were stacked outside the house prior to burial. Prisoner, Sgt. David Kennedy of the Ninth Ohio Calvary wrote in his diary, "Wuld that I was an artist and had the material to paint this camp and all its horrors or the tounge of some eloquent statesman and had the privleage of expressing my mind to our hon. Rulers in Washington, I should gloery to describe this hell on earth where it takes seven of its occupants to make a shadow" (*original spelling*).

As the years pass, there is a danger that we will forget what we were and where we were before the Lord saved us. All of us were held captive by sin and Satan. For many, their prison was a "hell on earth." But there was a glorious day when the Lord Jesus delivered us from our prison. Our difficulty is not in describing the awful conditions of our past life, but the blessedness of a life that has been set free. Today, let your mind reflect on your past condition and then let what you are and where you are warm your heart with praise to God.

February 28

1 Corinthians 4:2, "Moreover it is required in stewards, that a man be found faithful."

ON *THIS* DAY in 1638 the Scottish Presbyterians signed the National Covenant at Greyfriars Kirk in Edinburgh, Scotland. Today if you visit Greyfriars Kirk, one of Edinburgh's most historic churches, a large amount of attention is given to a dog that was named Greyfriars Bobby. Every day for 14 years, after the death of his master, this Skye terrier faithfully visited the grave of his master. The little dog was buried just inside the entrance to the churchyard and is memorialized for its fidelity to its master. Yet, the real story of faithfulness is told in those who were imprisoned on the church grounds and martyred just outside the church grounds as result of the backlash of the signing of the National Covenant. The Martyr's Memorial in one corner of the church graveyard tells the ultimate story of faithfulness. The real story of faithfulness is not to be found in a little dog that daily visited the grave of his master year after year, but in those who were willing to pay the ultimate price for their faith.

There are no greater examples of faithfulness than in those who were willing to give their life rather than deny the faith. We may not be called upon to give our life, but none-the-less, faithfulness is required of each of us. God always honors faithfulness. Regardless of who you are or what your role is in the work of God, be faithful. Be faithful no matter the cost. It will be worth it when you hear the words of Jesus, "*Well done, good and faithful servant*" (Matt. 25:23). Today, ask God to help you to be faithful. Meeting God each day is a good first step to being faithful.

February 29

1 Corinthians 3:15, "If any man's work shall be burned, he shall suffer loss: but he himself shall be saved; yet so as by fire".

ON THIS DAY in 1528, Patrick Hamilton, the Scottish reformer, was burned at the stake. While studying in Paris, Hamilton was introduced to the teachings of Martin Luther and later returned to Scotland preaching Luther's theology. Hamilton was arrested and sentenced to death for the crime of being a heretic and propagating heresies and was burned at the stake. Set in the cobblestones at the place where he was executed, outside St. Salvators College, St. Andrews, Scotland, is a simple marker with the letters "P.H." It is believed that standing on these initials will result in exam failure and other such salutary repercussions for those who would carelessly trespass his memory.

In the future of every believer is an examination time. *"For we must all appear before the judgment seat of Christ; that every one may receive the things done in his body, according to that he hath done, whether it be good or bad"* (2 Cor. 5:10). The Judgment Seat of Christ will be a time when the life of every believer will be reviewed. Both the good and bad will be examined. Tragically, Paul says that some will fail to get a passing grade. In light of all Christ has done for us, giving His life that we might have life, the believer ought to be motivated to live a life that is pleasing to the Lord and when reviewed will not get a failing grade. Today, live in light of the future. When the examination day comes, we don't want the result to be "exam failure."

March 1

2 Timothy 2:19, "Nevertheless the foundation of God standeth sure, having this seal, The Lord knoweth them that are his. And, Let every one that nameth the name of Christ depart from iniquity."

ON THIS DAY in 1790 Congress authorized the first U.S. census. Article 1, section 2, of the U.S. Constitution, established a nationwide population census on a regular basis in 1787. Congress assigned responsibility for the 1790 census to the marshals of the U.S. judicial districts and began enumeration in August of 1790. The law required that every household be visited. Information to be obtained consisted of the head of every household, the number of persons in each household of the following descriptions: free white males sixteen and over (for the purpose of assessing the countries industrial and military potential); free white males under sixteen, free white females, and all other free persons (by sex and color) and slaves.

Paul declared, "*The Lord knoweth them that are his.*" The Lord knows each one who is His. He knows each one by name. The Lord's family is large, but He knows each one personally and cares for each one equally. His knowledge of His children extends to every detail of their lives. The Psalmist declared, "*For he knoweth our frame*" *(Psalm 103:14)*, "*For the Lord knoweth the way of the righteous*" *(Psalm 1:6)*. He even "*knoweth the days of the upright. (Psalm 37:18)*. Jesus said, "*I am the good shepherd, and know my sheep*" *(John 10:14)*. Today, rejoice that you know Him, but even more that He knows you and He doesn't need to take a census every ten years to find out about you.

March 2

John 8:36, "If the Son therefore shall make you free, ye shall be free indeed."

ON THIS DAY in 1807 Congress abolished the African slave trade. The act was passed to "prohibit the importation of slaves into any port or place within the jurisdiction of the United States...from any foreign kingdom, place, or country." The first African captives brought to America arrived at Jamestown, Virginia in August of 1619, and by the time of the American Revolution it is estimated that English importers alone had brought some three million captives. The number had increased to over 12 million by 1865 with 1 million having died during the voyage across the Atlantic.

Slavery is a tragic chapter in any nations history. Yet, the Bible teaches us that we all were in slavery. We were all slaves to sin and Satan. The chains of our sin held us firmly in their grip, and Satan's power was humanly impossible to escape. Many can remember their futile attempts to escape their bondage only to find their enslavement worst than before. The conditions of slavery manifests itself in different conditions in different people, but none-the-less is evident. Thank God for the day when Jesus set us free. In the 19th century, a Judge Harrington, of Vermont, was asked to return a runaway slave and refused on the ground of insufficient evidence. "What would you regard as sufficient?" asked the claimant. "Nothing short of a bill of sale from Almighty God!" was the reply. Thank God there is a bill of sale from God and it is the blood of the Lord Jesus. Today give thanks that you have been delivered from the bondage of sin and Satan and the Son has made you free.

March 3

Acts 12:5, "Peter therefore was kept in prison: but prayer was made without ceasing of the church unto God for him."

ON *THIS* DAY in 1934 John Dillinger escaped from the County Jail in Crown Point, Indiana using a wooden gun. First F.B.I. Public Enemy number one, Dillinger was awaiting trial for the murder of an East Chicago police officer. From September, 1933 to July, 1934, Dillinger and his gang terrorized the Midwest by killing ten men, wounding seven, robbing banks, staging three jail breaks, killing a sheriff during one and wounding two guards in another. Authorities boasted that the Crown Point Jail was "escape proof." Dillinger escaped with what he claimed was a wooden gun he had whittled. He forced a guard to open his cell, and then grabbed two machine guns, locking up the guards and then fled.

Peter managed a jail escape but it was not due to a make believe gun, but because of the power of prayer. When Peter was arrested a group of believers began to pray, and God answered with Peter's "jail break". There is power in prayer! James declares, "*the effectual fervent prayer of a righteous man availeth much*" (James 5:16). Prayer brings us in contact with God who, "*is able to do exceeding abundantly above all that we ask or think, according to the power that worketh in us*" (Eph. 3:20). Martin Luther said that prayer is able to do anything, for God is able to do anything. Do you need a miracle from God? Have you prayed? James 4:2 reminds us, "*yet ye have not, because ye ask not.*" Today, take your need to the Lord in prayer. If God can get Peter out of prison, He can help you. There is power in prayer!

March 4

Psalm 27:1, "The Lord is my light and my salvation; whom shall I fear? the Lord is the strength of my life; of whom shall I be afraid?"

ON THIS DAY in 1933, Franklin D. Roosevelt was inaugurated as the 32nd president of the United States, and in his Inauguration Address, said to the American people, "the only thing we have to fear is fear itself." Elected in November to the first of four terms, Roosevelt assumed the presidency at a time when the United States was in the depths of the Great Depression. Over 13 million were unemployed, and almost every bank was closed. At his inauguration, pledging to pull the country out of depression, promising prompt and vigorous action, Roosevelt sought to help the American people regain faith in themselves and their country. His challenge was that the only thing Americans had to fear was fear itself.

The believer does not have to live in the grip of fear. David, as an old man, looked back over his life and said, "I will fear no evil." Many times we find in the Bible the words, "fear not." Someone has said there are 365 "fear not's" in the Bible, one for each day. Paul told Timothy, *"For God hath not given us the spirit of fear; but of power, and of love, and of a sound mind"* (2 Tim. 1:7). The believer does not have to fear the past, the present, or the future. The Psalmist declared, "The Lord is on my side; I will not fear"(Psalm 118:6). We do not have to fear "whom" or "what". We are in the Lord's care. Today, *"Fear not,"* for He that cares and provides for the little sparrows cares for you and you *"are of more value than many sparrows"* (Matt. 10:31).

March 5

Psalm 23:4, "Yea, though I walk through the valley of the shadow of death, I will fear no evil: for thou art with me; thy rod and thy staff they comfort me".

ON THIS DAY in 1982, actor and comedian John Belushi was found dead of a drug overdose in a rented Hollywood bungalow. John was in Chateau Bungalow #3 with some friends working on a movie script. That night he decided that he wanted something that would take him further than he had ever been, so he shot up a mix of heroin and cocaine. The mixture began slowing his breathing and resulted in respiratory failure. On March 9, Dan Ackroyd, dressed in a black leather jacket and black jeans, led the funeral procession to a cemetery on Martha's Vineyard on his motorcycle. As the snow began to fall, James Taylor sang, "That Lonesome Road."

I remember the day so well. I had just left the funeral of a preacher friend, and as I heard the details of Belushi's funeral on my car radio I thought of what a contrast to the funeral I had just attended. The church building had been packed with family, friends, and preachers from all over the country. I thought of how the congregation had stood and sung, "Heaven's Jubilee". There had been sad hearts and many tears, but much rejoicing as we sang victoriously our friends home-going. Death for a Christian is not a "lonesome road." One day each of us will have to walk through the valley of the shadow of death, but we know that we will not walk that valley alone. Our blessed Lord will walk that valley with us. A heavenly escort always accompanies the believer's death. Today, rejoice that the Lord is always with you and will be with you even till the end.

March 6

Mark 16:15, "And he said unto them, Go ye into all the world, and preach the gospel to every creature."

ON THIS DAY in 1981, Walter Cronkite signed off for the last time as principal anchorman of CBS news. Cronkite's career began with him writing for the Houston Press and included work as a war correspondent, reporting at the Nuremberg Trials, and he covered the first televised presidential convention. He was hired in 1950 by Columbia Broadcasting System (CBS) to develop the news department for its television station in Washington, D.C. It was not long before he was appearing on nationally telecast public affairs programs. He served as anchor of the "CBS Evening News with Walter Cronkite" from 1962 to 1981. He developed a reputation as "the most trusted journalist in the United States."

As believers, we are in the "news" business and the "good news" business. When Jesus returned to heaven He made every believer heavenly anchormen to inform the public of the good news that Christ had died for the sins of the world and that salvation is available to all. His plan is that the whole world will know what He has done for them, and believers are His means of getting that news out. When so much of the evening news is about tragedies, political scandals, and world problems, it should motivate us to let the world know there is good news. We may not be able to have millions tune in nightly to hear our news, but the neighbor next door, the friend at work, and the family up the street need to know about this good news. Today, ask the Lord to give you an opportunity to tell someone the "good news" and may we keep on telling it until it is time to "sign off."

March 7

Romans 8:28, "And we know that all things work together for good to them that love God, to them who are the called according to his purpose."

ON THIS DAY in 1876, Alexander Graham Bell received a patent for the telephone. He was born in Edinburgh, Scotland and from the age of eighteen, Bell worked on the idea of transmitting speech. Bell's telephone actually came about as the result of an accident. Bell had built an experimental telegraph that began to function strangely one day because a part had come loose. The accident gave Bell understanding in how voices could be transmitted over wires. He constructed his phone, a transmitter and receiver, and had it patented. His experiments were successful when the first complete sentence was transmitted, "Watson, come here; I want you."

Many a blessing has come from what appeared to be a tragedy. What first appeared to be an accident was later realized to be God's appointment. God has a way of taking the negative and making it positive. God is in charge of our life, and nothing comes our way that He does not allow or arrange—even the bad things. In His loving plan for our life He takes all things, including the bad, and sees to it that they work for our good. Handley C.G. Moule said, "There is no situation so chaotic that God cannot from that situation create something that is surpassingly good. He did it at the creation. He did it at the cross. He is doing it today." Today give thanks for God's promise that even the bad things turn out for our good.

March 8

Revelation 21:10, "And he carried me away in the spirit to a great and high mountain, and shewed me that great city, the holy Jerusalem, descending out of heaven from God."

ON THIS DAY in 1977, the Eisenhower Tunnel in Colorado was opened. Originally called the Straight Creek Tunnel but renamed in 1972 in honor of President Dwight D. Eisenhower, it is the highest tunnel in the world and the longest in the U.S. It took six years to complete the westbound side and four to complete the eastbound side. One million cubic yards of material were cleared and 190,000 cubic yards of concrete were used for each tunnel lining. 1,140 persons were employed in three shifts working twenty-four hours a day, six days a week. Each tunnel has 2,000 light fixtures with eight-foot bulbs in each. The utility bill is about $70,000 a month. The cost of construction was $108 million.

One can only imagine what the cost of constructing the heavenly city would be. It would be difficult to estimate the cost of building a city in which streets are paved with pure gold, gates made of pearl, walls made of jasper, and the foundations are garnished with all manner of precious stones. Then when you realize that the size of the city is 15,000 times the size of London, ten times bigger than Germany it would be almost impossible to determine a construction cost. Can you imagine what the utility bill would be for such a place? We may never be able to determine a cost for building such a city but we do know the cost for living there. It cost the Lord Jesus His life. Today give thanks that Christ loved you enough to die for your sins, and on top of that, is building you a new home to live in one day.

March 9

Acts 11:26, "And when he had found him, he brought him unto Antioch. And it came to pass, that a whole year they assembled themselves with the church, and taught much people. And the disciples were called Christians first in Antioch."

ON THIS DAY in 1959, the Barbie Doll debute at the American Toy Fair in New York City. In its first year on the market Barbie set new sales records selling over 357,000 at three dollars each. Since 1959 more than one billion have been sold, making the Barbie product line the most successful in the history of the toy industry. Today the Barbie Doll sells at a rate of two dolls every second and is sold in more than 150 countries. The creator of Barbie was Ruth Handler who named the doll in honor of her daughter, Barbie.

As Christians, we are honored with a name that has been given to us because of our relationship with the Lord Jesus Christ. The name was originally given to the disciples at Antioch as a term of contempt. Yet, no greater honor could have been bestowed upon the early church than to be called Christians, i.e. a follower of Jesus Christ. What an honor to be called a Christian. We should never be embarrassed when asked if we are Christians nor if someone calls us a Christian. It is a badge of honor. It is a wonderful privilege to be associated with the Lord Jesus Christ. Today give thanks that you are a "Christian" and ask God to help you to do nothing that would bring shame or harm to the name. Oh, by the way, in 1961 Ruth Handler introduced a male doll—named after her son Ken.

March 10

Joshua 24:15, "And if it seem evil unto you to serve the Lord, choose you this day whom ye will serve; whether the gods which your fathers served that were on the other side of the flood, or the gods of the Amorites, in whose land ye dwell: but as for me and my house, we will serve the Lord."

ON THIS DAY in 1971, the U.S. Senate approved the 26th amendment lowering the voting age to eighteen. Section one of the amendment reads, "The right of citizens of the United States, who are 18 years of age or older, to vote shall not be denied or abridged by the United States or by any state on account of age." Originally in the U.S. voting privileges were restricted to white men who met certain property qualifications. The 14th (1868) and 15th (1870) amendments forbid the disenfranchisement of African-American men, and the 19th (1920) amendment had conferred the right to women. Prior to the 70's, the voting age had been twenty-one although Georgia, Kentucky, Alaska, and Hawaii had lower age limits.

The ability to vote by the people of a nation is a privilege. It is a process by which a people choose the leaders of their government along with many other matters that affect their lives. Yet the most important choice that a person can make is not national but spiritual. Joshua called for the people to make a choice. The choice involved whom they would serve—false gods or the true God. It is a choice that we make each day of our life and not just once every four years. Today, say with Joshua, "*As for me and my house, we will serve the Lord.*" It is a choice that you do not have to wait until you're eighteen to make.

March 11

John 14:3, "And if I go and prepare a place for you, I will come again, and receive you unto myself; that where I am, there ye may be also."

ON THIS DAY in 1942 General Douglas MacArthur vowed to the people of the Philippines, "I shall return." After the bombing of Pearl Harbor and the American air bases in the Philippines, General MacArthur commanded the defense of the Philippines. Ordered by President Roosevelt to Australia to take command of the Allied Forces in the Southwest Pacific, he left the Philippines promising, "I came through—and I shall return." He did keep his promise, returning October 20, 1944.

As the Lord Jesus prepared His disciples for His death and leaving, He gave them the promise that He would return. When He will return is uncertain. Jesus said, *"But of that day and hour knoweth no man, no, not the angels of heaven, but my Father only"* (Matt. 24:36). But we can be certain it is a promise that He will keep. It has been said that there are 1,845 references to His coming in the Old Testament and a total of seventeen Old Testament books that give it prominence. Of the 260 chapters in the entire New Testament, there are 318 references to the Second Coming or one out of thirty verses. Twenty-three of the twenty-seven New Testament books refer to this great event. For every prophecy on the First Coming of Christ, there are eight on Christ's Second Coming. The return of Jesus Christ is a great subject of the Bible and will be a great event for the believer. Today, look up, for He may come today. He promises He will return, and He shall.

March 12

Revelation 22:12, "And, behold, I come quickly; and my reward is with me, to give every man according as his work shall be."

ON THIS DAY in 1904, Andrew Carnegie established the Carnegie Hero Fund Commission. The fund was established to recognize extraordinary heroism in the United States and Canada. For some time Carnegie had held the idea that ordinary citizens who performed extraordinary acts of heroism should be recognized. After an explosion at Harwick, Pennsylvania that claimed 181 lives, including two who had entered the mine in ill-fated rescue attempts, Carnegie set aside $5 million under the care of a commission to recognize "civilizations heroes" and to provide financial assistance for those disabled and the dependents of those killed. Since the establishment of the fund, 8,446 have received the bronze Carnegie Medal and $24.5 million has been given in grants, scholarship aid, and financial assistance.

Only a few in life will earn hero status and be rewarded for their heroism, but every Christian can earn a reward for their work and service to others. The Lord's promise is that when He returns He will reward every man according to his work. Paul declared, "*If any man's work abide which he hath built thereupon, he shall receive a reward*" (1 Cor. 3:14). A life that is invested in the Lord's work and in service to others will not go without reward. We are in the business of saving lives by telling others that Jesus saves. There may not be an earthly commission to honor such service, but there will be a rewarding day in heaven. Today, become a future medal honoree by serving the Lord and investing your life in helping others.

March 13

Ephesians 2:14, "For he is our peace, who hath made both one, and hath broken down the middle wall of partition between us."

ON *THIS* DAY in 1904, the "Christ of the Andes" was dedicated. Located in Uspallata Pass, high in the Andes, the "Christ of the Andes" is a statute of Christ commemorating a series of peace and boundary treaties between Argentina and Chile. The twenty-six foot statute holds out its right hand in blessing over the disputed nations that for years have quarreled about boundaries. The left hand clings to a cross, and under the feet is the western hemisphere. Sitting on a base of granite and fashioned from the very cannons that once were used to strike terror into the hearts of the Chileans, it stands at the point where the two countries meet, a symbol of peace. One plaque at its base reads, "He is our peace, Who hath made us one." At the dedication ceremony, the statue was presented to the world as a sign of the victory of good will.

The One who said to the waves "*peace, be still*"(Mk. 4:39), said to the woman with the issue of blood, "*go in peace*" (Mk. 5:34), stood in the midst of the troubled disciples and said, "*Peace be unto you*" (Lke. 24:36) is the "*Prince of Peace*" (Isa. 9:6). Real peace can be found in Christ alone. This world we live in is often absent of peace, but for those who have met the "Christ of the Ages," they have found a peace that only Christ can give or bring. He is more than a statue commemorating peace; He is a blessed person living in our hearts who says, "*My peace I give unto you*" (John 14:27). Today, give thanks that you personally know the Peacemaker.

March 14

Ezekiel 22:30, "And I sought for a man among them, that should make up the hedge, and stand in the gap before me for the land, that I should not destroy it: but I found none."

ON THIS DAY in 1950, the FBI's "Ten Most Wanted" fugitives program began. In late 1939 a reporter for the International News Service (now UPI) asked the FBI for names and descriptions of the "toughest guys" the FBI would like the capture. The names and descriptions were run in the newspaper, and there was so much appeal that J. Edgar Hoover implemented the program. The names on the list come from nominees from the fifty-six Field Offices of the FBI and are reviewed and selected by Special Agents of the Criminal Investigative Division. Final approval comes from the FBI's Deputy Director. As of December 2000, there have been 460 fugitives listed on the "Ten Most Wanted."

God has a couple of "Wanted" lists. There is His list of every unsaved person. God wants each unsaved person to come to Him and be saved. He also has His wanted list which includes the names of every believer. He wants them for His service to help Him seek those that are unsaved. Sadly, there are some who flee God's call as much as a fugitive flees the law. The best day of a person's life will be when he or she quits running and turns himself or herself in to the Divine "Authority." God wants you to serve Him and glorify Him in your life. Today, if you haven't already done so, give your life to God. You are on God's "Wanted List." He wants to use you. May it not have to be said by God, "*I found none.*"

March 15

Romans 3:25, "Whom God hath set forth to be a propitiation through faith in his blood, to declare his righteousness for the remission of sins that are past, through the forbearance of God."

On *This* Day in 1937, Bernard Fantus established the first blood bank. Director of therapeutics at Cook County Hospital in Chicago, Fantus found that blood treated with a 2% solution of Sodium Citrate would not clot and so could be stored in refrigerators. In creating a hospital laboratory that could preserve and store donor blood, Fantus originated the term "blood bank." Within a few years blood banks were established across the U.S. Some of the earliest were in San Francisco, New York, Miami, and Cincinnati. Today the Red Cross and other organizations collect more than 11 million units of blood a year.

The greatest "blood donor" was the Lord Jesus Christ. The Bible states that, "*Without the shedding*" of his "*blood is no remission*" or forgiveness of sin (Heb. 9:22). The Lord Jesus gave His life that we might have eternal life. Peter tells us that we, "*were not redeemed with corruptible things, as silver and gold, from your vain conversation received by tradition from your fathers; But with the precious blood of Christ, as of a lamb without blemish and without spot:* (1 Peter 1:18-19). There are many who owe their physical life to blood donors, but every believer owes their spiritual life to Christ who died and shed His blood. Our salvation rests in our "*faith in His blood.*" Today, thank the Lord that He loved you enough to shed His blood for you and that you have been to Heaven's blood bank—Calvary!

March 16

1 John 1:9, "If we confess our sins, he is faithful and just to forgive us our sins, and to cleanse us from all unrighteousness."

ON THIS DAY in 1850, Nathaniel Hawthorne's *Scarlet Letter* was first published. Born in Salem, Massachusetts, Hawthorne changed his name from Hawthorne because of an uncle's role in the Salem Witch Trials. For twelve years he lived in seclusion with his mother and devoted his life to writing. His novel, *Scarlet Letter* brought him success and fame as a writer. It is the story of a woman, Hester Prynne and the Rev. Dimmersdale, who fall in love, commit adultery, and Prynne becomes pregnant. The town shuns her and her punishment was to wear the letter "A" on her breast for all to see. The Rev. Dimmersdale hid his sin for sometime, but his guilt and shame became more than he could bear. He confessed his sin shortly before he died.

While only a novel, real life is not without the stories of those who fall into sin. Many wear a scarlet letter upon their heart for the guilt and shame of their sin. David confessed, "*my sin is ever before me*" (Psalm 51:3). Like the Rev. Dimmersdale, he tried to cover his sin, but he knew what he had done. Night and day, day and night, his sin haunted him. The answer to sin is not covering it, but confessing it. The promise of God is that if we confront our sin and confess our sin, God will forgive and cleanse us of sin. The sin we cover, God will uncover, but the sin we uncover, God will cover. We all fail the Lord, but when we do we should not attempt to hide the sin nor should we live under a load of guilt. Today give thanks that God is merciful and will forgive our sins. Trade your guilt in for His grace.

March 17

Titus 3:2, "To speak evil of no man, to be no brawlers, but gentle, shewing all meekness unto all men."

On This Day in 1906, President Theodore Roosevelt coined the name "muckrakers". Roosevelt had a talent for lively speech, and when angered he quickly let it be known how he felt. In a speech he lashed out at a group of journalists who had been investigating corruption in business and politics. Roosevelt agreed with many of the charges but felt they had gone too far and called them "muckrakers". He compared them to a character in Bunyan's *Pilgrim's Progress* who could look no way but downward with a "muckrake" in his hand and was interested in raking only the filth. The journalists, instead of being angry with the president accepted the name with pride.

Unfortunately there are "muckrakers" found in the Church. The greatest joy for some is digging up dirt on someone or always raking the filth. There is always one who you can find who always knows "the low-down" on everybody else. Paul's admonition was to speak evil of no man. Paul told the believers at Ephesus to put away "evil speaking" (Eph. 4:31). Someone gave wise advice when they said: "If you can't say something good about someone, don't say anything." It should never bring pleasure to the heart of the believer to hear something bad or negative about someone else. If we hear bad news about someone and it does not grieve us we need to examine our own hearts. James reminds us that the tongue, even though it is a little member, can stir up a destructive fire (James 3:5). Today, make your goal to speak only well of others. Remember, "muckrakers" are always raking in the filth. Who wants to be in such a nasty business?

March 18

Mark 4:37, "And there arose a great storm of wind, and the waves beat into the ship, so that it was now full."

ON THIS DAY in 1925, the worst tornado in U.S. history swept through three states. Known as the "Tri-State Tornado," it tore across Southeast Missouri, Southern Illinois, and Southwest Indiana. At an average speed of sixty-two mph, with winds that reached in excess of 300 mph, it left a 219 mile path that averaged one half mile in width. Lasting three and a half hours, 164 square miles were devastated, and 15,000 homes were destroyed. Damages amounted to seventeen million dollars; there were 2,027 injuries and 695 deaths—a record for a single tornado. In Murphysboro, Illinois, 234 deaths were recorded, a record for a single community from such a disaster.

There was a night when the disciples found themselves in a terrible storm. Their tiny ship was being tossed about by the wind and waves and was in danger of capsizing. Yet, the Master of the wind was aboard, and when they cried out to Him, He simply spoke the words, "Peace be still," and the angry sea lay down like whimpering puppies at His feet (Mark 4:39). There are times when we find ourselves in a storm. A report from the doctor, a knock at the door, or a phone call is all it takes to turn our calm seas into a raging storm. Yet, the believer is never without the presence of the Lord Jesus in the storm. The disciples asked, "*Master, carest not that we perish?*" (Mark 4:38) We never have to ask if He cares. We are assured of His care! Maybe you are going through a storm in your life right now. Perhaps your boat is full. Today, if you are in a storm, never forget that the Master of the sea sails with you, and He cares. He is able to calm the stormy seas of life.

March 19

2 Samuel 12:14, "Howbeit, because by this deed thou hast given great occasion to the enemies of the Lord to blaspheme, the child also that is born unto thee shall surely die."

ON THIS DAY in 1987, Jim Bakker resigned as head of PTL (Praise the Lord) after admitting to a sexual liaison with church secretary Jessica Hahn. Bakker had built PTL to a $129 million nationwide TV ministry with tens of millions of viewers. He had also built Heritage USA, which was then the third most popular theme park in America. Three years later Bakker was imprisoned on twenty-four counts of fraud for milking followers out of $158 million spent on oversold time-share apartments at Heritage USA. He would serve five years in prison. After his release he wrote his autobiography entitled *I Was Wrong.*

When Nathan the prophet confronted David for his sin of adultery with Bathsheba he reminded the leader of Israel that he had not only sinned against God but by his actions had given the enemies of the Lord an opportunity to scorn the name of the Lord. It is said that on one occasion Mahatma Ghandi said, "I would be a Christian if it were not for other Christians." There are many who are going to hell because of those who are going to heaven. The poor testimony and sins of some believers have often been the cause for some to frown on Christianity. No doubt you have heard someone give the argument that the reason they don't go to church is because of all the hypocrites. As a believer we can never take how we live lightly. Our practice must always match our profession. Today, ask God to help you walk worthy of your vocation (Eph. 4:1). There is always someone watching how we live.

March 20

1 Peter 1:25, "But the word of the Lord endureth for ever. And this is the word which by the gospel is preached unto you."

On This Day in 1852, Harriet Beecher Stowe's book *Uncle Tom's Cabin* was first published. Stowe wrote at least ten novels, but none which had the impact of *Uncle Tom's Cabin*. Sales were unprecedented; 500,000 were sold in the United States alone within five years, and it was translated into more than twenty foreign languages. The book focused public interest on the issue of slavery and did much to crystallize militant anti-slavery sentiment in the North, and therefore became an important factor in precipitating the Civil War. When she met President Lincoln, he greeted her as "the little lady who made this big war."

No book has touched more lives nor had greater impact on the world than the Bible—God's Word. A.T. Pierson said, "While other books inform, and some reform, this one book transforms." A.W. Pink said, ""God has given us His word that under its guidance we may regulate our beliefs, renovate our hearts, and reform our lives." While *Uncle Tom's Cabin* told of slavery, the Bible tells how men can be set free from the slavery of sin and Satan. It is indeed a life-transforming book. It is inspired. Its truths are life giving. Its promises are reliable. It is more than a collection of writings by various authors or a book of poetry and Hebrew history. It is the WORD OF GOD! Today, as you read the Bible take a moment to think of it as God's Word. As you read let God speak to you through His Word. If you do so you will never be the same.

March 21

James 3:16, "For where envying and strife is, there is confusion and every evil work."

ON THIS DAY in 1891, a Hatfield married a McCoy bringing to an end the long feud that had existed between the two families. The Tug Fork of the Big Sandy River divided the two families; the Hatfields on the West Virginia side and the McCoys on the Kentucky side. The feud lasted for nearly twelve years and cost twelve lives. The feud began in the fall of 1878 when Randolph (Ranel) McCoy accused Floyd Hatfield of his stealing his hog. McCoy took his complaint to the local judge, but when the court ruled against him bad feelings festered, and the hostilities reached a peak four years later when Ellison Hatfield was attacked and killed in 1882 by three of the McCoys.

The Bible speaks of the "confusion" (disorder) and "evil work" that envy and strife often cause. Families, friends, and even churches have been divided over some cause, and the words and deeds that have resulted have been far short of Christ-like. A heart which is full of anger and revenge is often vented through bitter words and cruel deeds. Years are often required for healing. Regardless of what the cause, we must always weigh the outcome against the desire to get even. Is it really worth it? The testimonies that are ruined and the relationships that are broken are never worth it. A heart full of bitterness and anger are never worth the joy and blessings that are lost. Today, ask God to help you to keep your heart clean of anger, bitterness, and a desire for revenge.

March 22

1 Peter 2:2, "As newborn babes, desire the sincere milk of the word, that ye may grow thereby."

ON THIS DAY in 1989, President George Bush vowed to never eat Broccoli again. At a news conference, the President upset the nations broccoli farmers of the United States when he said, "I do not like broccoli…I'm the president of the United States and I'm not going to eat anymore broccoli." The question of the president's dislike of broccoli arose after a report revealed that Bush had banned the vegetable from meals on the presidential plane. The California Broccoli Shippers Association protested by sending boxes of broccoli to the White House along with some gourmet recipes.

You may be like the president and hate broccoli. But whether you like broccoli or not, as believers, we should all have a love and hunger for God's Word. Peter speaks of having a spiritual appetite for God's Word. He describes our hunger for God's Word as essential to our spiritual growth. If you don't like broccoli, you can eat something else, but eat you must. Feeding ourselves is essential to growth and the sustaining of our physical life. There is a period of time that one can go without eating, but in time death is certain if we do not eat. We must feed on God's Word to keep our spiritual life healthy. Why do some believers not grow spiritually? Why are some Christian's spiritually weak? It is due to a lack of feeding from God's Word. Today, eat a good meal from God's Word. It is essential that you take time in God's Word each day of your life. That's what this book is all about.

March 23

Matthew 20:6, "And about the eleventh hour he went out, and found others standing idle, and saith unto them, Why stand ye here all the day idle?"

On This Day in 1775, Patrick Henry uttered his famous statement, "Give me liberty or give me death." Henry, a living symbol of the American struggle for liberty and self-government, speaking at the St. John's Church in Richmond, Virginia where the legislature was meeting at the time, urged his fellow Virginians to arm in self-defense. He challenged the delegation, "Why stand we here idle? What is it that gentlemen wish? What would they have? Is life so dear, or peace so sweet, as to be purchased at the price of chains and slavery? Forbid it, Almighty God! I know not what course others may take; but as for me, give me liberty or give me death!"

The Lord Jesus gave a parable of a master who hired laborers to work in his vineyard. His search for workers took him to the marketplace, and he found some standing around idle. He asked, "Why stand ye here idle?" (Matt. 20:6). Their answer: "No one has hired us" (Matt. 20:7). There is a great work to be done by the Christian. There is work to be done in the Father's vineyard. There are many who are unsaved, and the time is short to reach them. Sadly, there are many who are idle. There is none who can say, "We haven't been hired," for every believer has been placed in heavenly employment. Every believer is to be a worker in God's vineyard. Today, if you haven't already done so, go to work for God. He promises that at the end of the day, each worker will be paid for his or her labor. You can be sure that His pay is out of this world!

March 24

2 Timothy 2:4, "No man that warreth entangleth himself with the affairs of this life; that he may please him who hath chosen him to be a soldier."

ON THIS DAY in 1958, pop and movie idol, Elvis Presley traded in his rock and roll crown for a set of army fatigues. Presley, age twenty-three, reported to Local Draft Board Eighty-six in Memphis, arriving in the drizzling rain at 6:35 a.m., accompanied by his parents and manager. He was met by hordes of press as well as a throng of young teenagers who were distraught over losing their pop star and movie idol to the armed forces for the next two years. Now just US 53310761 rather than a star, Presley's earnings plummeted from more than $100,000 a year to next to nothing. Presley said, "I'm looking forward to serving in the army. I think it will be a great experience for me."

Paul, when writing to Timothy, spoke of believers as being soldiers. When we were saved we traded in the garments of the old life for heavenly fatigues in God's army. As a spiritual soldier we are now under the orders of our Heavenly Commander. We march under the flag of a heavenly country. Our weapons are not carnal but mighty through God (2 Cor. 10:4). Our fight is against evil principalities and powers, against the rulers of the darkness of this world, against spiritual wickedness in high places (Eph. 6:12). Our induction is for the rest of our lives, not just for a couple of years. Our ultimate objective is to be a good soldier and to please the One who has chosen us to be a soldier. Today, if you haven't done so already, report in as a soldier of Jesus Christ. Get your marching orders for the day. Fight the good fight of faith. All who have done so have found it to be a great experience. Oh, by the way, let me remind you once again that the pay is out of this world.

March 25

Amos 4:11, "I have overthrown some of you, as God overthrew Sodom and Gomorrah, and ye were as a firebrand plucked out of the burning: yet have ye not returned unto me, saith the Lord."

ON THIS DAY in 1911, the Triangle Shirtwaist Company factory in New York City caught fire. Five minutes before quitting time a young woman yelled, "Fire." Beginning on the eighth floor, a smoldering fire in a bin of fabric burst into flames. Within minutes the finished clothes overhead caught fire and sent flames spreading quickly through the building. Panic set in as hundreds of women tried to escape. Many jumped to their death. In an effort to save people, three male employees on the eighth floor made a human chain of their bodies and swung across a narrow alleyway to a building on the opposite side of the street, forming a human bridge for people to cross. So many crowded onto the human bridge the weight on the center man broke his back and he fell to the ground along with those trying to cross over him. The other two men lost their holds on the windowsills and fell to their deaths. A total of 146 lives were lost in the fire.

The prophet Amos spoke of those who were plucked from the burning. Thank God someone cared enough and became a bridge to save us from the fires of eternal hell. We owe our salvation to the Lord Jesus, yet we owe a great debt to those who preached the gospel and told us about Jesus. When we were in danger of an eternity in hell lost without God, they became a human bridge by which we were plucked from the burning. Today, be a bridge for someone to be saved from an eternal hell. We may not be able to save everyone, but we want to save as many as we can.

March 26

1 John 2:14, "I have written unto you, fathers, because ye have known him that is from the beginning. I have written unto you, young men, because ye are strong, and the word of God abideth in you, and ye have overcome the wicked one."

On This Day in 1937, the Spinach growers of Crystal City, Texas erected a statue to Popeye. By the 1930's, the city had gained the reputation for being the "Spinach Capital of the World." In 1936 the first annual spinach festival was held and the following year the statue of Popeye was erected across from the city hall in the city square. The cartoon sailor man, who gains his strength from eating spinach, was created by the Fleischer brothers in the 1930's.

Spiritual growth is an important part of our life in Christ. One of the complaints Paul had concerning the Corinthians was they had remained as babes in Christ (1 Cor. 3:1). John spoke of believers as being "little children" (1 John 2:13) and then as "young men" with the believers ultimately becoming "fathers." He describes stages of physical growth to illustrate the place of spiritual growth. One of the characteristics of spiritual growth is growing spiritually strong. Spiritual strength is needed to be able to stand against the attacks of the devil (Eph. 6:11), to stand fast in the faith (1 Cor. 16:13), and to stand fast in the will of God (Col. 4:12). Believers do not have to eat spinach to become spiritually strong, but they do have to have an appetite for the Word of God. A daily diet of God's Word builds our spiritual muscles so that we are strong in the Lord. Today, take the time to read and meditate in God's Word. You can't afford to skip one single "meal." If you want to be spiritually strong, it is essential.

March 27

Luke 8:18, "Take heed therefore how ye hear: for whosoever hath, to him shall be given; and whosoever hath not, from him shall be taken even that which he seemeth to have."

On This Day in 1977, the worst disaster in air travel occurred. KLM flight 4805 from Amsterdam with 248 passengers and Pan Am flight 736 from Los Angeles and New York with 396 passengers had been ordered to backtrack down the runway. KLM 4805 had been instructed to go to the end of the runway and to make a 180-degree turn. Pan AM 736 had been instructed to the third taxiway to the left. Then a series of mistakes occurred. Pan Am 736 proceeded to the fourth taxiway. Because of the heavy fog, the control tower did not know that the Pan Am jet was still on the runway. The other mistake was a misunderstanding by the KLM pilot. He had apparently failed to hear the controller's instruction to standby and began an unauthorized takeoff. Seconds later the two planes collided. Only 61 of the combined 644 passengers survived.

Jesus gave instructions to take heed how we hear. Listening to God and His word is important to each believer. Many have failed to hear His word, and the end result of not listening to God always leads to spiritual disaster. Jesus also said that it was not only important how we hear but what we hear: "*And he said unto them, Take heed what ye hear*" (Mark 4:24). When God tells us to "standby" it is essential that we listen. When making important decisions, only when God gives us "clearance" should we move. Today, take heed how you hear and what you hear. Listen closely to what God says. It can prevent a spiritual tragedy in your life.

March 28

Psalm 58:11, "So that a man shall say, Verily there is a reward for the righteous: verily he is a God that judgeth in the earth."

ON THIS DAY in 1990, President George Bush posthumously awarded Jesse Owens the Congressional Gold Medal. During Owens' collegiate days at Ohio State University, Owens broke several world records in track and field. In 1936 he participated in the Olympics which were held in Nazi Germany. Known to many as the "Hitler Olympics," Hitler sought to prove to the world that the German "Aryan" people were the dominant race. Owens was triumphant in the 100-meter dash, the 200-meter dash and the broad jump. He was also a key member of the 400-meter relay team that won the gold medal. In all but one of these events he set Olympic records and had the German fans cheering for him. He died on March 31, 1980 from cancer, and ten years later was awarded the nations highest expression of national appreciation for distinguished achievements and contributions.

When this life is over the believer who lives for God and serves God faithfully is promised a reward. One of the things that encouraged the heart of the Psalmist was that there was a reward for the righteous. The believer does not have to participate in the Olympics or thrill a crowd with their achievements to win a heavenly reward. All that is required to receive a heavenly reward is to live a life that pleases God. During his college days, just prior to a broad jump, Jesse put a handkerchief at twenty-six feet two and a half inches, the distance of the world record and then shattered the old world record by nearly six inches. Today, make it your goal that a heavenly reward will be yours. The righteous will be rewarded!

March 29

Genesis 26:18, "And Isaac digged again the wells of water, which they had digged in the days of Abraham his father; for the philistines had stopped them after the death of Abraham: and he called their names after the names by which his father had called them."

ON THIS DAY in 1848, the Niagara Falls stopped flowing for thirty hours due to an ice jam. With a width of 3,600 feet and a height of 180 feet, more than 5 billion gallons of water flow over the edge of the falls per hour or 35 million gallons of water per minute. The massive volume of water that flows over the Horseshoe Falls gives it, its green color. About half of the water is diverted for electric power by the United States and Canada, making Niagara Falls the largest producer of electric power in the world. The water that flows over the falls comes from four of the five Great Lakes. Niagara Falls attracts millions of visitors per year and is the "honeymoon capital" of the world.

Once in a while the believer finds something "blocking the flow" in their life. Isaac found the wells that had been dug by Abraham blocked. The Philistines had filled the wells, stopping them from flowing. If we are not careful and watchful, debris in our life can build up and stop the flow of God's blessings in our life. What had been a wonderful flow of power and blessings is blocked and cut off in our life. Like Isaac, we have to clean out what has blocked the flow so that once again we can enjoy God's blessings. Sin has to be confessed and cleansed. Today, if something is blocking the flow of God's blessings in your life, confess it to God and ask for His forgiveness. Once again you can enjoy the flow of God's blessings. Always keep a spiritual shovel near to keep the well open.

March 30

Hebrews 12:15, "Looking diligently lest any man fail of the grace of God; lest any root of bitterness springing up trouble you, and thereby many be defiled."

ON THIS DAY in 1984, Gaeton Dugas, known as "Patient Zero" died of AIDS. In the late 1970's and early 1980's, American doctors began noticing that some of their homosexual patients were developing a disease that attacked the immune system. Epidemiologists with the U.S. Center for Disease Control in Atlanta, Georgia began searching for the causes and the source of the disease. In early efforts to track the disease, attention was drawn to Dugas, a homosexual Air Canada flight attendant. He was nicknamed "Patient Zero" and became the first person to be recognized as a major transmitter of AIDS. He was reported to have had 250 sexual partners a year as he traveled across the country. He died at the age of thirty-two.

We often forget that our sins affect others. The writer of Hebrews spoke of the sin of bitterness and how its presence in a life affects others. Would you not agree that Adam and Eve's sin affected more than just them? Just ask the children who carry a life-long scar in their heart because they came from a home broken by sin. Just ask the members of a church who were crushed when it was revealed that a pastor had committed a moral indiscretion. Sin always affects one personally, but unfortunately sin often also affects others. As a parent, we should view our sin in light of our children. As a church leader, we should view sin in light of those who follow us. Do you want to crush their dreams and break their hearts? Today, look at sin not only as something that will affect you but also something that will affect others.

March 31

Romans 8:16, "The Spirit itself beareth witness with our spirit, that we are the children of God."

ON THIS DAY in 1987, the biological mother of "Baby M" was denied custody and all rights to her child. In the controversial "Baby M" surrogate case, a judge gave custody to "Baby M's" biological father, William Stern, and his wife Elizabeth, a pediatrician. Mary Beth Whitehead had been promised a fee of $10,000 to bear a child for Mrs. Stern who had multiple sclerosis and had been advised that a pregnancy would worsen her condition. After giving birth to the child, Whitehead reneged on the surrogate contract refusing to give up the baby. She fled to Florida taking the baby with her. The Stern's hired a private investigator to find her and then sued for custody of the child.

One of the blessings of being a Christian is that we are the children of God: "*But as many as received him, to them gave he power to become the sons of God, even to them that believe on his name*" (John 1:12). God is our Father and we are His sons. What a privilege to be called God's child. John declared, "*Behold, what manner of love the Father hath bestowed upon us, that we should be called the sons of God*" (1 John 3:1). The earthly relationships of some children may involve a custody battle, but our relationship to God is settled for eternity. We never have to worry about being separated from Him. Instead of an attorney fighting to take us away from God, we have a heavenly advocate who assures us that we are God's throughout eternity. Today, rejoice that you are a child of God. You are His child and that will never be in dispute. No one can pluck you out of his hand (John 10:28).

April 1

2 Corinthians 5:2, "For in this we groan, earnestly desiring to be clothed upon with our house which is from heaven."

On This Day in 1973, John Lennon and his wife, Yoko announced the birth of a new country. Following a decision by the Immigration and Naturalization Service ordering Lennon to leave the United States because of a 1986 conviction in England for the possession of hashish, Lennon said at a press conference, "We announce the birth of a conceptual country, NUTOPIA." Reading from a prepared statement Lennon continued, "Citizenship of the country can be obtained by declaration of your awareness of Nutopia." He described it as a country in which there were no laws, no land, no boundaries, and no passports, only people. Its national anthem was silence and its flag was Kleenex tissue of which "you can blow your nose in it."

The believer is looking forward to a land that is more than a concept. It is a land that is more than wishful thinking and one's imagination. It is a glorious reality. You could say it is a land out of this world. Citizenship is open to anyone, yet it takes more than awareness. To become a citizen a person must accept Christ as their Lord and Saviour. The national anthem will not be silence but the "Hallelujah Chorus." Throughout the land will be heard praise of its citizens as they praise the One who made it all possible. The flag of the land is inscribed with the words, "His banner over me is love" (Song of Solomon 2:4). No, it is not a dream but a land that one day will become the home of every believer. Today, give thanks that you have a home in heaven. The longer we live in this world, the more we look forward to living in the next.

April 2

John 12:32, "And I, if I be lifted up from the earth, will draw all men unto me."

ON THIS DAY in 1931, a teenage girl struck out Babe Ruth and Lou Gehrig back to back. Joe Engel, one of the most colorful baseball promoters of all time, staged everything from elephant hunts to giving away a house to bring people into his Engel Stadium in Chattanooga, Tennessee. One of his gate attractions was seventeen year-old Jackie Mitchell pitching for his Chattanooga Lookouts, a farm team of the Senators, against the New York Yankees. Ruth waved wildly at two pitches and watched the third strike go by. Gehrig gallantly timed his three swings to miss the ball. She then walked Tony Lazzeri and left the game. The Yankees won the game 14-4.

As believers we are constantly seeking to bring people to Christ. Most have a deep desire to see the churches full. However, we do not have to resort to publicity stunts or stage unusual events to attract people. The greatest method of "Church Growth" is lifting up the Lord Jesus. Jesus said that if He were lifted up, He would draw people unto Himself. As churches we must never forget that Jesus is the One who does the drawing. Our part is to see that we do nothing to hinder His attraction. Christ must be lifted up in every church service and in every life. He must be honored, worshiped, exalted and obeyed. There is an amazing power of attraction when Jesus is Lord and is lifted up in all His glory. If we use human means to draw people, we will only get human results. If we want divine results, Christ must be lifted up. Today, lift Jesus up in all you do and everywhere you go. It's the way people are attracted to Him.

April 3

Psalm 129:8, "Neither do they which go by say, The blessing of the Lord be upon you: we bless you in the name of the Lord."

ON THIS DAY in 1962, it was argued before the Supreme Court that the reading of a nondenominational prayer in a state school violated the "establishment of religion" clause of the First Amendment. The Board of Regents for the State of New York had authorized a short, voluntary prayer for recitation at the start of each school day: "Almighty God, we acknowledge our dependence upon Thee, and beg Thy blessings upon us, our teachers, and our country." In Engel v. Vitale, it was later ruled that neither the prayer's nondenominational character nor its voluntary character saves it from unconstitutionality. The Court stated that by providing the prayer, New York officially approved religion. This was the first in a series of cases in which the Court used the establishment clause to eliminate religious activities of all sorts in public schools.

In my personal opinion, 1962 was a turning point in our nation and sent us in a direction where God has become outlawed in about every area of our public life and national life. As individuals and a nation we must acknowledge our dependence on God. We need God's blessings and should, as a needy people, beg that God's blessings be upon us. The Psalmist spoke of those who have no interest in God's blessings. As for the believer, we should have great interest in the blessings of God. Today, ask God to bless you, your church, and your nation. The highest court in the universe has ruled that such praying is acceptable.

April 4

1 Kings 19:16, "And Jehu the son of Nimshi shalt thou anoint to be king over Israel: and Elisha the son of Shaphat of Abel-meholah shalt thou anoint to be prophet in thy room."

ON THIS DAY in 1841, Vice President John Tyler ascended to the presidency because of the death of president William Henry Harrison. Under the campaign slogan "Tippecanoe and Tyler too," Harrison and his running mate, Tyler gained the first Whig nomination for president. Harrison died thirty-one days after assuming office. At his inauguration, a bitterly cold day, Harrison declined to wear a jacket or hat, made a two-hour speech, and attended three inauguration balls. Shortly thereafter, he developed pneumonia. Tyler became the first individual in U.S. history to become president through the death of a president.

The ministry of the great man of God, Elijah, was drawing to an end. Elijah was instructed by God to anoint Elisha to take his place when his ministry concluded. One great servant would go home but God had another servant to take his place. It has been said that God buries His workers, but His work goes on. Each believer of our day is God's replacements for the servants of yesterday. They served God in their own time and we that are living are their replacements. We are to take up where they left off. This is our day! This is our hour! While we honor those who are no longer with us, we must realize that in their leaving they passed the baton on to us. We are to serve God as they served God. When our race is finished, the next generation will take our place. Today, realize that what will be done for God in this day, is what will get done through us. This is our time to serve God. The dead have left the work to us.

April 5

Matthew 14:25, "And in the fourth watch of the night Jesus went unto them, walking on the sea."

ON THIS DAY in 1943, Poon Lim was rescued after 133 days drifting on a raft in the South Atlantic. Lim holds the world record as a survivor at sea alone on a life raft. The twenty-four year old seaman was a second steward on the British merchant ship Ben Lomond that was torpedoed by a Nazi U-boat on November 23, 1942. Jumping from the sinking ship, Lim swam to an eight-foot square raft made of timbers. Tied to it were some tins of British biscuits, a ten-gallon water tank, some flares, and an electric torch. As his food and water supply began to run out, he used the canvas of his life jacket to catch rain water, used a wire from the torch as a fish hook, a hemp rope as a fishing line, and a piece of biscuit as bait to catch fish. On the morning of the 133rd day, he spotted a sail on the horizon and began jumping up and down until he was seen.

At times in life we find ourselves thrust into difficult situations. The burden of those trials depletes our human resources and each day becomes a struggle for survival. Days go by and it seems that no help is in sight. The disciples found themselves in desperate conditions on the sea. All seemed hopeless, but then Jesus came walking on the water to save them. As the old song says, "Just when I need Him most," Jesus always comes to the aid of His children. Today, you may find yourself fighting to survive. Watch the horizon for the Lord's arrival. You don't have to jump up and down to get His attention, but you may do a little jumping when He shows up. When you know the Lord, help is always on the way.

April 6

Ephesians 2:8, "For by grace are ye saved through faith; and that not of yourselves: it is the gift of God."

ON THIS DAY in 1888, the Kodak camera went on sale for the first time. George Eastman, judged "not especially gifted," founded a photographic dry plate business that became the world renowned Eastman Kodak company that ranks today as a premier multinational corporation and one of the twenty-five largest companies in the United States. Eastman took the cumbersome and complicated process of picture taking and created a simple camera that was easy to use and accessible to nearly everyone. The name "Kodak" was born with the slogan, "You push the button, we do the rest."

Salvation is a simple matter and available to everyone. Salvation does not require that one achieve certain standards or accomplish certain things. The Bible is clear, "*Not of works, lest any man should boast*" (Eph. 2:9). A person can live his or her whole life doing good things but never be able to obtain salvation. It cannot be earned with the best we have to offer. A good life is commendable but insufficient to merit or earn salvation. All that is required is "faith." You could say that all one has to do is believe and God does the rest. God alone does the saving. Salvation is His work, not ours. God does not ask us to turn over a new leaf or go to work doing good deeds for others. All He asks is that we come to Him and accept Christ by faith and He does the rest. Salvation is His gift. Salvation is not a matter of DO but DONE. Today, give thanks that God has provided a salvation that is simple and accessible for all. We could have never been saved otherwise.

April 7

John 1:42, "And he brought him to Jesus. And when Jesus beheld him, he said, Thou art Simon the son of Jona: thou shalt be called Cephas, which is by interpretation, A stone."

ON THIS DAY in 1940, Booker T. Washington became the first black to appear on a U.S. postage stamp. Born a slave, Booker Taliaferro Washington went on to lead the Tuskegee Institute in Tuskegee, Alabama and gain national fame as an educator. He once told how he got his name. As a child he had always been called simply Booker. When he began school and the roll was being called, he noticed that most of the students had at least two names. When the teacher came to him and asked what his full name was, he replied, "Booker Washington," as if he had been called the name all his life. It was the name by which he would forever be known. He later learned that his mother had given him the name "Booker Taliaferro" shortly after he had been born.

Several times in the Bible,we find those who gained an additional name. For example, the Lord Jesus told Simon that he would be known as Peter. Saul, the persecutor of the church, became Paul the apostle. These name changes or additional name given to these individuals were often reflective of their new life in Christ or a turning point in their life. When we accepted the Lord Jesus as our Saviour, we gained several new names. We were in the past, sinners, but now in Christ, we are called saints, Christians, believers, to name a few. Today, gives thanks that one day you were given several additional names. They are names that tell what Jesus has done for you and all that you have in Him. They are names given to us by our Heavenly Father.

April 8

Exodus 4:10, "And Moses said unto the Lord, O my Lord, I am not eloquent, neither heretofore, nor since thou hast spoken unto thy servant: but I am slow of speech, and of a slow tongue."

ON THIS DAY in 1989, one-handed pitcher Jim Abbott made his Major League debut. Born without a right hand, Abbott bypassed the minors to the starting rotation of the California Angels after being a star for the University of Michigan. On the mound, Abbott wore a right-hander's fielder's glove over the stump at the end of his right arm. While completing his follow-through after delivering a pitch, he quickly switched the glove to his left hand so he could handle any balls hit to him. In his first game in the Major Leagues, he went 4 2/3 innings and ended the season with a 12-12 record and a 3.92 ERA. In 1991, he won 18 games for the Angels while posting a 2.89 ERA. Probably his most impressive stat, given that he could only swing with one arm, was his two hits in twenty-three career at-bats.

When the call of God came to Moses, an excuse that he offered was his speech impediment. Moses probably felt that because he could not talk plainly, it would limit him from serving God. There are times when we feel that we are inadequate to serve God. Like Moses, we come up with reasons why we would not be a good choice. Yet, the lack of an education, certain skills or talents, or even a handicap does not limit one from doing something for God. God can take anyone and do something special with his or her life. As it has been said, it is not our ability but our availability that is the key to doing something for God. Today, give what you have to God. That's all He wants anyway. You may be surprised by what He does through you.

April 9

2 Chronicles 7:14, "If my people, which are called by my name, shall humble themselves, and pray, and seek my face, and turn from their wicked ways; then will I hear from heaven, and will forgive their sin, and will heal their land."

ON THIS DAY in 1865, General Robert E. Lee surrendered to General Ulysses Grant, bringing to an end the American Civil War. It was a Sunday afternoon when the two met in the parlor of the McLean House in Appomattox, Virginia. The two shook hands and then seated themselves at a small marble topped table in the center of the room. Grant made an attempt at a friendly conversation and Lee finally interrupted him and said, "I suppose, General Grant, that the object of our present meeting is fully understood. I asked to see you to ascertain upon what terms you would receive the surrender of my army." The terms were discussed and agreed upon. As Grant's aide began to write out the formal document, he started with, "I have the honor to reply to your communication," but Lee interrupted, "Don't say 'I have the honor.' Just say, 'I accept the terms'."

We often hear about the subject of revival. One may speak on the need of revival and another on what revival will do for the church. History records revivals that changed believers, churches, and even nations. Our generation has yet to experience a revival as previous generations. Why is that? Could it be that we have not accepted the terms for revival? God's terms are that His people must humble themselves, pray and seek His face, and deal with sin in their life. These are the terms. Today, pray for revival. While you pray, say to the Lord, "I accept the terms." At least you can have revival!

April 10

Proverbs 27:1, "Boast not thyself of tomorrow; for thou knowest not what a day may bring forth."

ON THIS DAY in 1912, the *Titanic* set sail from Southampton, England for New York City on its maiden voyage. At the time the great ship was the largest and most luxurious afloat. Designed and built by William Pirrie's Belfast firm Harland and Wolff, it had a double-bottomed hull that was divided into sixteen presumably watertight compartments. Because four of these could be flooded without endangering the liner's buoyancy, it was considered unsinkable. On April 14, about 400 miles south of Newfoundland, it struck an iceberg and five of its watertight compartments were ruptured. At 2:20 a.m. on the 15th, the great liner sank to its watery grave. Approximately 1,500 lives were lost.

When the *Titanic* pulled out of Southampton, no doubt everyone aboard the "unsinkable ship" expected to arrive in New York City in a few days. Who among the more than 1,500 that perished in cold waters of the Atlantic boarded the great ship with the thought that in a few days their life would come to an end? It is true that we cannot boast of another day, for we know not what tomorrow may bring. The only moment we are assured of is this very moment. We don't know what the next hour will bring, much less a day. Because tomorrow is filled with so much uncertainty, today becomes ever so important. What we do with God and for God becomes a matter that we must consider today. We can't afford to put it off another day, for we do not know what tomorrow may bring. Today, whatever you need to do with God and for God, do it. You have today, but you can't be sure about tomorrow.

April 11

Revelation 22:17, "And the Spirit and the bride say, Come. And let him that heareth say, Come. And let him that is a thirst come. And whosoever will, let him take the water of life freely."

On This Day in 1890, President Benjamin Harrison designated Ellis Island as an immigration station. Located in New York Harbor in New York City, it officially opened in 1892. More than twelve million immigrants passed through Ellis Island between 1892 and 1954. Over 100 million Americans can trace their ancestry in the United States to a man, woman, or child whose name passed from a steamship manifest sheet to an inspector's record book in the Registry Room at Ellis Island. Each was scrutinized for disease or disability and about ninety-eight percent of immigrants were admitted to America. The station closed its door in 1954. Because of its unique historical importance, it was declared part of the Statue of Liberty National Monument in 1965 and after a six-year, $162 million renovation, it reopened to the public in 1990.

Throughout the years, millions have come through Calvary. They have come from every country and from all conditions of life. As many who came through Ellis Island to find in America a new life, all who have come through Calvary have found a new life. As many who came to America to escape an oppressive society and dictator, many have come through Calvary to be free from the power of sin and Satan. Not one that ever came to Calvary was turned away and Calvary has never shut its doors. The invitation is extended to all regardless of who they are or what they have done. Even the diseased and disabled are welcome. Today, rejoice that you have been accepted as a citizen of the kingdom of heaven.

April 12

Revelation 4:1, "After this I looked, and, behold, a door was opened in heaven: and the first voice which I heard was as it were of a trumpet talking with me; which said, Come up hither, and I will shew thee things which must be hereafter."

ON THIS DAY in 1981, the first space shuttle was launched. The space shuttle *Columbia* was launched from Cape Canaveral, Florida, becoming the first reusable manned spacecraft to travel into space. Robert L. Crippen and John W. Young piloted the shuttle. Launched by two solid-rocket boosters, the *Columbia* entered into orbit around the earth, orbiting the earth thirty-six times before touching down at California's Edward Air Force Base on April 14. To date, there have been more than 100 space shuttle flights since the inaugural flight of the *Columbia.*

One of these days the believer is going to take a space flight. As John heard the voice of the Lord saying, "Come up hither," the Lord will descend from heaven with a shout and both the living and the dead will be taking a heavenly flight and we won't even need a shuttle for the trip. We won't spend our flight orbiting the earth but will fly straight to our new home in heaven. We won't need a space suit for we will have glorified bodies. We won't need solid-rocket boosters to get off the ground for at the sound of the Lord's voice, earth's gravitational hold on the believer will be broken and we will be caught up into the air. If someone wanted to track our flight, they would not be able to do so for it will all happen in the twinkling of an eye (1 Cor. 15:52). Today, rejoice that this may be the day that we hear the Lord say, "Come up hither" and we take our heavenly flight. We don't have to be a member of NASA, just one of the Redeemed.

April 13

1 Corinthians 15:3-4, "For I delivered unto you first of all that which I also received, how that Christ died for our sins according to the scriptures; And that he was buried, and that he rose again the third day according to the scriptures."

On This Day in 1860, the Pony Express delivered its first mail. The Pony Express rider Tom Hamilton clattered into Sacramento, California, delivering forty-nine letters and three newspapers posted in St. Joseph, Missouri, eleven days earlier. Hundreds cheered as Hamilton galloped up to the post office and handed over the mail satchel. The new mail service, which involved a run of over 1,966 miles had been organized by the Central Overland Company that had bought 500 horses and advertised for "skinny, expert riders willing to risk death daily." Each horse was galloped at speed for about twelve miles before the horseman changed mounts.

Paul described himself as one who delivered wonderful news. Each believer has "good news" to deliver. It is the news that Christ has died for sinners and rose again that men might be saved. God is looking for believers that will be a part of delivering this wonderful news. He doesn't care if you are not skinny. One of the items that every Pony Express rider carried was a Bible. As believers, we are to deliver the good news of God's word to every person. Aren't you glad that one day someone delivered you the message that Jesus loved you and could save you from your sins? Why not answer God's call and become a part of getting the good news to others. Today, tell God you want to be a heavenly postman. God will put you to work today. Saddle up and deliver the good news to everyone you meet today. Did I tell you the pay is out of this world?

April 14

Proverbs 30:5, "Every word of God is pure: he is a shield unto them that put their trust in him."

ON THIS DAY in 1828, the first edition of Noah Webster's dictionary was published. His great dictionary, *An American Dictionary of the English Language*, appeared in two volumes. It included 70,000 entries, 12,000 words, and 40,000 definitions that had never before appeared in a dictionary. Webster gave a total of twenty-eight years in preparation for his dictionary. He learned twenty-six languages in order to research the origins of his country's own tongue. He traveled through all the American states to listen to what people said and how they said it. He was the first to document distinctively American vocabulary such as *skunk*, *hickory*, and *chowder*. He urged altering many words such as *musick* to *music*, *centre* to *center*, and *plough* to *plow*.

The greatest book of words ever written is the Bible. As Solomon declares, every word of the Bible is pure. It is a book without error or contradiction. Webster's dictionary has gone through revisions because words change over time. Samuel Johnson, another famous dictionary marker, once said, "No dictionary of a living tongue can ever be perfect, since while it is hastening to publication, some words are budding, and some are fading away." Dictionaries may need revising because words and languages change but the Bible will forever be perfect for it is the Word of God. The Psalmist says, "*For ever, O Lord, thy word is settled in heaven*" (Psalm 119:89). Today, take a few moments to cherish your Bible. It is the only perfect and pure book that has ever been written. It is also the most valuable book that has ever been written, for it is God's eternal word. As you read it, listen, for it is God speaking.

April 15

2 Peter 1:5, "And beside this, giving all diligence, add to your faith virtue; and to virtue knowledge;"

ON *THIS* DAY in 1970, Canon Business Machines introduced the calculator. The announcement was made in Tokyo of the Pocketronic Printing Calculator. The Pocketronic cost $150 and gave you an answer on paper tape. Even though designed for the pocket, it weighed two and one-half pounds. Jack Hilly, Jerry Merryman, and James Van Tassel of Texas Instruments had patented this "miniature electronic calculator". For the first time, people could multiply, divide, and add without using their brains.

The Christian life consists of adding, subtracting, and multiplying. Peter spoke of several things that needed to be added to the Christian life, such as virtue and knowledge. The Christian life is to be one of spiritual growth. As we grow, there will be the adding of certain things to our life. Peter also spoke of that which should be multiplied in our life: "*Grace and peace be multiplied unto you through the knowledge of God, and of Jesus our Lord*" (2 Peter 1:2). As we grow spiritually, there are certain things such as grace and peace that should not only be added but multiplied in our life. Of course, there are some things that should be subtracted such as: "*Take away all iniquity*" (Hosea 14:2). Sin, bitterness, hatred, and lying, to name a few, are things that need subtracting from our life. Today, get out your spiritual calculator and check out your adding, multiplying, and subtracting. Check to see if the numbers are correct or if you need to make some adjustments or corrections. The Bible is your calculator. Check your math by what it says.

April 16

Proverbs 14:9, "Fools make a mock at sin: but among the righteous there is favour."

ON THIS DAY in 1964, nine men were sentenced twenty-five to thirty years for Britain's "Great Train Robbery." On August 8, 1963, Ronald Biggs and twenty-nine other bandits pulled off a daring robbery of the Glasgow to London Royal Mail train and looted it of nearly $3 million. Biggs and all but one of the gang were eventually caught. Afterwards, members of the gang expressed how they felt pulling off one of the largest robberies in history. Carles Wilson said, "It wasn't worth it." His wife: "The nagging fear of discovery gave me a permanent headache." James White was "at the end of his tether" and stated that he was "glad it was all over." When Ronald Edwards surrendered, he stated that it was like living "a crazy, unnatural life." Bruce Reynolds probably summed it up best for the whole gang: "Anyone who thinks crime pays must be mad."

Solomon declared that anyone who thinks they can sin without consequences is a fool. Those who have laughed at sin and the consequences for their sin will be the first to tell you that sin never pays. David is a good example (Psalm 51). We only deceive ourselves to think that sin is without a payday. Paul spoke of the wages of sin (Roman 6:23). The word that he used for "wages" was a term that described a soldier's rations or pay. Paul defined the wages of sin as being death. In other words, sin will always bring a heavy cost. Sin will cost you far more than you wanted to pay. Sin always presents itself as that which will bring you joy, pleasure, and even wealth. But in the end, it never pays. Today, don't laugh at sin. It has a way of turning your smile into a frown.

April 17

Acts 1:14, "These all continued with one accord in prayer and supplication, with the women, and Mary the mother of Jesus, and with his brethren."

ON THIS DAY in 1492, Christopher Columbus signed a contract with Spain to find the Indies. Columbus believed that land could be reached by sailing west and was determined to realize his dream. Although repeatedly rejected, he continued seeking support for his "Enterprise of the Indies." Finally, after eight years of supplication, Ferdinand and Isabella of Spain decided to risk the enterprise. His persistence had paid off and on August 3, 1492, Columbus sailed from Palos, Spain to make his dream come true.

When it comes to prayer and getting things from God, persistence is often the key. Like the disciples gathered, we must continue in prayer and supplication until we get an answer from God. The words of Jesus, *"Ask, and it shall be given you; seek, and ye shall find; knock, and it shall be opened unto you"* (Matt. 7:7) ring with the thought of persistent praying. We are to come to God in prayer and ask Him for things. We are to seek these things from Him as we pray. We are to keep coming to God and knocking until He answers. The testimony of some dear saints is that they prayed for years before God answered their prayer. Just because we don't get an answer the day after we pray is not an indication God is not going to answer our prayer. Keep praying! Like the disciples, continue daily in prayer and supplication. Don't give up and quit bringing your petitions to God. There may be a Pentecost just around the corner. Today, as you pray, thank God for answered prayer—regardless of when that answer may come.

April 18

Matthew 27:51, " And, behold, the veil of the temple was rent in twain from the top to the bottom; and the earth did quake, and the rocks rent."

ON THIS DAY in 1906, the city of San Francisco was hit with a major earthquake. At precisely 5:12 a.m., the city experienced a quake felt from Coos Bay, Oregon to Los Angeles, to central Nevada. Called the worst disaster ever to befall a North American city, 3,000 were left dead, 250,000 were homeless, and 28,000 buildings were destroyed. Although lasting only 50 seconds, pressure that had been building up in the San Andreas Fault gave way at 12,000 times more energy than the atomic bomb that was dropped on Hiroshima.

Not all earthquakes in history are associated with devastation and death. When Jesus died, there was an earthquake that announced salvation and life. Simultaneously with the quake was the renting of the veil of the Temple from top to bottom. Matthew Henry says, "The renting of the veil signified that Christ, by his death, opened a way to God. We have an open way through Christ to the throne of grace, or mercy-seat now, and to the throne of glory hereafter." The Bible tells us in Hebrews 10:19-20, *"Having therefore, brethren, boldness to enter into the holiest by the blood of Jesus, by a new and living way, which he hath consecrated for us, through the veil, that is to say, his flesh."* The earthquake that occurred when Jesus died signified that the price for sin had been paid and a new and living way had been opened to the Father. Most earthquakes, like the San Francisco quake, usually take lives. Today, give thanks for the quake that announced that man could have life.

April 19

Philippians 4:21, "Salute every saint in Christ Jesus. The brethren which are with me greet you."

On This Day in 1909, Joan of Arc was declared a saint. Jeanne d'Arc, as she was known in France, was a simple peasant girl who became a French national heroine. She grew up as a devout Catholic and by age 13 claimed to have religious visions and heard the voice of saints. These voices persuaded her that God had chosen her to help King Charles VII of France drive the English from French soil. The English saw her as an agent of the devil and after her capture, tried her for witchcraft and on May 30, 1431, burned her at the stake. In 1456, Pope Callistus III pronounced her innocent. Pope Benedict XV beatified her in 1909, which is a preliminary step toward canonization (becoming a saint).

When it comes to the matter of being a saint, one does not have to be a national hero or heroine or be beatified or canonized. It is not a matter that is bestowed upon you by the hands of man or a church. Every person that has come to the Lord Jesus and accepted Him as his or her Lord and Saviour is a saint. Have you ever trusted Christ as your Saviour? If so, then congratulations for you are a saint! God Himself has declared you a saint. To be a saint simply means that you have been set apart as God's property and are separate from the world. A saint is one who in Christ is made holy. Understanding that we are saints motivates us to live a life that is reflective of who we are in Christ. Since we have been made holy in Christ, we should live a consecrated and holy life (See 2 Peter 3:11). Today, let your life be a reflection of who you are in Christ. You are a saint!

April 20

1 Corinthians 16:13, "Watch ye, stand fast in the faith, quit you like men, be strong."

ON THIS DAY in 1990, one teacher and twelve students were killed at Columbine High School in Jefferson County, Colorado. At 11:21 a.m., two students, Eric Harris and Dylan Klebold, walked into Columbine High School and opened fire with a semi-automatic pistol, two sawed-off shotguns, and a semi-automatic rifle. Along with the thirteen killed, twenty-three were injured. Harris and Klebold took their own life. One of the students killed was seventeen year-old Cassie Bernall. One of the killers walked up to her and asked if she believed in God. She told him she did and he shot her. Two days before she died, Cassie had a part in a church video where teens spoke of their faith: "I just try not to contradict myself, to get rid of all the hypocrisy and just live for Christ." At her funeral, attended by nearly 2,500, she was praised for the stand she took for Christ, even when it cost her life.

Living for Christ means many things for the believer. It involves daily fellowship with Him through prayer and the reading of His Word. To live for Christ is to seek to glorify Him in all we do and to do His will for our lives. It also means that we must stand for Him. The Christian must never be ashamed of being a Christian or of Christ their Lord. In Cassie's case, one may never know in this life if denying the Lord would have spared her life, but even in the face of death she would not deny her faith in Jesus Christ. A heart-searching question we could ask ourselves today is whether or not, if faced with death, would we stand for Jesus Christ? How we stand today would be a good test of how we would face the ultimate test of standing for Christ. It is something to think about.

April 21

2 Timothy 2:8, "Remember that Jesus Christ of the seed of David was raised from the dead according to my gospel."

ON THIS DAY in 1836, Sam Houston and the Texas militia defeated the Mexican forces of Santa Anna at San Jacinto. The victory, near present-day Houston, gave Texas their independence from Mexico. Shouting, "Remember the Alamo," Houston, with a small force of about 800 men, made a surprise attack on the Mexican army of about 1,300 men. In less than twenty minutes, the outnumbered army had killed or captured nearly all of Santa Anna's men, with Santa Anna being among those captured. In exchange for his freedom, Santa Anna signed a treaty recognizing Texas's independence. Within the year, Houston became the first president of the Republic of Texas. On December 29, 1845 Texas entered the United States as the twenty-eighth state.

The rallying cry of the church of Jesus Christ is, "Remember that Jesus Christ was raised from the dead." The Texas militia was motivated by the massacre of their comrades at the Alamo, but the believer is motivated by both the death and resurrection of the Lord Jesus Christ. We march under the banner of a living Lord and Saviour. The constant theme and message of the early church was that Jesus Christ was alive. It was their rallying cry as they fought the good battle of their faith. As we war against the world, the flesh, and the devil, we fight in His resurrection, life, and power. The assurance of our own victory is victory over the grave. As believers, it may appear that we are fighting with the odds stacked against us, but in Christ, we are more than conquerors (Rom. 8:37). Today, as you face the enemy, let your cry be, "Jesus is risen from the dead!"

April 22

Romans 5:18, "Therefore as by the offence of one judgment came upon all men to condemnation; even so by the righteousness of one the free gift came upon all men unto justification of life."

On This Day in 1889, two million acres of the Oklahoma district was claimed by a land race. At precisely noon, a government official raised his gun and fired a single shot and the race was on for 160 acres of free land. It is estimated that more than 200,000 people swarmed over the borders of Texas and Kansas in covered wagons, carriages, hacks, on horseback, on bicycles, and on foot. By nightfall, almost all of the two million acres had been claimed. The idea of the land race was to ensure fair play. Law enforcement officers were present to make sure the "sooners" who tried to beat the gun had not snatched up the prime lots. It was a race for first come first serve.

The offer of free land was obviously appealing to many. Yet the greatest offer ever made was the offer of salvation, for it was offered as a free gift to all. When you throw in eternal life, a home in heaven, the forgiveness of sins, and the numerous other blessings it includes, it is an offer no one should turn down. However, it is an offer that is spurned and rejected by multitudes. Even many of us were slow in accepting the offer. We look back now and think of how foolish we were to risk hell for heaven and to have been so blind to the many blessings our salvation has brought us. But thank God there was a day when we accepted God's wonderful offer and the free gift of salvation. Today, give thanks that salvation was a free gift from God. I wouldn't trade it for any amount of free land. Would you?

April 23

Isaiah 37:16, "O Lord of hosts, God of Israel, that dwellest between the cherubims, thou art the God, even thou alone, of all the kingdoms of the earth: thou hast made heaven and earth."

ON THIS DAY in 1992, astronomers announced that they had discovered the seeds from which the sun, stars, and planets evolved. The announcement was made at a meeting in Washington D.C. of the American Physical Society. The team responsible for NASA's Cosmic Background Explorer satellite (COBE) reported the existence of "ripples" in the microwave background radiation, which they believed to be the dying echo of the Big Bang. According to their theory, the Big Bang was the method by which the universe was to have begun between ten and twenty billion years ago. Dr. George Smoot of the University of California proudly announced, "What we have found is evidence for the birth of the universe."

If you really want to know how the universe came into existence, the best way is not by "ripples" but by simply asking the One who created it all. If God were given the platform, He would simply say, "*In the beginning God created the heaven and the earth*" (Gen. 1:1). This universe is not the result of a Big Bang but rather a Big God. We may not be scientists or understand all their theories, but as far as I am concerned, the Bible is the real source of information. We may be called "unenlightened" but when it is all said and done, it will be proven that we were not as uninformed as it was thought. Today, worship your heavenly Father. After all, He is the Creator of the universe.

April 24

John 21:25, "And there are also many other things which Jesus did, the which, if they should be written every one, I suppose that even the world itself could not contain the books that should be written. Amen."

On This Day in 1800, the Library of Congress was established. President John Adams approved legislation to appropriate $5,000 to purchase "such books as may be necessary for the use of Congress." The first books for the Library were ordered from London. The first library catalog listed 964 volumes and nine maps. When the British burned the library twelve years later, it had grown to 3,000 volumes. Former President Jefferson responded to the loss by selling his personal library of 6,487 volumes to Congress. A second fire in 1851 destroyed about two-thirds of its 55,000 volumes. After the Civil War, the library was greatly expanded and by the 20th century was one of the largest in the world. Today, the library is housed in three large buildings, containing more than seventeen million books, as well as millions of maps, manuscripts, photographs, films, audio and video recordings, prints and drawings.

As John thought on the life of the Lord Jesus, his summary was that if everything He had done was written in books, the world could not contain the number of volumes that would be required. Imagine a library covering 196,951,000 square miles (the total surface area of planet earth) and each volume recording the life of the Lord Jesus. Even then, the library would be too small to hold the books that would have to be written and would only contain what He did while He was on earth. Today, give thanks that if His works through the ages were recorded, there would be a chapter that would be about what He did for you.

April 25

John 16:13, "Howbeit when he, the Spirit of truth, is come, he will guide you into all truth: for he shall not speak of himself; but whatsoever he shall hear, that shall he speak: and he will shew you things to come."

ON THIS DAY in 1928, Buddy, a German Shepherd, became the first guide dog for the blind in the United States. Dorothy Harrison Eustis of Switzerland received a letter from Morris Frank in Tennessee: "Thousands of blind people like me abhor being dependent on others. Help me and I will help them. Train me and I will bring back my dog and show people here how a blind man can be absolutely on his own." She invited her young correspondent to Switzerland and while he was there, picked and trained Buddy that became the first "Seeing Eye Dog" in the United States. In 1929, Dorothy Eustis returned to the United States and with the help of Morris Frank and Buddy, *The Seeing Eye*, the pioneer guide dog school in the U.S. was started in Nashville, Tennessee.

It has been my privilege to know those who were blind and their courage and abilities have never ceased to amaze me. They serve as an inspiration to me and all whose lives they touch. Yet, the need for a guide is not limited to those who have not their physical sight. Every believer stands in need of a spiritual guide. There are times when the way is unclear and we need a guide to help us to make the right decision. Within every believer is that guide. He is the person of the Holy Spirit that indwells each believer. The promise of Jesus was that He would guide us into all truth. Today, if you need guidance, all you have to do is ask the Holy Spirit. He is in you and waiting to guide you.

April 26

John 15:13, "Greater love hath no man than this, that a man lay down his life for his friends."

ON THIS DAY in 1986, the Chernobyl tragedy occurred. At 1:23:58 a.m., two massive explosions blew away the roof and sides of Reactor Number Four of the Chernobyl Nuclear Power Facility. A plume of radioactive material was sent 36,000 feet into the air, leading to the loss of 125,000 lives. In an act of unparalleled heroism, Aleksandr Lelechenko tried to restart the reactor cooling systems by going unprotected through piles of radioactive debris and through knee-deep radioactive water, sparing his younger co-workers the deadly task. He was exposed to 2,500 rads, enough to kill five people instantly. He later died an agonizing death.

It has been said that love is best displayed than defined. The ultimate demonstration of human love is one giving his life in order to help or save others. It is the ultimate act of selflessness. Occasionally, we hear of those who pay the ultimate price by willingly sacrificing their lives that others might live. Calvary is the greatest demonstration of love. The proof of God's love for all men is found in His willingness to give His life that others might live: *"Hereby perceive we the love of God, because he laid down his life for us"* (1 John 3:16). People often say, "If God really loved me, He would not have allowed this to happen to me." We do not measure God's love by what we have or by what happens in life. We measure God's love by the cross. Calvary is the proof of His love. Today, give thanks that God loves you. No one ever loved us more or proved their love more than Him.

April 27

2 Timothy 1:12, "For the which cause I also suffer these things: nevertheless I am not ashamed: for I know whom I have believed, and am persuaded that he is able to keep that which I have committed unto him against that day."

On This Day in 1937, the first U.S. Social Security payment was made. President Franklin D. Roosevelt, in response to the Great Depression, developed the Social Security program in 1935. He stated to Congress that there was a need for the government to secure the future of the American citizen with a social insurance program. The first reported applicant was a retired Cleveland motorman named Ernest Ackerman, who retired one day after the Social Security program began. During his one day of participation in the program, a nickel was withheld from his pay for Social Security and upon retiring, he received a lump-sum payment of seventeen cents.

The greatest form of security for the future is the assurance that the Lord Jesus Christ is your personal Lord and Saviour. If, with Paul, you can say, "I know in whom I have believed," then you have assurance that your future is secure. Involved in President Roosevelt's Social Security plan was benefits for the unemployed, the elderly, aid to dependent children and spouses, and federal aid to state and local government for public health. The benefits of God's eternal security program are too numerous to count! We not only have the assurance that we have a heavenly home, but we have a source for every need in our life to be met. You could say that these benefits are out of this world! Today, give thanks that your future is secure.

April 28

Psalm 34:17, "The righteous cry, and the Lord heareth, and delivereth them out of all their troubles."

On This Day in 1906, W.H. Carrier patented the air conditioner. Willis Haviland Carrier called the device he patented "An Apparatus for Treating Air." His device was originally created for the comfort of machines or industrial processes rather than people. One of the first users of Carrier's new system was the Chronicle Cotton Mill in Belmont, N.C. A lack of moisture created static electricity that made cotton fibers fuzzy and hard to weave. The air-conditioner was first designed in 1902 and his customer was a frustrated Brooklyn, New York printer who couldn't print a decent color image because changes in the heat and humidity kept changing the paper's dimensions and misaligning the colored inks.

The next time you enjoy the comfort of an air-conditioned room or home on a hot day, give thanks that it is the result of someone's problem being solved. All of us at times in life find ourselves having to deal with problems. Life is not without its problems. Our problems can be very frustrating at times, yet when problems come, we can take them to the Lord. He is a master at solving problems. The Psalmist found that he could turn to the Lord in the time of trouble with the assurance that the Lord would hear his prayer and solve his problems. Are you facing a problem in your life? Have you talked to the Lord about your problem? Oftentimes we take our problems to the Lord as a last resort. The Lord wants to help us with our problems. He is only waiting for us to ask Him to help us. Today, take all your problems to the Lord. Tell him about your problems. He has never met a problem that He couldn't solve.

April 29

Proverbs 16:32, "He that is slow to anger is better than the mighty; and he that ruleth his spirit than he that taketh a city."

On This Day in 1992, riots broke out in Los Angeles, California when four Los Angeles police officers were acquitted. On March 31, 1991, Rodney King led police on a high-speed chase through the streets of Los Angeles County before surrendering. Intoxicated and uncooperative, King was dragged out of his car and beaten by the four officers. Someone with a personal video camera filmed the arrest and the beating of King by the officers. When their trial concluded with not guilty verdicts, violence broke out at the intersection of Florence Boulevard and Normandie Avenue in South-Central Los Angeles. Rioting continued for the next three days, leaving 55 people dead, almost 2,000 injured, 7,000 arrests, and one billion dollars in damage, including the burning of nearly 4,000 buildings.

When we feel that we have been mistreated, it is easy to become angry. Oftentimes in a moment of rage, we vent our anger in destructive ways. We say things that hurt others and even behave in ways that do us as much harm as it does others. Solomon spoke of the one that is slow to anger as being better than mighty or powerful. When we vent our anger in destructive ways, we are no different than the one who hurt us and we lower ourselves to their level. Solomon also described the one who is able to rule his anger is greater than the one who takes a city by force. Those who in the face of great hurt are able to control their anger, lift themselves to a level that the one who initiated the hurt had never reached. Today, instead of venting your anger, live on a higher plain. It makes you a much better person!

April 30

Titus 2:7, "In all things shewing thyself a pattern of good works: in doctrine shewing uncorruptness, gravity, sincerity."

ON THIS DAY in 1789, the first Presidential Inauguration was held. George Washington, standing on the balcony of the Senate Chamber at Federal Hall located on the corner of Wall and Broad Streets in New York City, took his oath as the first president of the United States. On February 4th, all sixty-nine presidential electors had unanimously elected Washington as the first president of the United States. After taking his oath with his hand resting on a Bible, he spoke of "the experiment entrusted to the hands of the American people." In a letter to James Madison, Washington wrote: "As the first of every thing, in our situation will serve to establish a Precedent. It is devoutly wished on my part, that these precedents may be fixed on true principles." Washington's integrity in office set a pattern for all other Presidents to follow.

The Apostle Paul spoke of every believer as being a pattern in good works, an incorruptible character, honesty, and genuineness. In our situation, we are children of God and representatives of the Lord Jesus Christ. This world ought to be able to look upon the life of each believer and see modeled a loving, compassionate, and committed life. In a world that is characterized by a lack of character, integrity, dishonesty, and hypocrisy, the believer is to be the exception. As President Washington wanted to set an example for all who would follow him, may we as believers be an example to those around us. Today, let someone see in you the real thing. In our day and time, we need a good example.

May 1

Matthew 16:18, "And I say also unto thee, That thou art Peter, and upon this rock I will build my church; and the gates of hell shall not prevail against it."

ON THIS DAY in 1931, President Hoover pressed a button in Washington, D.C., turning on the lights of the Empire State Building and officially opening the world's tallest building at the time. The 102-floor building stands 1,860 feet from street level to the 102nd floor. It consists of 6,500 windows, 73 elevators, 70 miles of pipe to provide water to tanks at various floor levels, and 2,500,000 feet of electrical wire. It took one year and forty-five days, including Sundays and holidays to complete the construction (7,000,000 man-hours). Construction of the building began on March 17, 1930 and the framework rose at a rate of four and a half stories per week. The total cost was $40,948,900 (including land). Its total weight is 365,000 tons and its foundation reaches fifty-five feet below ground. John Jakob Raskob (creator of General Motors) built the Empire State Building as part of a competition between Walter Chrysler (Chrysler Corp.) to see who could build the tallest building.

The Lord Jesus announced to Peter that He had a building project of His own—the church. Its foundation was the apostles and prophets and Jesus Himself was the cornerstone (Eph. 2:20). It is a building that has been under construction for nearly 2,000 years. Construction on the building goes on night and day, seven days a week, 365 days a year. What makes this building so unique is that it is made up of sinners saved by grace. Today, give thanks that you are a part of the greatest building that has ever been built—actually it is being built. When the building is completed, there will be a dedication service like none other.

May 2

1 Peter 2:7, "Unto you therefore which believe he is precious: but unto them which be disobedient, the stone which the builders disallowed, the same is made the head of the corner,"

ON *THIS* DAY in 1863, General Thomas (Stonewall) Jackson was shot by his own men. At the Battle of Chancellorsville, Jackson and a small reconnoitering escort advanced in front of his own lines who, mistaking the party for a body of Federal Calvary, opened fire upon them. General Jackson's right hand was pierced by a bullet and his left arm was shattered by two balls above and below the elbow, breaking the bones and severing the main artery. Several of the escorts were also killed and wounded. Jackson's left arm had to be amputated and he died eight days later from his wounds. General Robert E. Lee, when he heard that Jackson had been wounded, sent the message through a friend, "He has lost his left arm, but I have lost my right arm." Upon his death, Lee said, "I know not how to replace him."

In our verse for today, Peter gives us some wonderful descriptions of the Lord Jesus. He speaks of the Lord Jesus as being the "stone, which the builders disallowed" and Him as being the "head of the corner." In summary of who Jesus is and all He means to the believer, Peter describes Him as being "precious." The word "precious" speaks of that which has such value there is no replacement. Peter is declaring that there is no one like the Lord Jesus and there could never be a replacement for Him in our life. The Lord Jesus means so much to the believer, no one could ever take His place. Today, give thanks that He will never have to be replaced. As each believer has discovered, there is no one like Him.

May 3

Psalm 16:7, "I will bless the Lord, who hath given me counsel: my reins also instruct me in the night seasons."

ON THIS DAY in 1988, Donald Regan, ex-chief of staff, claimed that President Ronald Reagan consulted the stars for guidance. Regan claimed in a new book that the president consulted his wife's astrologer before almost every important event. His claims included that the stars and planets dictated the date of the nuclear arms talks with Soviet leader, Mikhail Gorbachev. The astrologer, who lived in California, according to Regan, advised the Reagans whether the timing was right for several major summits. If not, Regan alleged, the President would insist that meetings be moved to a more auspicious time. Responses to the revelations ranged from shock to ridicule.

As believers, we have a heavenly guide but it is not the stars and planets. Our guide is the One who made the stars and planets. When we need advise or counsel, we can go to our heavenly Father. God says, "*I will instruct thee and teach thee in the way which thou shalt go: I will guide thee with mine eye*" (Psalm 32:8). God gives us guidance by His Word. The Psalmist declares, "Thy testimonies also are my delight and my counselors" (Psalm 119:24). When the king sought his astrologers, he failed to find the answers he sought. But when Daniel sought his God, he received guidance and instruction (Dan. 2). We do not have to read our horoscope each day to gain guidance. Our "sign" or the stars are a false source for guidance. It's a good thing for I don't even know what my sign is. Do you need guidance? Do you need to seek advise about a certain matter? Today, turn to God's Word. Let God direct your paths. Look to Him in prayer. It's a toll free call!

May 4

2 Peter 1:3, "According as his divine power hath given unto us all things that pertain unto life and godliness, through the knowledge of him that hath called us to glory and virtue:"

ON THIS DAY in 1942, food was first rationed in the United States. During the war, the federal government began the rationing systems to ensure a fair division of essential items and to keep inflation from skyrocketing. Sugar was the first item to be rationed and Americans received their first supply of ration coupons based on their estimation—recorded in the sworn dispositions—of how much sugar they had at home. Other items were quickly added: coffee and meat; gasoline, because petroleum was needed for the war effort; canned goods, because tin was needed for soldier's c-ration cans and armament. Ration books with coupons, red for butter, fats, and meats, and blue for canned goods, bought Americans an average of ten ounces of sugar per week, twenty-eight cents of meat per week, a pound of coffee every thirty-five days, and three to five gallons of gasoline per week.

Jesus promises that all who come to Him will never experience a spiritual "rationing." His promise is that those who receive Him as Saviour will always have available to them all that pertains to life and godliness. All that the believer needs to live for God, to serve God, and to please God is made available to us in an unlimited quantity. We can come as often as we like and get all that we need or want. Today, give thanks that heaven's resources are never restricted to the believer, but that all we need is available whenever we need it. What is your need today? There is a plenteous supply available to the believer. There is no limit on heaven's resources.

May 5

Psalm 92:10, "But my horn shalt thou exalt like the horn of an unicorn: I shall be anointed with fresh oil."

On This Day in 1821, Napoleon Bonaparte died while in exile. At two in the afternoon, as his household gathered around him, he muttered, "*France. Armee. Tete d'armee. Josephene*," and then fell into a coma. He was fifty-one and had spent the last six years like a caged lion on the island of St. Helena which was nothing more than a volcanic mass far from the fields of Europe where he had ruled with mastery and the courts where he made and unmade kings. His approaching end became apparent in October when he fainted and his vomiting and lack of appetite weakened him. Shortly before his death, he told his faithful court chamberlain Monotholon, "There is no more oil in the lamp."

It has been said that at times we get tired in the work but not of the work. There are times when we feel "there is no more oil in the lamp." We find ourselves weary, discouraged, and spiritually depleted. The pastor whose labors seem to bear so little fruit, the missionary who labors with so little results, or the church worker who sees so little accomplished, at times finds himself running on empty and feels there is no more oil in the lamp. What is our need in such times? It is to be anointed with fresh oil. We need our lamps filled once again, filled with oil from the oil cellars of heaven. Are you running on empty today? Do you feel there is no more oil in your lamp? Today, bring your empty lamp to the Lord and ask Him to give you fresh oil. He will refill your lamp with fresh oil. Also, He will not only refill your lamp but will also light your lamp that it may burn brighter than before. Let Him refill and refire you today.

May 6

James 1:2, "My brethren, count it all joy when ye fall into divers temptations."

ON THIS DAY in 1937, the German airship *Hindenburg* exploded and crashed. The luxury airship and pride of Hitler's Germany, carried seven million gallons of highly flammable hydrogen. As it approached an airport in New Jersey, the rear of the airship exploded into a ball of flame and in a matter of thirty-two seconds burned out leaving only its twisted metal frame. Hebert Morrison was reporting for WLS Chicago and as the great airship arrived, with great excitement he said, "Here it comes, ladies and gentlemen, and what a sight it is, a thrilling one, a marvelous sight." Then suddenly Morrison screamed, "Oh, oh, oh…it's burst into flames…Oh, my this is terrible." Morrison then broke down into tears.

It only takes a matter of seconds for our joy to be turned into sorrow. A phone call or a knock at the door can turn a beautiful day into a nightmare. James speaks of falling into various kinds of trials. The word "fall" is descriptive of that which can happen suddenly and without warning. The word was used of the man traveling along the Jericho Road, where suddenly and without warning he was attacked by thieves (See Luke 10:30). The trials we find ourselves in never seem to give us warning of their arrival. They just seem to barge into our lives without sympathy or invitation. Yet James tells us that even when unexpected trials come, we can rejoice. Why? He tells us that our trials, even the unexpected ones, are working in our favor (James 1:3). Today, rejoice that your trials have a purpose, even the trials that come unexpectedly.

May 7

Matthew 13:46, "Who, when he had found one pearl of great price, went and sold all that he had, and bought it."

ON THIS DAY in 1934, the world's largest pearl was found. An anonymous Filipino diver found the pearl off the Philippine island of Palawan. Known as the "Pearl of Allah" and later officially named the "Pearl of Lao-tze," it weighed fourteen pounds (6.4 kg) and a circumference of twenty-five inches shaped much like a brain. In 1936, Wilbur Dowell was given the pearl as a gift by a chieftain of Palawan for having saved the life of his son. In 1980, Cobb's heirs sold the pearl to a jeweler in Beverly Hills, California for $200,000. In 1997, it was appraised at over $59 million.

Jesus gives the parable of a man who sold all he had in order to buy a pearl that had been found. The buyer apparently recognized the worth of the pearl and felt that whatever the cost, it was a wise investment to secure the pearl. Jesus gives the parable to illustrate the value of the kingdom of heaven and those who are citizens of that kingdom. As believers, we know that we cannot purchase our way into the kingdom of heaven, for salvation is a gift through the grace of God (Eph. 2:8-9). However, the greatest decision that a person can ever make is to be a citizen of that heavenly kingdom. To be a citizen of God's kingdom is so wonderful that if necessary, one should be willing to do anything to become a citizen. To turn down the invitation to be a citizen of heaven is like turning down an opportunity to be the owner of the "Pearl of Lao-tze." God offers this pearl to you at no cost. Today, rejoice that you have found the greatest pearl the world has ever known and that it didn't cost you anything. It was free for the taking.

May 8

John 4:14, "But whosoever drinketh of the water that I shall give him shall never thirst; but the water that I shall give him shall be in him a well of water springing up into everlasting life."

On This Day in 1886, Coca-Cola was sold for the first time. Dr. John Pemberton, the inventor of Coca-Cola, delivered the first gallon of Coca-Cola syrup to Jacob's Pharmacy in Atlanta, Georgia. The name Coca-Cola was suggested by Dr. Pemberton's bookkeeper, Frank Robinson. He penned the name in the same flowing script that is famous today. During the first year, sales at the soda fountain of Jacob's Pharmacy sold an average of nine drinks a day. Today, Coca-Cola products are consumed at the rate of more than one billon per day. In 1886, that first gallon of Coca-Cola syrup was carried by hand to Jacob's Pharmacy. Today, Coca-Cola trucks are the largest commercial fleet in the world and travel more than one million miles a day delivering their products.

The greatest "drink" the world has ever known is the one Jesus offers. One drink and you are forever satisfied and you become an eternal customer. There is a thirst in this world that no soft drink can quench, a thirst deep in the soul of every man. There is a drink that can quench that thirst. It is the water that Jesus offers. Today, give thanks that one day you took a drink that has turned into a well springing up into everlasting life. Oh, by the way, Dr. Pemberton first sold his invention as a brain tonic and was used for medicinal purpose. The drink that Jesus offers has cured many a spiritual ailment. The water Jesus offers is indeed the "real thing."

May 9

Exodus 20:12, "Honour thy father and thy mother: that thy days may be long upon the land which the Lord thy God giveth thee."

ON THIS DAY in 1914, President Wilson made the official announcement proclaiming "Mother's Day" as a national holiday that was to be held each year on the second Sunday of May. All across the world, over forty-six countries honor mothers with a special day. Julia Ward Howe, the writer of "The Battle Hymn of the Republic," first suggested Mother's Day in the United States. However, it was largely due to the efforts of Anna Jarvis that Mother's Day became a national holiday in the United States. In 1907, Miss Anna began a campaign to establish a national Mother's Day. She persuaded her church in Grafton, West Virginia to celebrate Mother's Day on the second anniversary of her mother's death, which was the second Sunday of May. The campaign she then launched led to President Wilson proclaiming that the second of May would be recognized as Mother's Day throughout the United States.

Speaking of mothers reminds me of a small boy who walked into the lingerie section of a big California department store and shyly presented his problem to a woman clerk. "I want to buy my mom a slip for a present," he said, "but I don't know what size she wears." "Is she tall or short, fat or skinny?" asked the clerk. "She's just perfect," beamed the small boy. So she wrapped up a size ten for him. Two days later, mom came to the store herself and changed it for a thirty-two. To many, their mother is "just perfect." Today, honor your mother and don't wait for the second Sunday of May each year to do so. Someone that is "just perfect" deserves to be honored. Do I hear an "Amen?"

May 10

2 Corinthians 5:8, "We are confident, I say, and willing rather to be absent from the body, and to be present with the Lord."

On This Day in 1863, General Thomas (Stonewall) Jackson died from the wounds received at Chancellorsville. Known for his devout Christian faith, the final hours of Jackson's life bore tribute to the hope of every believer. On the morning of May 10, his attending physician told his wife that he had a few hours to live at the most. Mrs. Jackson sat down beside him and told him that the doctors thought he would soon be in heaven. At first, he did not seem to comprehend what she was saying, but upon repeating it and asking him if he was willing for God's will to be done, he looked at her calmly and said, "Yes, I prefer, I prefer it." She then told him that "before the day was over, he would be with the blessed Saviour in His glory." He responded, "I will be an infinite gainer to be translated." They talked about the place of burial before he sank into unconsciousness. Occasionally, he murmured disconnected words, but all at once he spoke out cheerfully and distinctly his last sentence: "Let us cross over the river, and rest under the shade of the trees."

Every believer lives with the knowledge that life, as we know it, is not forever. We know that we have an appointment with death (Heb. 9:27), yet we know that to be absent from the body is to be present with the Lord. Death is not an enemy of the believer; it is a blessed friend that takes us to be with the Lord. Today, give thanks that when it is our time to "cross over the river," each of us will be "an infinite gainer." Death is to be absent from the body, but to be with the Lord!

May 11

Mark 5:20, "And he departed, and began to publish in Decapolis how great things Jesus had done for him: and all men did marvel."

ON THIS DAY in 1751, the first hospital in the United States was founded. Dr. Thomas Bond and Benjamin Franklin founded the Pennsylvania Hospital in Philadelphia "to care for the sick, poor, and insane who were wandering the streets of Philadelphia." The idea for the hospital originated with Dr. Bond, who had studied medicine in London and had spent time at the famous French hospital, the Hotel-Dieu in Paris, and had been impressed with the continent's new hospital movement. Bond and Franklin were long-standing friends. When Bond approached the Philadelphians for support, they asked him what Franklin thought of the idea. He approached Franklin who became a strong supporter of the idea and the major fundraiser for the hospital. The first hospital was housed in the home of the deceased John Kinsey, a Quaker and speaker of the Assembly.

Mark chapter five has been called, "A Hospital for Incurables." The chapter gives us the story of three hopeless cases; the man of Gadara possessed with demons, the death of the daughter of Jairus, and the woman with an issue of blood who had spent all trying to find a cure for her problem. It is a chapter in which we see the men's, the women's, and the children's ward of this hospital for incurables. All were hopeless until the Lord Jesus—the Great Physician—paid a visit to the hospital. Jesus has never met a hopeless case. Many of us are testimonies that Jesus can cure the worst of the worst. Today, give thanks that one day Jesus passed by your way and made a difference in your life. He does great things and we are all living proof.

May 12

Acts 27:14, "But not long after there arose against it a tempestuous wind, called Euroclydon."

ON THIS DAY in 1978, the Commerce Department announced that hurricanes would no longer be only female names. The giving of short, distinctive names to hurricanes originated to make communications quicker and less confusing than the older more cumbersome latitude-longitude identification methods. In the past, confusion and false rumors had arisen when storm advisories broadcasted from radio stations were mistaken for warnings concerning an entirely different storm hundreds of miles away. An Australian meteorologist began giving women's names to tropical storms before the end of the nineteenth century. That practice came to an end in 1978 and in 1979, male and female names were included in the lists for the Atlantic and Gulf of Mexico.

I would assume that some women were not fond of a storm always being identified with a woman (I have known a few men whose name would have been a good one for a storm, if you know what I mean). Speaking of the names of storms, the Apostle Paul found himself in a storm called "Euroclydon" that means "southeast wind raising mighty waves." It is described as a "tempestuous wind." Paul found himself in such a terrible storm that shipwrecked the ship on which he was a passenger. There are times when we find ourselves sailing the stormy seas of life, but like Paul, we will find that the Lord does not abandon us but will be with us (Acts 27:23). Today, give thanks that in the storms of life the Lord stands with us. It doesn't matter if the storm is named Bob or Sue; He will be there.

May 13

James 2:25, "Likewise also was not Rahab the harlot justified by works, when she had received the messengers, and had sent them out another way?"

On This Day in 1983, Reggie Jackson became the first major league baseball player to strike out 2,000 times. During his career, Jackson struck out 2,597 times, a first all-time. However, during his twenty-one seasons, he played on eleven divisional winners, six pennant winners, and five World Champions. He has a .357 lifetime World Series average and the best career World Series slugging average at .755. His 563 homeruns was sixth all-time when he retired. In 1969, he led the league in strikeouts for the second of four straight years with 142. Yet, when the name Reggie Jackson is mentioned, no one speaks of his strikeout record but only of his other accomplishments.

One of the greatest stories of saving faith and how God's grace can transform a life is that of Rahab (Joshua 2). When you find her name in the Bible, her former profession of a harlot is most always attached to her name like in our verse for the day. It is as if the Holy Spirit wants to remind us that no matter what one has done in the past, God can give them a new life. However, when we speak of Rahab and call her a harlot in the same breath, our focus is not on what she used to be but on what she became. Many things can stain a person's past but they can still be remembered for the many good things in their life. Today, live a life that pleases God and you will not be remembered for the times you struck out, but for the many good things you have done. Don't let past failures keep you down. When it is all said and done, it is the rest of the record that will be remembered.

May 14

Jeremiah 30:3, "For, lo, the days come, saith the Lord, that I will bring again the captivity of my people Israel and Judah, saith the Lord: and I will cause them to return to the land that I gave to their fathers, and they shall possess it."

ON THIS DAY in 1948, Israel became a nation. After two millenniums of wandering, shortly after sunrise, the Union Jack was lowered from its staff over the Government House in Jerusalem. This region had been administered by Britain under the auspices of the League of Nations since 1922. Finally, a long cherished dream was realized —the first Jewish state since Biblical times. At 4 p.m. David Ben-Gurion, longtime leader of the Jewish settlers, (Zionists) proclaimed "the establishment of the Jewish State in Palestine to be called Israel." One of the first actions of the new Israeli government was to open its door to all Jews. A proclamation invited Jews to join "the struggle for the fulfillment of the dream of generations, the redemption of Israel."

Israel becoming a nation and the returning of the Jews to their homeland was more than the fulfillment of a dream for the Jewish people; it was also the fulfillment of Biblical prophecy. Through the prophet Jeremiah, God tells of a day when He will cause the Jewish people to return to the land He had given to them. While Prime Minister Gurion read the proclamation as the Israeli flag, the Star of David, flew over his head, Bible prophecy was literally fulfilled. One of the greatest signs of the nearness of the Lord's return is the prophecy of Jeremiah. Today, rejoice that the return of the Lord Jesus is near. If you have any doubts, think of Jeremiah's prophecy when you hear someone speak of Israel as a nation.

May 15

Colossians 3:24, "Knowing that of the Lord ye shall receive the reward of the inheritance: for ye serve the Lord Christ."

ON THIS DAY in 1929, Hollywood presented its first academy awards. The Academy of Motion Pictures Arts and Sciences gave the film industry's first awards for outstanding achievement by actors, directors, producers, and technicians. A twelve-inch tall model of a gold plated naked man symbolized the award. The academy president, Douglas Fairbanks, presented the first statuette to Janet Gaynor. Other winners were actor Emil Jannings, directors Frank Borsage and Lewis Milestone, screenwriter Ben Hecht, and producer Jack Warner. It was announced that the awards would be annual.

For the believer, there is no earthly ceremony in which they are given awards for a job well done. There are many believers who are faithful and do an outstanding job in God's work, yet they never receive any kind of award or recognition. But you can mark it down that one day Heaven will put on an awards ceremony which will surpass any earth has ever known. For every believer who has served God, been faithful to His will and done a good job for the Lord, they will hear the Lord say, "Well-done," and they will be rewarded. Occasionally there are some who are recognized by a school or a church for outstanding Christian service, but for the most part, those who serve faithfully week after week, are never honored. Maybe you are one of those. Today, remember that you are not home yet. One day you will attend the greatest award ceremony ever held, and you will be one of those who will be recognized. Until then, keep serving the Lord.

May 16

Exodus 3:11, "And Moses said unto God, Who am I, that I should go unto Pharaoh, and that I should bring forth the children of Israel out of Egypt?"

ON THIS DAY in 1888, President Andrew Johnson was acquitted of impeachment by one vote. A fascinating fact of history is how on many occasions one vote made the difference. Oliver Cromwell won control of England in 1645 by one vote when Parliament voted ninety-one to ninety in his favor. During the American Revolution when anti-British sentiment was high in the colonies, a bill was defeated by one vote which would have abolished English as the official language in favor of German. Rutherford B. Hayes was elected president of the United States by the electoral vote of 185 to 184. Texas was admitted into the Union by one vote. An Indiana senator changed his mind and voted in favor of admission. He had won the election to his office by one vote! On November 8, 1923, Adolph Hitler was elected leader of the Nazi party by the margin of one vote. One vote changed France from a monarchy to a republic. These are only a few examples of how just one vote made the difference.

When Moses was called by God to deliver the Jewish people from Egyptian bondage, he asked the question, "Who am I?" He was questioning both his ability and God's choice. You can almost hear him say, "But God, I am just one person. What can one person do, especially me?" Yet, there are no unimportant people in the family of God. Each believer has been given a certain work to do by God and each person has a certain place in God's plan. Today, realize that you are just as important as anyone else in God's family. You may be the one that will make the difference.

May 17

Zechariah 4:10, "For who hath despised the day of small things? for they shall rejoice, and shall see the plummet in the hand of Zerubbabel with those seven; they are the eyes of the Lord, which run to and fro through the whole earth."

ON *THIS* DAY in 1792, the New York Stock Exchange was founded. A group of stock and bond brokers gathered under a tree located on what is now called Wall Street and agreed to meet daily at that location to trade stocks and bonds. By 1794, they had moved indoors to the Tontine Coffee House, on the corner of Wall and Water Streets. In 1817, the group moved closer to its present location and drew up a constitution and named itself the New York Stock and Exchange Board. It changed its name to the New York Stock Exchange (NYSE) in 1863 and has become one of the most important financial trading centers in the world. In 1999, the Exchange listed the stocks of about 3,750 companies valued at approximately $12 trillion.

History is replete with story after story of great things that had small and humble beginnings. I wonder if those men who met under a tree in New York City dreamed that one day what they were starting would affect the financial equilibrium of not only the United States but also the world. As the prophet Zechariah declared, "For who hath despised the day of small things?" Every great church had its small beginnings. Every great work for God started with one person or a handful of believers. Many of God's greatest servants came from humble beginnings. Today, take heart that God can take that which is small and do something that can shake the world. A small beginning or even a small person may one day be something great for God.

May 18

2 Peter 3:3-4, "Knowing this first, that there shall come in the last days scoffers, walking after their own lusts, And saying, Where is the promise of his coming? for since the fathers fell asleep, all things continue as they were from the beginning of the creation."

ON THIS DAY in 1980, Mount St. Helen's in Washington State erupted. Mt. St. Helen's had remained dormant for 123 years, but in March of 1980, scientists began to record seismic tremors from the mountain. When it erupted at 8:32 on a Sunday morning, the explosion blew off 1,300 feet of the mountain's top and sent ash and debris more than twelve miles into the sky. Nearly 150 square miles of forest were devastated and about 540 million tons of ash fell over an area of more than 22,000 square miles. State officials had begun ordering residents to evacuate the area. However, not everyone heeded the warning. Harry Truman was one of those who refused to leave his lodge at Spirit Lake. Harry said, "I'll never leave the mountain, never, never...yes, this mountain shakes a lot and pours out steam and ash, but I got me a cave nearby, and for that I'll make a dash." When the mountain blew, there was no time for flight for Harry Truman.

Peter speaks of those who scoff at the idea of the Lord's return. They talk of how they have heard this "second coming stuff" and "doomsday prophecy" for years and nothing has happened. Just because He hasn't come is no indication that He will not come as He promised. It is a dangerous thing to ignore the warning signs of the nearness of the Lord's return. When He returns, it will happen so quickly that there will be no time to get ready. Today would be a good day to get ready, if you are not ready. Don't ignore the warnings.

May 19

Luke 12:43, "Blessed is that servant, whom his lord when he cometh shall find so doing."

ON THIS DAY in 1780, near total darkness descended upon New England. What happened still remains unexplained. It began with a strange haze spreading across the sky, and then a thick darkness settled over much of New England. By one o'-clock, panic had begun to set in among the people. Thousands crowded into the churches thinking that the Day of Judgment had come. In Hartford, Connecticut, both houses of the legislature were meeting. One quickly dismissed since its members thought the world was coming to an end. In the other body, a man made the motion to dismiss since the day of reckoning was thought to have come. A Mr. Davenport objected saying, "Mr. Speaker, this is either the Day of Judgment or it is not. If it is not, there is no need for adjourning. If it is, I desire to be found doing my work. I move that candles be brought in and that we proceed to business." The meeting went on.

If the Lord Jesus were to return today, would He find you doing His work? Jesus gives a parable that illustrates how the believer is to watch for the Lord's return and be faithful to the work God has given us. The heart and soul of the parable is, *"Be ye therefore ready also: for the Son of man cometh at an hour when ye think not"* (Luke 12:40). The Lord Jesus could return at any moment and in light of His imminent return, like Mr. Davenport, it should be our desire that when He returns, He should find us doing our work. Today, live with the awareness that Jesus could come at any time. He could come today! If He does, will He find you doing the work He has given you to do? Understanding He could return, I move that we all proceed to business.

May 20

1 Peter 5:5, "Likewise, ye younger, submit yourselves unto the elder. Yea, all of you be subject one to another, and be clothed with humility: for God resisteth the proud, and giveth grace to the humble."

ON *THIS DAY* in 1873, Levi Strauss and Jacob Davis were granted a patent for a garment called "waist overalls" which is now called blue jeans. Born in Butteheim, Bavaria, Strauss immigrated to New York and then during the California Gold Rush moved to San Francisco. He established a dry goods business and in 1872 received a letter from Jacob Davis, a Reno, Nevada tailor. Davis, who purchased cloth from Strauss to use for his business, told him of a unique way he made pants for his customers—placing metal rivets at the points of strain. He didn't have the money for the patent and asked Strauss if he could help and they would share the patent. Today, Levi Strauss and Company is one of the world's largest brand name apparel manufacturers with twenty-one production facilities and twenty-five customer service centers around the world, with 1999 sales of $5.14 billion.

Peter speaks of humility as a garment that believers are to make a part of their wardrobe. It has been said that humility is recognizing that God and others are responsible for the achievements in our life. The proud person takes the credit for what he or she has and who he or she is, whereas, the humble person recognizes that he or she owes everything to the Lord. A.W. Tozer said, "Because Christ Jesus came to the world clothed in humility, He will always be found among those who are clothed with humility. He will be found among the humble people." Today, put on the garment of humility. It is a garment the Lord loves to see on His people.

May 21

1 Corinthians 12:25, "That there should be no schism in the body; but that the members should have the same care one for another."

On This Day in 1881, Clara Barton founded the American Red Cross. During the American Civil War, Barton worked with the Union armies "for the purpose of distributing comforts for the sick and wounded and nursing them." After the war, she went to Europe to rest and while there heard about the International Committee of the Red Cross that had been formed in Switzerland. She worked closely with the committee and watched them in action during the Franco-Prussian War of 1870-71. Upon returning to the United States, she began speaking out about the Red Cross and the need for such an organization in America to help people during the time of war or a natural disaster. At first the American State Department refused to be involved, but finally the Senate ratified the Red Cross Treaty. Barton served as the first president of the American Red Cross until her retirement in 1904.

The Apostle Paul describes believers as being members of "Heaven's Red Cross." He speaks of the believer as being a member of a spiritual body that cares for others in times of suffering and need. The word "care" speaks of someone who is moved by the needs of others and reaches out to minister to them. As we look upon the battlefield of life, we see those who are hurting and suffering. Today, seek to reach out to someone who could use a word of encouragement. Give them a call or send them a note. A visit may even be needed. Knowing that someone really cares may be just what someone needs today.

May 22

Hebrews 11:8, "By faith Abraham, when he was called to go out into a place which he should after receive for an inheritance, obeyed; and he went out, not knowing whither he went."

On This Day in 1843, the first large wagon train known as the "Great Emigration" departed for Oregon. The large wagon train consisted of a thousand settlers and a thousand head of cattle. They left Independence, Missouri and began its 2,000-mile journey, reaching Oregon five months later. Glowing reports of fertile valleys attracted the settlers to the Oregon region with the dream of a better life. The "Oregon Trail" was soon crowded with wagon trains of pioneer settlers, cattle and sheep ranchers, and families leaving their homes in search of a better home. The journey was not without its hardships. The journey required strength and endurance. Many lost their life from cholera, smallpox, accidents, and Indians yet to those pioneers, what was ahead was worth the sacrifice.

One day Abraham and his family packed up all their earthly possessions and began a journey that would take them to a new home. He became an earthly pilgrim in search of *"a city which hath foundations, whose builder and maker is God"* (Heb. 11:10). As believers,we are in this world but are not of this world. We are pilgrims merely passing through this world enroute to a "land that is fairer than day." Our journey is not without its hard times and difficult days, but the thought of what is ahead fills our heart with delight. The number on this heavenly trail is many and all along the way, we are picking up more who are interested in a better life. Today, remember that this world is not your home. We are on our way to our new home.

May 23

Leviticus 23:22, "And when ye reap the harvest of your land, thou shalt not make clean riddance of the corners of thy field when thou reapest, neither shalt thou gather any gleaning of thy harvest: thou shalt leave them unto the poor, and to the stranger: I am the Lord your God."

ON THIS DAY in 1761, the first insurance policy in the United States was issued. It was issued in the city of Philadelphia, a city which gave Americans many of their firsts, such as the first public school, the first public library, the first volunteer fire department, the first novel printed in America, the first hospital, the first commercial bank, the first stock exchange, and America's first paved turnpike. Getting back to our subject, the first insurance policy issued was the Corporation for the Relief of Poor and Distressed Presbyterian Ministers and of the Poor and Distressed Widows and Children of Presbyterian Ministers. In a world in which there are more life insurance companies than can be imagined, the first insurance company was the Presbyterian Minister's Fund and the first policies issued were to "poor" preachers.

God has always had a policy that provided "relief" for the poor, whether they are preachers or not. Under the law, God gave the instruction that when the fields were harvested, the corners were to be left for the poor to glean. In times of distress, grief, loss, and hardship, God always has His ways of caring for us. The Psalmist testifies, "*But I am poor and needy: make haste unto me,* O *God: thou art my help and my deliverer*...(Psa. 70:5). Today, remember that in times of need, God is your help and deliverer. It is stated so in your heavenly insurance policy.

May 24

1 Samuel 12:24, "Only fear the Lord, and serve him in truth with all your heart: for consider how great things he hath done for you."

On This Day in 1844, the first instant communication between two cities was successfully sent. That communication was sent by a code developed by Samuel Findlay Morse over a wire he had created called the telegraph line. In a factory room of the Speedwell Ironworks at Morristown, New Jersey, Morse had worked on a wire that he believed electrical impulses could be sent from point to point. Later in a basement room of New York University, where he had strung one mile of his wire around and around that limited room, he was successful. Congress had appropriated enough money for forty miles of the same wire, enough to reach from Washington, D.C. to Baltimore. From the chambers of the Supreme Court, Morse sent the message: "What hath God wrought!"

When believers begin to consider all that God has done for them, they have to exclaim, "Glory to God, He hath done great things!" Every believer can join with Mary and say, "*For he that is mighty hath done to me great things; and holy is his name*" (Luke 1:49). When we think of the great things God hath wrought, we also join with the Psalmist and say, "*The Lord hath done great things for us; whereof we are glad*" (Psalm 126:3). How should all that the Lord has done for us affect us as believers? It should fill our hearts with awe and inspire us to serve the Lord all the days of our life. All that the Lord has done for us is deserving of all that we can do for Him. Even then, we could never repay Him for all that He has done. Today, take time to think of some of the great things the Lord has done for you. They are many!

May 25

Psalm 145:4, "One generation shall praise thy works to another, and shall declare thy mighty acts."

ON THIS DAY in 1927, the "Movietone News" was shown for the first time. The primary source of news before the age of television was newspapers and magazines. To view an event, people relied on Movietone News, which were news segments played before movies shown in theaters. Movietone News had cameramen all over the world to capture footage of breaking stories. The "newsreel camera" of Movietone News captured great events like Amelia Earhart's flight and the bombing of Pearl Harbor, as well as speeches by Winston Churchill, Benito Mussolini, and Herbert Hoover. Today, the Movietone archives make up the world's largest collection of historic news footage. The first Movietone News footage was shown at the Sam Harris Theater in New York City and featured Charles Lindbergh's epic flight aboard the "Spirit of St. Louis."

In every generation, God has had people who provided their day with the best news that the world has every heard. God's method of informing the world what He could do for them has always been His people. One generation would tell the next and that generation would tell the next, and so on. God's plan of getting the good news out has always been by those who had experienced His saving power to tell another about His glorious works and mighty acts. God has always had His "witnesses" around the world to tell about Him and what He can do for a person. That is how each one of us learned that God loved us and could save us. Today, tell someone the wonderful news that Christ died for his sins and how he can be saved. It is news that everyone needs to hear.

May 26

Philippians 3:20, "For our conversation is in heaven; from whence also we look for the Saviour, the Lord Jesus Christ."

ON THIS DAY in 1827, Robert Owen's commune on the banks of the Wabash collapsed. Owens, a Welsh born and self-made millionaire, had bought 30,000 acres of land in Indiana and founded a "model" village that he named New Harmony. His human treatment of his employees in Britain had made him a noted reformer and educator. He dreamed of creating an idealistic, socialist community in the United States, where all property was to be held in common and where there was to be "absolute freedom of action for the individual" and equality of the sexes. Nine hundred disciples followed him there, pledging to make "an empire of common sense." In spite of Owen's dream of creating the perfect place to live, he overlooked human greed and jealousy, lost four-fifths of his fortune, and his commune collapsed from internal anarchy.

All of us would like to have a perfect world in which to live. It would be great if we lived in a town where everyone worked together, shared, and lived for one another. Yet, we know that this world is an imperfect place stained by sin. We live in a world where greed, jealousy, selfishness, and strife are the norm. However, the believer looks forward to a new home, in which such things do not exist and will never exist. Our citizenship (conversation) is in heaven, which is a perfect world and community to live in. Today, as you are reminded of things that make this present world imperfect, remember that there is a perfect home awaiting you. It will be a great place to live throughout all eternity.

May 27

Psalm 103:19, "The Lord hath prepared his throne in the heavens; and his kingdom ruleth over all."

ON THIS DAY in 1931, Swiss physicist Auguste Piccard and his assistant became the first to reach the stratosphere. They ascended in a pressurized balloon with one side painted black to absorb the sun's rays and the other side white to repel them. Piccard had planned on using an electric motor to rotate away from the sun or toward it, but the motor froze. Temperatures rose and they were only able to descend when the temperatures fell and the balloon's gas contracted. Their balloon ride carried them to a height of 52,000 feet.

The Psalmist tells us that the heavens are the dwelling place of God's throne. The stratosphere is the space ten to thirty miles above the earth and is only a small part of the heavens that stretch for endless miles out into the universe. Somewhere in the heavens God occupies His throne and rules over the universe He has created. As believers, we can look up into the heavens with the assurance that God is on His throne. It fills our heart with great assurance and peace to know that He is in charge. With the Psalmist we can, "*Sing unto God, sing praises to his name: extol him that rideth upon the heavens by his name Jah, and rejoice before him*" (Psa. 68:4) The Bible declares, "*Thy throne, O God, is for ever and ever: the sceptre of thy kingdom is a right sceptre*" (Psa. 45:6) One of these days we will ascend to heights man has never traveled. We will bow before His throne in the heavens and worship Him in all His glory. We won't even need a pressurized balloon to get there. Today, rejoice that God is on His throne and He is in charge.

May 28

Romans 8:39, "Nor height, nor depth, nor any other creature, shall be able to separate us from the love of God, which is in Christ Jesus our Lord."

On This Day in 1934, on a small farm in the backwoods of Ontario, Elzire Dionne gave birth to five identical girls. The birth of the Dionne quintuplets made instant headlines around the world and was regarded as a miracle of human fertility. Within forty-eight hours, representatives of the Chicago's World Fair had telephoned the Dionnes inviting them to place the infants on exhibit at the fair for twenty-three percent of the gate receipts. Already supporting six children on a monthly income of barely $100, the Dionnes agreed. Yet the Canadian government stepped in and made the quintuplets wards of the states. It was only in 1941 that the Dionnes regained custody of their daughters.

As a child of God, we never have to fear of being separated from our heavenly Father and His love. Through our faith in Christ, we have been brought into an eternal relationship with God, and there is no power in heaven or earth that can sever that relationship. Later, the Dionne girls, after being reunited with their parents, wrote a book telling how harshly their parents treated them, and how they had been deprived of a yearly $30,000 income from movie appearances and endorsements. They wrote that they had "a painfully unhappy childhood." The testimony of the believer is that being a child of God and a member of God's family is a glorious experience. Today, rejoice that you are God's child and that nothing can ever separate you from Him or His love.

Revelation 21:1, "And I saw a new heaven and a new earth: for the first heaven and the first earth were passed away; and there was no more sea."

ON THIS DAY in 1942, the biggest selling record of all time was recorded. The song was "White Christmas" recorded by Bing Crosby. Irving Berlin had written the song for the movie *Holiday Inn*. When Crosby first heard the song, he told Berlin that he had a winner. "Winner" was an understatement. Before the year's end, "White Christmas" topped the charts where it stayed for eleven weeks. It topped the charts again in 1947. Crosby recorded the song again in 1947 with the John Trotter's Orchestra because the original masters had been worn out in all the pressings. The song won the Academy Award for the Best Song of 1942. More than thirty million copies of Crosby's recording have been sold and a total of nearly seventy million, including all versions of the standard, have been sold. The original popularity and impact of the song seems to have been due to the separation of loved ones that WW II brought.

As John saw the new Heaven and earth, one of the things that caught his attention was that there was no sea. The sea in the Bible speaks of separation such as the seas separate continents one from the other. John saw a place where there would no longer be a separation of loved ones. Many are "dreaming" of a day "just like the ones" we "used to know." They are looking forward to the day when they will be with their loved ones again. There are days when we remember the times we were together, and our hearts long to be together again. One day, we will live in a place where there will be no more separation. Today, rejoice that we will see our loved ones again. In my opinion, that day is not far away.

Philippians 1:3, "I thank my God upon every remembrance of you,"

On This Day in 1868, Memorial Day became an officially sanctioned holiday. First called "Decoration Day," the day was established to honor the soldiers who had died in the Civil War. The day was eventually extended to commemorate all U.S. soldiers killed in war. General John A. Logan, commander-in-chief of the Grand Army of the Republic, (an organization of Union veterans of the Civil War) named May 30th as a special day to honor the graves of Union soldiers. The location of the first Memorial Day has often been disputed, but in 1966, the U.S. Government proclaimed Waterloo, New York as the birthplace of Memorial Day. In 1971, the last Monday in May was made a federal holiday in honor of those who died serving the country.

When I think of those who paid the ultimate price serving our country to preserve our values and freedom, I think of the words of Sir Walter Scott:

"Solider, rest! Thy warfare o'er,
Sleep the sleep that knows not breaking,
Dream of battled fields no more.
Days of danger, nights of waking."

Today, may each of us give thanks for those who gave their lives on our behalf. To them, we owe a great debt and our heartfelt gratitude. Even more, may we stop in our busy day and kneel before our Lord and Saviour and give thanks that He gave His life so that we might be free. For His ultimate sacrifice, we could never thank Him enough. To our nation's heroes and our Saviour, we say "Thank you."

May 31

Revelation 1:3, "Blessed is he that readeth, and they that hear the words of this prophecy, and keep those things which are written therein: for the time is at hand."

On This Day in 1859, London's "Big Ben" began telling the time. Possibly London's most famous landmark, Big Ben is the clock tower of the Houses of Parliament. The nickname "Big Ben" was originally given to the thirteen-ton "Great Bell of Westminster," but the term came to include the clock and St. Stephen's Tower. The bell was named after the first commissioner of works, Sir Benjamin Hall. The four dials of the clock are twenty-three square feet, the minute hand is fourteen feet long, and the figures are two feet high. Minutely regulated with a stack of coins placed on the huge pendulum, Big Ben has proven to be an excellent timekeeper and has rarely stopped. During the second World War, the House of Commons was destroyed, but the clock tower remained in tact and Big Ben continued to keep time. Its unique sound was broadcast to the nation as a welcome reassurance of hope to all who heard it.

The book of Revelation gives us a description of the things that will come to pass in the future. It describes the events that will take place on earth and in heaven. At the very beginning of the book, we are told, "*the time is at hand.*" All that the future holds will happen according to God's plan and in His time. God's Prophetic Clock keeps the time and at the appointed hour, will chime the arrival of each event. For those who have trusted Christ as their Saviour, we are closer to many glorious events with each tick of the clock,. Today may be the day when God's clock rings out, announcing the arrival of the Lord Jesus. "The time is at hand."

June 1

Jeremiah 32:17, "Ah Lord God! behold, thou hast made the heaven and the earth by thy great power and stretched out arm, and there is nothing too hard for thee:"

ON THIS DAY in 1938, the first issue of the comic book "Superman" appeared in newsstands. Highschool classmates Jerry Seigel and Joe Shuster originally created the super hero as a villain that had been granted super-powers by a mad scientist. But later they turned him into a hero. They set out to recreate *Superman* as a comic strip. Siegel came up with almost all of the *Superman* legend as we know it, wrote the comic strips, and Shuster did the drawing. Together they chose the primary colors for his costume because, as Shuster recounted, they were "the brightest colors we could think of." After being rejected by several publishers over a period of three years, DC Comics found "Superman" just what they wanted for their new *Action Comics*. In order to meet the first issue's deadline, Shuster cut, pasted, and redrew *Superman's* daily strips into thirteen comic book size pages. The super-human being that could "leap tall buildings in a single bound" was born.

As believers, we have more than a superhuman comic book character. We have a God that is great and glorious and there is nothing He cannot do. Our God is not from some distant planet, but He is the Creator of all planets. There is nothing too hard for God! Not even Kryptonite can hinder or limit what He can do. Our childhood friend *Superman* may have thrilled us with his great exploits, but our God is more than a comic book character. He is real! He is able! He is our God! Today, worship One that is more than superhuman. He is supernatural!

June 2

Romans 15:20, "Yea, so have I strived to preach the gospel, not where Christ was named, lest I should build upon another man's foundation."

ON *THIS* DAY in 1953, Queen Elizabeth II knighted Edmund Hillary for conquering Mt. Everest. The highest mountain known to man, its official height is 29,028 feet. Before 1953, thirteen expeditions had attempted Everest and failed to reach the peak. Fifteen men had died in efforts to be the first to conquer Everest. At half past eleven on May 29, Hillary and Tenzing Norgay reached the top of Everest. The two men shook hands and then threw their arms around each other. They had done what no other person had ever done. They had reached the earth's highest point.

Believers are to be climbers, always striving to reach greater heights and accomplish great things for God. Paul says that his great ambition *(striving)* was to preach the gospel and to carry the message of Christ to where it had never been heard before. What is your ambition as a believer? What heights are you trying to reach in your Christian life? We may not reach every goal we set in our Christian life, but as one has said, "It is better to shoot at something than nothing." No matter where you have gotten in your Christian life or what you have done, there are greater heights to climb. While we rejoice at every peak that we have reached, let us reach forth for greater heights and see greater things. The climb itself is thrilling, although at times challenging. One day the King will reward those who were spiritual climbers. The epitaph of one climber reads, "He died climbing." Today, ask God to make you a climber. The view from the top of the mountain is breathtaking.

June 3

Joshua 21:45, "There failed not ought of any good thing which the Lord had spoken unto the house of Israel; all came to pass."

ON THIS DAY in 1888, Ernest Lawrence Thayer's poem "Casey at the Bat" was first published. When it first appeared in the *San Francisco Daily Examiner,* no one hailed its greatness. It was totally ignored by the public until Archibald Clavering Gunter gave the poem to comedian De Wolf Hopper to read at the Wallack Theater in New York. Gunter had read that both the New York and Chicago baseball clubs would be attending Hopper's show so he thought it would be a good poem for Hopper to read. As they say, the rest is history. May I refresh your memory? The game in Mudville had but one inning to play and the score was four to two. Yet all was not despair for "Casey, mighty Casey, was advancing to the bat." The crowd of 5,000 stood and cheered as Casey stepped to the plate. They watched as he took two strikes but they "knew Casey wouldn't let that ball go by again." What about the next pitch?

Oh, somewhere in this favored land the sun is shining bright;
The band is playing somewhere, and somewhere hearts are light:
And somewhere men are laughing, and little children shout;
But there is no joy in Mudville—great Casey has struck out.

The mighty Caseys of this world may fail us, but we know that our Lord will never fail. As with Joshua, the believer finds that every promise the Lord has made is true and not one will ever fail. Today, trust in God's wonderful promises. There will always be joy in the heart of those who trust Him—He never strikes out.

June 4

Galatians 5:1, "Stand fast therefore in the liberty wherewith Christ hath made us free, and be not entangled again with the yoke of bondage."

ON THIS DAY in 1989, the Chinese army massacred students in Tiananmen Square. Thousands of pro-democracy protestors gathered in Beijing's Tiananmen Square in what had become the symbol and focus of China's democratic movement. To clamp down on the protestors, the People's Liberation Army swept through the streets of the capital, firing automatic weapons indiscriminately into the crowd. The 300,000 strong army advanced towards Tiananmen Square. Armored vehicles smashed their way through burning barricades into the square to confront protesting students. Troops lined up for their assault and up to a thousand protestors were massacred as soldiers opened fire.

I think of the picture shown hundreds of times of the student standing before a tank in the street. The student stood there defiant of the tank's advance. It was a demonstration of how the desire and dream of freedom for some has known no cost. Many who have lived under a suppressive dictatorship have been willing to pay the ultimate cost just to be free. On the other hand, there are many who live in a country of democracy and freedom, yet live in bondage—spiritual bondage. They are slaves to Satan and sin. The believer rejoices that he has been delivered from the bondage of Satan and sin. Oh, blessed day it was when our chains of sin were broken by God's saving grace. Today, rejoice that you are free. We need not live in bondage again for whom the Son sets free is free indeed (John 8:36).

June 5

Joshua 10:14, "And there was no day like that before it or after it, that the Lord hearkened unto the voice of a man: for the Lord fought for Israel."

ON THIS DAY in 1967, the Six-Day War began. Responding to the Egyptian reoccupation of Gaza and the closure of the Gulf of Aqaba to Israeli shipping, Israel launched military offences against Egypt, Syria, and Jordan. During the so-called Six-Day War, Israel gained control of territory three times its original size, driving Arab armies from the Sinai Peninsula, Gaza Strip, West Bank, the Golan Heights and Jerusalem, reunited under Jewish rule. The speed and scope of Israel's victory was astounding. Egypt, Syria, and Jordan lost almost all of their air forces and much of their armed weaponry. Nearly 10,000 Egyptians were killed in Sinai and Gaza alone, compared with 300 Israeli casualties. In all, Egypt lost about 11,000 troops, Jordan nearly 6,000, and Syria about 1,000. Israel lost a total of 700.

The history of Israel is not without several amazing victories in the face of great odds. A Biblical example of an amazing victory was Joshua and the children of Israel's victory over a coalition of five kings. Against great odds, they came forth victorious. Yet, the secret to their victory was not their military might but that "*the Lord fought for Israel.*" The Lord fighting for Israel was demonstrated in the sun standing still and the total destruction and conquering of the coalition of kings. As believers, we do not have to fight our battles in our own strength and ability. The same Lord that fought for Israel is our Lord and He will fight our battles. Today, are you fighting some battle? Give the battle to the Lord. The God who caused the sun to stand still is still in the miracle business.

June 6

Luke 24:23, "And when they found not his body, they came, saying, that they had also seen a vision of angels, which said that he was alive."

ON THIS DAY in 1985, authorities in Brazil exhumed the remains of Dr. Josef Menegele. Known as the "Angel of Death" because of his role as a Nazi doctor at the German concentration camp at Auschwitz, Menegele had fled Germany assuming a fake identity and spent the next thirty-years hiding from international authorities. During his time at Auschwitz, Menegele had supervised the "selections" of incoming transports. These selections determined which would be sent to the gas chambers and which would become prisoners in the camp. As a doctor, he symbolizes the manner in which medicine became a tool for genocide by the Nazi's. The Israeli government was committed to his capture, trial, and execution for the crimes he had committed against the Jewish people, but he always managed to escape capture. In 1985, while in Brazil, he suffered a stroke while swimming and drowned. Through letters confiscated at a friend's house, they learned where he had been hiding and exhumed his skeletal remains to verify he was dead.

When the disciples arrived at the grave of the Lord Jesus, they found that the tomb was empty. His body was not to be found. Furthermore, they had an encounter, not with an angel of death, but with an angel that announced Jesus was alive. What a difference it would have made if the body of the Lord Jesus had been found or it ever was found. If the body of the Lord had been found, it would mean that our faith is in vain and we are still in our sins (1 Cor. 15:17). Today, rejoice that His body was not found. He was not missing—He was alive!

June 7

Isaiah 1:16, "Wash you, make you clean; put away the evil of your doings from before mine eyes; cease to do evil."

ON THIS DAY in 1899, Carry Nation walked into a saloon and announced, "Men, I have come to save you from a drunkard's fate." In her hatred and fight against alcohol, fifty-two year old Carry Nation decided to take things into her own hands. After a period of prayer, she claimed to have heard a voice from above that said, "Take something in your hands and throw at those places and smash them." She gathered up some bricks and stones from her backyard, wrapped them in newspapers, hitched up her buggy, and drove to Kiowa, Kansas. She walked into a saloon and after announcing her purpose, she began throwing the bricks and stones. Within minutes, every bottle in the place had been smashed, as well as the mirror behind the bar and the two front windows. It became the first of many saloons she dedicated her life to smashing up.

Isaiah heard a voice from above that called for the people to put away all evil things and to cleanse themselves. Of course, nothing was said about throwing bricks at the people. As believers, we must have a hatred for any sin in our life and with great passion seek the removal of that sin. I don't believe that God would tell us to smash up saloons or bomb abortion clinics, but God does tell us to put away all sin in our personal lives. Have you declared war on sin in your life? Today, ask God to give you a hatred for sin in your life. I would not recommend smashing up places you don't like, but I would recommend cleaning up your own life.

June 8

Psalm 33:12, "Blessed is the nation whose God is the Lord: and the people whom he hath chosen for his own inheritance."

ON THIS DAY in 1794, France celebrated what was termed "The Supreme Being and Nature." Because of the fear that France would become an atheistic society, the entire country celebrated a day recognizing the Supreme Being. From early morning, the residents of Paris decorated their houses with flowers and leaves and joined a procession through the streets.

It is always a tragic stage in any nation when God is no longer recognized and acknowledged as Lord. The Psalmist declares that a blessed nation is a nation whose God is the Lord. It is more than recognizing a Supreme Being. It is acknowledging and accepting Him as Lord. It is not enough to have a day to say, "In God We Trust." The secret to a nation being blessed is when God is Lord of that nation 365 days of the year, who He is honored and revered as Lord. For believers, it deeply grieves the heart to see your nation that has been so blessed of God and in its history acknowledge God as Lord, push God out of its affairs and make it almost a crime to allow God to have part in the affairs of that nation. When a nation begins to legislate God out of its affairs and makes Him nothing more than a token of its heritage, the need is more than decorating our houses with flowers and leaves. We need a revival that will shake the very foundations of the nation, bringing people to their knees in repentance. Today, pray for your nation. Pray that God will send a revival that will change the course in which we are heading. When God is Lord of a nation, that nation will be blessed. When He is not Lord, those blessings are removed.

June 9

Judges 8:23, "And Gideon said unto them, I will not rule over you, neither shall my son rule over you: the Lord shall rule over you."

ON THIS DAY in 1898, Britain was granted a nintey-nine-year lease on Hong Kong. At the outbreak of the First Opium War in 1839, Britain had invaded and occupied Hong Kong. Two years later, China formally ceded Hong Kong to the British with the signing of the Chuenpi Convention. As a British colony, Hong Kong flourished as an East-West trading center and as the commercial gateway for southern China. After the granting of an additional lease of ninety-nine-years, in 1984, the British and Chinese Communists signed a formal agreement that approved the 1997 return of the island back to the Chinese with the promise that China would preserve Hong Kong's capitalist system. On July 1, 1997, in ceremonies attended by Chinese and British officials, including Prince Charles, Hong Kong reverted back to Chinese rule.

Because of Gideon's leadership in leading the children of Israel out from under the rule of the Midianites, the children of Israel requested that Gideon rule over them. His response was simple and to the point; he nor his sons would rule over them, for the Lord was the only one who deserved the right to rule over them. As believers, we have come under the Lord's authority and control. We are to submit to His rule and Lordship. Unfortunately, some believers revert back to a control by their former ruler: the world, the flesh, and the devil. Yet, the Lord's rule over our life is not a lease agreement. It is not negotiable. It is to be a final and eternal rule. Today, let the Lord rule your life. Submit to His rule for time and eternity.

June 10

Psalm 121:1-2, "I will lift up mine eyes unto the hills, from whence cometh my help. My help cometh from the Lord, which made heaven and earth."

On This Day in 1909, the "SOS" signal was used for the first time. The "SOS" signal was adopted as a wireless telegraph maritime signal for distress. At the second Berlin Radiotelegraphic Conference of 1906, "SOS" was chosen. The Germans had used "SOE" as a general inquire call, but the "E" was changed to "S" because the final letter of "SOE" was a single dot, hard to copy in adverse conditions. The letter "S" was substituted for three dots. Three dashes and three dots (...– – –...) could not be misinterpreted. In spite of popular interpretations of "SOS" meaning "Save Our Ship," "Save Our Souls," or "Send Out Succour;" the "SOS" signal was adopted simply on account of its easy radiation and its unmistakable character. The first ship to use the "SOS" signal was the *S.S. Slavonia* that wrecked off of the Azores.

Many believers sailing on a stormy sea have sent up an "SOS" to the Lord. They have found that when they cried for help, He was "a very present help in trouble" (Psa. 46:1). Our cries for help are always heard. The Psalmist sent out his "SOS": *"Make haste, O God, to deliver me; make haste to help me, O Lord"* (Psa. 70:1) and he found that the Lord swiftly responded. In our case, our "SOS" does mean "Send Out Succour" and "Save Our Souls." Today, do you need His help? Send up an "SOS." You will find with the Psalmist that the Lord will help you. With the Psalmist you will be able to say, "My help cometh from the Lord." He always responds to your "...– – –..."

June 11

John 18:36, "Jesus answered, My kingdom is not of this world: if my kingdom were of this world, then would my servants fight, that I should not be delivered to the Jews: but now is my kingdom not from hence."

ON THIS DAY in 1982, the movie "E.T.: The Extra-Terrestrial" opened in theaters. The story is of the love that develops between a ten-year old boy named Elliott who is in need of a friend, and a little alien that is lost on earth after being separated from its mother ship that is on a mission studying earth plant life. They meet when Elliot hears sounds coming from near his home's backyard tool shed. He casually tosses his ball into the shed, and the little alien playfully throws it back at him. The story builds around the desire of E.T. to get back home. One of the box-office champion films of all time, the movie grossed over $100 million in its first thirty-one days. The movie went on to win Best Original Score, Sound, Sound Effects, and Special Visual Effects, as well as being nominated for Best Picture, Directing, Writing, Cinematography, and Film Editing in 1982.

Do you believe that aliens exist on earth? I do! I happen to be one. You see, each believer is a citizen of a kingdom that is not of this world. As it has often been said, we are in this world but are not of this world. As Jesus stood before Pilate, He describes His kingdom as being not of this world, and every person that has been saved is a citizen of that kingdom. His great mission on earth was to invite all to become citizens of that kingdom. So, you see, we are all aliens. The good news is that one day Jesus will come back for us to take us home. Today, look upon this world as but a temporary residence. Oh, by the way, if you need to "call home" you can.

June 12

Psalm 18:30, "As for God, his way is perfect: the word of the Lord is tried: he is a buckler to all those that trust in him."

On This Day in 1897, Karl Elsener patented his "Officers Knife" that became known as the "Swiss Army Knife." In 1881, Elsener designed a multi-function knife called the "????", which he sold to the Swiss Army and soon around the world. In the 1940's, the U.S. army began using them and the American soldiers actually gave the knife the name "Swiss Army Knife" because they could not pronounce its German name *Offizermesser*. The purpose of the knife was to give the soldiers an all-in-one tool that would meet many needs. It has a can opener, a screwdriver, scissors, and, of course, a knife. Today, that simple pocketknife is available in many styles and combinations and Elsener's cutlery company, which was founded in 1884 in Schwyz, Switzerland, is the largest cutlery manufacturer in Europe and is recognized in more than 100 countries around the world.

A certain Christian traveler was packing his suitcase, about to proceed on a journey. He remarked to a friend: "There is still a little corner left open in which I desire to pack a guidebook, a lamp, a mirror, a telescope, a book of poems, a number of biographies, a bundle of old letters, a hymnbook, a sharp sword, a small library containing thirty volumes—all these articles must occupy a space of about three by two inches." "How are you going to manage that?" queried his friend. The reply was, "Very easily, for the Bible contains all these things." The Bible is the Christian soldier's Swiss Army Knife. Today, use your knife. It has all that you need to be a good soldier of Jesus Christ.

June 13

1 John 2:1, "My little children, these things write I unto you, that ye sin not. And if any man sin, we have an advocate with the Father, Jesus Christ the righteous."

ON THIS DAY in 1966, the Supreme Court ruled that police could not interrogate individuals without notifying them of their right to counsel. In *Miranda verses Arizona*, the court considered the constitutionality of several instances in which defendants were questioned "while in custody or otherwise deprived of [their] freedom in any significant way." Ruled on jointly, the Court specifically outlined the necessary aspects of police warnings to suspects, including warnings of the right to remain silent and the right to have counsel present during interrogations.

John tells us that the believer is guaranteed of counsel. The believer is to attempt to live a life as free from sin as possible. Yet, when we sin, we have an Advocate. The idea of an advocate is one who pleads our case. Jesus is the believer's advocate! When we sin, the Lord Jesus represents us to the Heavenly Father. He does not argue our guilt or innocence. That is a settled issue. We are guilty! We have sinned! His single argument is His blood. God declares us forgiven through the merits of the Lord Jesus. When God looks at us, He looks at us through the blood of Jesus Christ and sees us clean. As believers, we do not have the right to be silent before God. We must confess our sins (1 John 1:9). Yet, when we do sin, we are assured that our Heavenly Advocate will represent us. We may not be able to live sinless, but we should try to sin less. Today, give thanks that when you sin, you have an advocate. That is your right as a believer.

June 14

Ruth 2:12, "The Lord recompense thy work, and a full reward be given thee of the Lord God of Israel, under whose wings thou art come to trust."

ON THIS DAY in 1954, the words, "under God" were added to the "Pledge of Allegiance" of the United States of America. The pledge was first published in the magazine "The Youth's Companion." Both James B. Upham and Francis Bellamy claimed to have written the pledge and in 1939, the United States Flag Association ruled that Bellamy was the author of the original pledge: "I pledge allegiance to the flag of the United States of America and to the Republic for which it stands, one nation, indivisible, with liberty and justice for all." I like "one nation under God" much better.

Ruth found a special place under God—under His wings. There she found a place of blessing and reward. The Psalmist says, "*How excellent is thy lovingkindness,* O God! *therefore the children of men put their trust under the shadow of thy wings*" (Psa.36:7). When we put our trust in Him, "*He shall cover thee with his feathers, and under his wings shalt thou trust: his truth shall be thy shield and buckler*" (Psa.91:4). What a blessed place to be during the trials of life. David found this blessed place during one of the darkest periods of his life: "*yea, in the shadow of thy wings will I make my refuge, until these calamities be overpast*" (Psa.57:1). His testimony was, "*Because thou hast been my help, therefore in the shadow of thy wings will I rejoice*" (Psa.63:7). As we proudly pledge allegiance to the flag of our nation, today may we humbly pray, "*Keep me as the apple of the eye, hide me under the shadow of thy wings*" (Psa.17:8).

June 15

Job 38:25, "Who hath divided a watercourse for the overflowing of waters, or a way for the lightning of thunder;"

ON THIS DAY in 1752, Benjamin Franklin performed his famous kite experiment with electricity. Even as a child, Franklin had a predilection for natural phenomena. The study of electricity became a great part of the inventor, politician, and author's life. To prove his hypothesis that lightning and electricity are manifestations of the same force, tied an iron wire to the top of his kite and let it sail. Tied to the end of the line by which he flew his kite was a silk ribbon and a metal key. His idea was that any electricity overhead would be attracted to the wire on top of the kite. As the lightning began to flash, he put his hand near the key and sparks flew. Franklin used his discovery to create the lightning rod. Words that pertain to electricity such as armature, charged, discharged, electrician, electrified, condense, and battery are a few associated with Franklin. It was a night in which he flew a kite that proved to be definitive in his research and studies of electricity.

Job speaks of God as the creator of lightning. In Franklin's case, he did not invent electricity as is sometimes misstated, but merely advanced his knowledge in that which existed. Lightning, as well as all of creation, is a marvel that man is continually learning about. Man is ever learning and discovering things about that which God has done. As believers, our knowledge of what God has given us and done for us is to be constantly expanding. We never get to the place where we have learned all that there is to learn about God. Today, sail your spiritual kites and discover more of the wonderful things God has given you in Christ.

June 16

Psalm 56:3, "What time I am afraid, I will trust in thee."

On This Day in 1933, President Franklin D. Roosevelt persuaded the Congress to pass the National Industrial Recovery Act. In the hold of a failing economy, the act was an unprecedented move that many would have thought unthinkable in a capitalistic society. The act gave President Roosevelt power to control industry, bring unions and bosses together, shorten working hours, fix wages, and regulate production. He made it clear that he was prepared to adopt near-dictatorship powers to save the country. He closed banks, allowing federal aid only to the efficient. Three billion dollars were ploughed into public works programs throughout the states. A civilian "conservation corps" was created to employ young people to plant trees, along with many other bold steps. The president kept in touch with the American people in regular "fireside chats" on the radio, which was listened to by millions. He told Congress, "I think this would be a good time for a beer."

The Psalmist has a different recommendation for dealing with hard times. Instead of having a beer, he put his trust in the Lord. Life is not always easy. There are times when we find our personal world rocked by trials and disturbing times. The hard times can be a fearful experience. Yet, in those times we can put our trust in the Lord. We can look to Him for help and place our troubles in His hands. The Psalmist declares, *"Commit thy way unto the Lord; trust also in him; and he shall bring it to pass"* (Psalm 37:5). Today, put your trust in the Lord. When hard times come, you will find that trusting Him will be far better than a beer. A peaceful soul is far better than a headache.

June 17

2 Corinthians 9:15, "Thanks be unto God for his unspeakable gift."

On This Day in 1885, the Statue of Liberty arrived in New York City. French sculptor Frederic Auguste Bartholdi was commissioned to design the sculptor. He began work on his form of a woman with an uplifted arm in 1875 and completed it in 1884. The statue was reduced to 350 individual pieces, packed in 214 cases, and shipped to the U.S. aboard the French frigate "Isere. It was reassembled on Ellis Island and set on its base. Its twenty-five windows in the crown symbolize gemstones found on earth and the heaven's rays shining over the world. The seven rays of the statue's crown represent the seven seas and continents of the world. The tablet that the statue holds in her left hand reads in Roman numerals, "July 4, 1776." There are 354 steps to reach the crown, and the total weight of the statue is 31 tons. It is the world's tallest statue standing 152 feet on a 150 ft. high pedestal. Originally known as *Liberty Enlightening the World*, the statue was a gift to the United States from France in recognition of their friendship established during the American Revolution.

When one thinks of gifts that have been given, the greatest gift is the gift God gave that we might have eternal life. The world's greatest gift was the gift of God's Son to purchase our salvation. Paul speaks of our salvation. He describes it as an "unspeakable gift." There are no words to describe the measure of God's gift to man. What is so amazing about God's gift is that it was given to those who were his enemies (Rom. 5:10). Today, give thanks for God's "unspeakable gift." It was a gift that represents our liberty!

June 18

Mark 16:6, "And he saith unto them, Be not affrighted: Ye seek Jesus of Nazareth, which was crucified: he is risen; he is not here: behold the place where they laid him."

On This Day in 1815, Wellington defeated Napoleon at Waterloo. The defeat was catastrophic for Napoleon and the beginning of the end for the French leader. Wellington, on his horse, Copenhagen, coolly directed his soldiers in the face of the French cannonade. The battle raged with terrible ferocity all day, but by end of the day Napoleon was defeated. All of England waited for news of the outcome of the battle. The message was signaled across the channel, "W-E-L-L-I-N-G-T-O-N D-E-F-E-A-T-E-D N-A-P-O-L-E-O-N." Yet due to a heavy fog, only the words "Wellington defeated" were received. All of England went into mourning. Then the fog lifted and the entire message was received and people celebrated throughout England.

When the Lord Jesus died, to the disciples and others, it was like receiving a message of defeat. But three days later, they received another message. The Lord Jesus was alive. He had risen from the dead! The combined powers of the religious leaders, Roman leaders, and military guards, along with Satan, could not keep the Lord Jesus in the tomb. The power in the tomb was greater than the powers outside the tomb. As the songwriter declares, *"Up from the grave He arose, with a mighty triumph ore His foes; He arose a victor over the dark domain and lives forever with His saints to reign."* Today, rejoice that Jesus rose from the dead. I join with another songwriter in saying, *"You ask me how I know He lives. He lives within my heart."*

June 19

Ephesians 6:2-3, "Honour thy father and mother; (which is the first commandment with promise;) [3] That it may be well with thee, and thou mayest live long on the earth."

On This Day in 1910, Father's Day was celebrated for the first time. In 1909, Sonora Smart Dodd of Spokane, Washington campaigned for a Father's Day celebration after listening to a sermon on the merits of Mother's Day. Her mother had passed away and her father had served as both father and mother to his six children for twenty-one years. In 1910, the first Father's Day was observed in Spokane. It was originally scheduled to be celebrated on June 5, her father's birthday, but it was moved to June 19 because there was not enough time to prepare for the celebration. Eventually, annual celebrations were held throughout the U.S. and Canada. In 1972, the U.S. Congress officially recognized Father's Day.

The Ten Commandments give the instruction that fathers and mothers were to be honored, and it was also reiterated in the New Testament. The New Testament describes this command as the first commandment with promise. In other words, it was the first of the Ten Commandments that included the promise that honoring parents brought blessings on those who kept the promise. There is a period of time in all of our lives when we are to obey our parents. When we leave father and mother and begin our own family, we are no longer obligated to obey our parents but we are still to honor them. Today, if you still have your father, do something to honor him. A hug and the words, "I love you" would be a good start. If the miles separate you, a call or note will work. Make many a day "Father's Day."

June 20

Psalm 33:18, "Behold, the eye of the Lord is upon them that fear him, upon them that hope in his mercy;"

ON THIS DAY in 1782, Congress approved the design of the Great Seal of the United States. The Continental Congress first commissioned the designing of a seal of the U.S. immediately after the signing of the Declaration of Independence. Charles Thomson, secretary of the congress, prepared the design. It is two-sided, having both an obverse and a reverse. The dominant figure on the obverse of the seal is an American eagle, shown with wings spread. On its breast, the eagle bears a shield having thirteen narrow vertical stripes, seven white alternating with six red, which are surmounted by a broad horizontal stripe of blue. The eagle holds an olive branch in its right talon, a cluster of thirteen arrows in its left, and in its beak a scroll on which appears the Latin motto *E pluribus unum* (from many, one). A cluster of thirteen five-pointed stars appears above the eagle. A pyramid is the central figure on the reverse side. The base of the pyramid is inscribed with the date 1776 in Roman numerals: MDCCLXXVI. At the zenith of the pyramid appears the all-seeing eye of Divine Providence. Above the eye is the motto *Annuit coeptis* (He has smiled on our undertakings).

The believer lives with the assurance that the all-seeing eye of God's Divine Providence is upon them. There is never a moment when we are not under His watchful care. We are the "*apple of His eye*" (Psa. 17:8). Today, give thanks that God is always watching over our lives and because He is watching, may He always be able to smile on our undertakings.

1 Corinthians 3:9, "For we are labourers together with God: ye are God's husbandry, ye are God's building."

On This Day in 1893, the world's first Ferris Wheel was opened to the public. It was opened at the World's Columbian Exposition. Designed by George Washington Gale Ferris, it stood 264 feet high. It had 36-pendulum cars that carried 60 passengers each (a total of 2,160 riders), weighed 1,200 tons, and was powered by two 1,000 horsepower engines. The cost of its production was $350,000. It was so popular that the cost was recovered within a few weeks at the exposition. Since it was so large, no single steel company could produce it. Therefore, Ferris contracted a dozen steel companies for its production.

As believers, we are in a great work and have a great task. Jesus tells His disciples, "*Go ye therefore, and teach all nations, baptizing them in the name of the Father, and of the Son, and of the Holy Ghost*" (Matt. 28:19). The gospel of the Lord Jesus is a message to be preached to the whole world. To carry out such a commission requires that every believer be involved. It is a task too large for just one or two. Paul describes a believer as a "laborer." He calls for a laboring together, or to put it another way, every believer getting involved in God's work. Are you involved in God's work? Are you aware of the greatness of the task before us? Today, if you are not involved, ask God where He would have you to serve. You are needed, for the task cannot be done with just a few. Everyone is needed. If you are involved, pray that God would give us more workers. We need as many as we can get.

June 22

Job 10:1, "My soul is weary of my life; I will leave my complaint upon myself; I will speak in the bitterness of my soul."

On This Day in 1969, Judy Garland was found dead in her bathroom from what doctors described as "an incautious self-over dosage of sleeping pills." At the age of seventeen, her role in *The Wizard of Oz* made her a superstar. By 1948, she was the leading musical actress. Yet by the age of eighteen she was seeing a psychiatrist, attempted suicide at twenty-eight, had four failed marriages and had been addicted to uppers to perform and downers to sleep since her early years as an actor. Living with her fifth husband in London, she was found locked in her bathroom, sitting with her head slumped over in her lap. Doctors said it was not suicide but that she had taken her usual dose of Seconal to sleep, then awakened and, confused, swallowed more pills. Her daughter Liza Minnelli said in a statement soon after, "It wasn't suicide, it wasn't sleeping pills, it wasn't cirrhosis. I think she was just tired, like a flower that blooms and gives joy and beauty to the world and then wilts away."

It may surprise you to know that certain great Bible characters were tired of living. Job is one such example. He confessed to being weary of life. All the things Job found himself going through made him tired of living. Maybe you have been there. The problems of life have a way of making us weary of life. Isaiah states, "*Even the youths shall faint and be weary*" (Isa. 40:30), but then gives us the antidote for such weariness: "*But they that wait upon the Lord shall renew their strength; they shall mount up with wings as eagles*" (Isa. 40:31). Today, if things have left you tired of life, God has just what you need to make your life worth living.

June 23

Psalm 121:4, "Behold, he that keepeth Israel shall neither slumber nor sleep."

ON THIS DAY in 1860, the United States Secret Service was created by an act of Congress. The Secret Service officially began in July 1865, for the purpose of protecting against the counterfeiting of U.S. currency. Following the assassination of President William McKinley in 1901, the role of the Secret Service was extended to protecting the president of the U.S. Through the years, the responsibilities of the Secret Service have taken on the role of protecting the president's family, the vice-president, major presidential and vice presidential candidates, past presidents, their wives, widows, and children sixteen and under. It also guards visiting heads of foreign governments and, at the request of the president, other foreign dignitaries.

As believers, we have our Protector. He is on guard and protecting us every minute of every day. As the Psalmist declares, "He is never asleep on the job. Day and night, from all elements and enemies, He protects us. His protection preserves us from evil" (Vs.7), and we are assured that *"The Lord shall preserve thy going out and thy coming in from this time forth, and even for evermore"* (Vs.8). Because we are His children, our Lord gives us His undivided attention. Our welfare is His ultimate concern. How comforting it is to the believer to know that we have "Someone" watching over us and out for us. With the Psalmist we can say, *"Thou art my hiding place; thou shalt preserve me from trouble; thou shalt compass me about with songs of deliverance. Selah"* (Psa. 32:7). Today, give thanks that the president of the United States is not the only one who has special protection.

June 24

Revelation 19:1, "And after these things I heard a great voice of much people in heaven, saying, Alleluia; Salvation, and glory, and honour, and power, unto the Lord our God."

ON THIS DAY in 1947, American search and rescue pilot, Kenneth Arnold had an experience which gave us the term, "flying saucers." Arnold was flying a mission over the Cascade Mountain when suddenly a bright flash lit the inside of his plane. He claimed to have seen, flying in a diagonal formation, nine bright objects flying close to the mountaintops at a speed he calculated to be 1,200 mph—twice the speed of any aircraft at that time. He described the aircraft as silvery on top and black on the bottom. His description of them flying, "like you'd take a saucer and skip it across the water," was picked up by newspaper reporters who wrote of "flying saucers" for the first time.

Quite often we hear discussions of whether there is life "out there." I am not sure of life on other planets, but I am certain that there is life "out there." Somewhere out there is a place called heaven, and it is the home of every person who has put their faith and trust in God's Son. John got a glimpse of heaven and saw that there were many people there. I personally have many friends and family there. I know that one day I will live there. I have no explanation for what Arnold saw during his mission, and I must confess that I have doubts that he encountered life forms from another world. Yet, I know that there is a place somewhere and many I know inhabit it. Today, rejoice that there is a place called heaven and that one day we will live there, along with our many loved ones who are already there.

June 25

Psalm 85:8, "I will hear what God the Lord will speak: for he will speak peace unto his people, and to his saints: but let them not turn again to folly."

ON THIS DAY in 1876, General George Armstrong Custer and the Seventh Calvary was killed at the Little Bighorn. Custer was involved in a campaign to force the Indians to leave the plains and return to their reservations. The buckskin clad general had expected to find no more than a handful of Sioux Indians as he led his force of 265 cavalrymen along the Little Bighorn River. Instead, he found an entire army of Sioux, Cheyennes, and Crows prepared to fight. In less than an hour, the general was dead and so was every one of his men. Custer and his men were so overwhelmed that they shot their horses for cover and formed a square on a pinnacle for defense. Custer's body was found with the flag of the Seventh Calvary still flying over him. The Indians took scalps from many of the men but not Custer's. However, his eardrums were pierced with a shaft so that he might be able to hear better in the next life and learn from the folly of his ways.

Listening to God is essential to the Christian life. Many mistakes have been made when we failed to listen to God. In many cases, much heartache could have been avoided if we had listened to God. The Psalmist speaks of those who, "*have ears, but they hear not*" (Psalm 115:6). There are times when we are no different. We refuse to listen to God and fail to hear His voice. I guess you could say that there are times when we need our eardrums spiritually pierced so that we can hear better. Today, ask God to give you ears to hear what He says. With the Psalmist say, "*I will hear what God the Lord will speak.*"

June 26

Ecclesiastes 5:4-5, *"When thou vowest a vow unto* God, *defer not to pay it; for he hath no pleasure in fools: pay that which thou hast vowed. Better is it that thou shouldest not vow, than that thou shouldest vow and not pay."*

ON THIS DAY in 1284, according to legend, the Pied Piper of Hamelin charmed the children and led them out of the city never to be seen again. The story is told of a strange and wondrous figure attired in a coat of many colors who arrived in the town of Hamelin, Germany. He pretended to be a rat catcher and promised to rid the town of rats and mice for a fixed sum of money which the citizens promised to pay. The stranger produced a pipe and began to play. Soon all the rats and mice came running out of the home, and the Pied Piper led them to the River Weser where they drowned. Hamelin was in a bitter mood. The historicity of the Pied Piper cannot be proven, but according to legend, it was on this date that he returned and once again played his pipe. Only this time, it was not rats and mice that came out but children. He led them through the Ostertor gate into the very heart of a hill, where they all disappeared.

Legend or fact, this story reminds us that vows are not to be broken. The wise man Solomon states very plainly that if we make a vow, God expects us to keep that vow. In fact, we are told that it is better not to make a vow than to make God a promise and break it. The Psalmist echoes the same thought when he says, "*Offer unto God thanksgiving; and pay thy vows unto the most High*" (Psa. 50:14). Have you made any promises to God? Today would be a good day to begin paying those vows. God keeps His promises and expects nothing less from us.

June 27

Luke 17:32, "Remember Lot's wife."

On This Day in 1829, English scientist James Smithson died leaving a will that aroused attention on both sides of the Atlantic. His will stated that in the event that his only nephew died without any heirs, the whole of his estate would go to "the United States of America, to found at Washington under the name of the Smithsonian Institution, an establishment for the increase and diffusion of knowledge." Six years later when his nephew died without any children, President Andrew Jackson sent diplomat Richard Rush to England to negotiate the transfer of funds. Two years later, Rush returned to the U.S. with 11 boxes containing a total of 104,960 gold sovereigns, 8 shillings, and 7 pence, as well as Smithson's mineral collection, library, scientific notes, and personal effects. After the gold was melted down, its worth amounted to over $500,000. On August 10, 1846, President James K. Polk signed an act establishing the Smithsonian Institute into law. What was so surprising to many about Smithson's clause in his will is that he had never been to the United States.

The Smithsonian Institute stands as a testimony to what one man left behind. Have you ever thought about what you will leave behind and how you will be remembered? Jesus speaks of remembering Lot's wife. When we remember Mrs. Lot, we think of a woman who was turned into a pillar of salt because her heart was tied to this world. Hers is a case of leaving a bad testimony. What kind of testimony will you leave behind? Today, ask God to help you to leave behind a testimony that will be a blessing to others and bring glory to God. You may not be able to bequeath thousands of dollars to a cause, but you can be remembered as one that pleased God.

June 28

Psalm 94:1, "O Lord God, to whom vengeance belongeth; O God, to whom vengeance belongeth, shew thyself."

ON THIS DAY in 1914, Archduke Franz Ferdinand was shot and killed while on an official visit to Bosnia. The archduke and his wife, the Duchess of Hohenberg, were driving down a narrow street when two shots rang out. One hit the archduke in the neck while the other struck his wife in the stomach. The duchess died almost immediately and the archduke died about ten minutes later. Nineteen year old Gavrilo Princip surrendered immediately. A member of a nationalist group from neighboring Serbia, Princip stated that he was avenging the oppression of the Serbian people. The assassination triggered WWI.

The desire for revenge is not uncommon.When someone feels that they have been unjustly mistreated, a spark ignites on the inside that grows into a flaming inferno. Hatred fills the heart and a desire to get even drives them to actions with no thought of personal consequences or how it will affect others. People can be cruel and our hurts legitimate. Yet, revenge is never an action for our taking, but a matter to be put into the hands of God. Vengeance belongs to God and God alone. As difficult as it may be, our step of action when wronged is to forgive. As Jesus says, "*Bless them that curse you, and pray for them which despitefully use you*" (Luke 6:28). Our human nature cries for revenge, but the divine nature calls for forgiveness. Today, put all your hurts and bitterness into God's hands. Leave vengeance to Him. When we take things into our own hands, we are liable to start a war in which many will be affected.

June 29

1 John 5:16, "If any man see his brother sin a sin which is not unto death, he shall ask, and he shall give him life for them that sin not unto death. There is a sin unto death: I do not say that he shall pray for it."

On This Day in 1972, the U.S. Supreme Court ruled that capital punishment was unconstitutional. In a vote of five to four, it was ruled that the death penalty as it was currently employed was in violation of the Eighth Amendment as "cruel and unusual punishment", primarily because states carried out executions in "arbitrary and capricious ways." It was the first time that the nation's highest court had ruled against capital punishment. However, the Supreme Court suggested that new legislation could make the death penalty constitutional again and in 1976, with sixty-six percent of Americans in favor of the death penalty, the Supreme Court acknowledged progress made in jury guidelines and reinstated the death penalty under a "model of guided discretion."

It may surprise some to know that God has His own "death penalty." The Bible plainly declares, *"There is a sin unto death."* God's death penalty is the ultimate expression of God's dealing with sin in the life of the believer. Speaking of the Corinthians, Paul declares, *"For this cause many are weak and sickly among you, and many sleep"* (1 Cor. 11:30). Paul is describing those who had died because of their refusal to deal with sin in their life (1 Cor. 11:31). A person can go so far in sin and refuse to repent, in spite of all God does to bring that person to repentance, that death is the outcome. Today, realize that God takes sin seriously in the life of a believer. He will forgive of all sin, but if we don't deal with sin, He will.

June 30

2 John 1:8, "Look to yourselves, that we lose not those things which we have wrought, but that we receive a full reward."

ON THIS DAY in 1994, the U.S. Figure Skating Association stripped Tonya Harding of her 1994 National Championship and banned her from the organization for life. The decision of the five-member panel stemmed from a January 6th attack on Nancy Kerrigan. A 1992 Olympic bronze medallist and one of the favorites to win the gold medal in the Winter Olympics, Kerrigan was attacked and hit on the right knee by a man wielding a blunt object. Harding did not show up for the two-day hearing, but the panel came to the decision that she had prior knowledge and was involved in the incident. Harding had earlier pled guilty to the felony of conspiracy to hinder the prosecution in the Kerrigan attack and had resigned from the USFSA. The panel that met for nine hours stated, "Ms. Harding's actions, as they related to the assault on Nancy Kerrigan, evidenced a clear disregard for fairness, good sportsmanship, and ethical behavior."

One of the great tragedies of the Christian life is to live for God and then let something happen that would strip the believer of his heavenly reward. John's words admonishing us to guard our life lest we lose a full reward remind us that the rewards we have earned in life can be lost. The believer who lives for God and serves Him faithfully is promised eternal rewards. No believer should want to go to heaven with no reward awaiting him or with less than what could have been received. Today, set your goal that when you stand before the Lord, you will have a full reward.

July 1

James 5:11, "Behold, we count them happy which endure. Ye have heard of the patience of Job, and have seen the end of the Lord; that the Lord is very pitiful, and of tender mercy."

On This Day in 1903, the Tour de France was held for the first time. The first winner of the Tour de France was the French cyclist Maurice Garin. Often called "the Tour," more than 150 competitors race along a course that covers nearly 3,200 km (about 2,000 miles) of European roads. The event is held each July and lasts about twenty-five to thirty days. The course lies mostly in France, but changes each year. The final stretch of the course always runs along the Champs-Élysées, a famous avenue in Paris. The race is run in stages. Certain stages emphasize a particular cycling skill, such as climbing hills, sprinting, or performance in the time-trial races. Cyclists are timed for each stage and during the race, the cyclist with the lowest cumulative time wears the *maillot jaune* (yellow jersey) that indicates the current leader. The winner of the race receives the yellow jersey as a trophy in a ceremony in Paris. The Tour de France is the most popular bicycle race in the world and one of the most challenging in professional cycling competition.

The Bible often speaks of the Christian life as a race. Although the imagery is that of a runner rather than a bicyclist, it is a race that requires endurance. Our race is not a short sprint but a lifelong race that takes us over a course of varied conditions. In the Tour de France, only about half of the cyclists who enter finish the race. Unfortunately, there are those who fall by the wayside in the race of life. Today, keep on keeping on for the Lord. Whatever stage of the race you are in, to wear the Lord's *maillot jaune* is worth every mile.

July 2

Psalm 144:15, "Happy is that people, that is in such a case: yea, happy is that people, whose God is the Lord."

ON THIS DAY in 1961, writer Ernest Hemingway committed suicide at his Ketchum, Idaho home. A best selling author throughout his adult life, Hemingway continues to be recognized by critics as one of the most important figures in 20th century literature. A.E. Hotchner, a close friend of Hemingway, in his biography entitled "Papa Hemingway," admitted that he was perplexed as to why Hemingway took his own life. In the foreword, the biographer listed what Hemingway had going for him: He had won both the Nobel and Pulitzer Prizes, he had a home in Idaho's Sawtooth Mountains; an apartment in New York, a yacht to fish the Gulf, apartments available at the Ritz in Paris, and the Gritti in Venice, a sturdy marriage, and fine friends everywhere."

Why someone takes his or her life is often a mystery. However, Hemingway's friend and biographer would seem to suggest that if a person has certain things in life and has achieved certain things, it would be a reason to be happy and find personal fulfillment. The opposite is often the case. Many who have had much of this world's goods, have in a moment of honesty admitted that these things did not make them happy. On the other hand, there are those who have little that this world has to offer, yet they possess happiness that eludes those who have much. Where does real happiness come from? The Psalmist declares that happiness is something one finds in a relationship with the Lord. Happiness is never found in things, it is only found in a person—the Lord Jesus Christ. Today, rejoice that you have found the real source of joy and happiness. To know the Lord Jesus is to know the real source of happiness.

July 3

Daniel 6:4, "Then the presidents and princes sought to find occasion against Daniel concerning the kingdom; but they could find none occasion nor fault; forasmuch as he was faithful, neither was there any error or fault found in him."

ON THIS DAY in 1988, the U.S. Navy ship *Vincennes* accidentally shot down an Iranian passenger plane, killing all 290 people aboard. The attack came near the end of the Iran-Iraq war. At first the U.S. denied being at fault but one month later, they admitted that there had been error on their part. When an official report was released, it stated that "stress, task fixation, and unconscious distortion of data", due to the *Vincennes* combat earlier in the day, may have contributed to the mistaken identification of the passenger plane as hostile. In December, a probe by the U.N.'s International Civil Aviation Organization found the U.S. Navy primarily responsible for the downing of Flight 655. Acknowledged as an "error," regardless of why it happened, it was an error that cost 290 innocent lives.

As believers, our "errors" can have drastic consequences. How we live is very important because our mistakes and errors can bring harm to those around us. Only heaven will reveal those who have been hurt because of the failures and mistakes of others. Daniel is a good example of a believer whose life was not marked by *"error or fault."* There was not one negative thing in his life that you could point a finger at. Today, realizing that our mistakes can bring great harm to others, ask God to help you to live a life without *"error or fault."* Too many have already been hurt by the failures of others. Another Daniel is just what our day needs.

July 4

2 Corinthians 9:11, "Being enriched in every thing to all bountifulness, which causeth through us thanksgiving to God."

ON THIS DAY in 1939, Lou Gehrig was honored in a special ceremony at Yankee Stadium. "Lou Gehrig Day" was perhaps one of the most famous ceremonies in baseball history. Gehrig had been diagnosed as having a rare, almost unknown, and incurable disease, amyotrophic lateral sclerosis, forever after known as Lou Gehrig's disease. He played in 2,130 consecutive games, holds the American League (AL) season record for RBI's, hit a Major League record 23 grand slams, one of two players to hit four homers in a nine-inning game, and led the AL five times in RBI's and four times in runs. When he retired, only Babe Ruth had hit more home runs. As he stood before the crowd, his voice broke with emotion as he said, "Today, I consider myself the luckiest man on the face of the earth."

There is so much that we have and do enjoy as believers. We have been blessed in so many ways. We are daily loaded with blessings (Psa. 68:19). The Lord's mercies are new every morning (Lamentations 3:23). Our blessings are so numerous that it would be impossible to name or number them. Paul describes how we have been enriched with bountiful blessings, and how a realization of how much we have been blessed leads to thanksgiving. Thinking always leads to thanking. Today, take the time to think about the number of ways you have been blessed. It will not be long before you find yourself saying, "I am the most blessed person on the face of the earth." But then, all of God's children feel that way.

July 5

Romans 15:20, "Yea, so have I strived to preach the gospel, not where Christ was named, lest I should build upon another man's foundation:"

ON THIS DAY in 1865, William Booth founded the Salvation Army. First known as the Christian Mission, the mission reached out to the poor and downcast of London's East End. Booth modeled his ministry after the British army, calling his ministers "officers" and new members "recruits." Today, the Salvation Army is established in 80 countries, has 16,000 evangelical centers, and operates more than 3,000 social welfare institutions, hospitals, schools, and agencies. In the United Kingdom, the Salvation Army is the largest supplier of social services apart from the government. On one occasion, King Edward VII invited Booth to Buckingham Palace and when the king asked him to write in his autograph album, he wrote:

Your Majesty,
Some men's ambition is art,
Some men's ambition is fame,
Some men's ambition is gold,
My ambition is the souls of men.

Paul states that his ambition *(strived)* in life was to preach the Gospel and win others to Christ. What is your great ambition in life? Is it to make more money or to have certain earthly possessions? These things in themselves may not be wrong, but the greatest ambition one could have is the souls of men. Today, make your great ambition in life to be that someday there will be someone in heaven because of you. Having such ambitions is a great way to meet the King of kings!

July 6

Matthew 17:16, "And I brought him to thy disciples, and they could not cure him."

ON THIS DAY in 1885, Louis Pasteur first gave his rabies vaccine to a human. Pasteur had spent years working on the causes of various diseases and their prevention by means of vaccination. After experimenting with the saliva of animals suffering from rabies, he concluded that the disease rests in the nerve centers of the body. He found that when an extract from the spinal column of a rabid dog was injected into the bodies of healthy animals, symptoms of rabies were produced. By studying the tissues of infected animals, Pasteur was able to develop an attenuated form of the virus that could be used for inoculation. His first human experiment was a peasant boy named Joseph Meister, who had been bitten by a mad dog. His parents brought the boy to Pasteur. They begged Pasteur to save their son. Pasteur hesitated to use his new vaccine on the boy because it had never been used on a human. Finally, he gave in. After several weeks of treatment, the vaccine proved successful and the boy's life was saved.

There was a day when a boy possessed with demons was brought to the disciples. Jesus had given them the power to cast out demons but on this occasion, they were unable to cast the demons out. Jesus attributed the cause to their lack of faith and admonished them that *"this kind goeth not out but by prayer and fasting"* (17:21). What is the cause of powerlessness in our lives as believers? It can always be traced to a lack of faith, prayer, and yes, even fasting. These are essential to effective service. Today, pray for an effective life. You never know when someone may come our way who needs the cure we have discovered.

July 7

1 Corinthians 12:18, "But now hath God set the members every one of them in the body, as it hath pleased him."

ON THIS DAY in 1891, Marcellus F. Berry was granted four copyrights for what he called "The Traveler Cheque." It all began when James C. Fargo, president of the American Express Company, couldn't get his checks cashed during a trip to Europe in 1890. Berry, an employee of American Express, came up with the solution. He later wrote, "There's one thing that every person does in a distinctive way. That is writing his signature. Therefore the foolproof device for taking money to strange places must carry the signature of the bearer. It must declare that it will only be cashed when a second and matching signature is signed before witnesses." A few weeks later William Fargo, James Fargo's son, traveled to Germany. Using the "Traveler Cheque", he had no difficulty when he wanted fifty dollars.

Every believer has not only a distinctive signature but a distinctive role in God's work. Each Christian is a gifted child of God. There is a diversity of spiritual gifts (1 Cor.12:4). God equips and uses people in different ways. Not every believer is a pastor or a teacher. There are many more roles in God's work than these. God has a specific plan for each believer, and His gifts are distributed to believers according to the role and plan He has for each life. This makes every believer an important person in God's work. Everyone has their place and therefore, a distinctive role in God's work. Today, remember that what sets you apart from everyone else is not just your signature, but also your place in God's family. Your gifts can be used anywhere.

Ephesians 4:27, "Neither give place to the devil."

ON THIS DAY in 1776, Colonel John Nixon gave the first public reading of the Declaration of Independence. The Declaration of Independence, written primarily by Thomas Jefferson with slight changes by Ben Franklin and John Adams, was made up of five distinct parts: the introduction, the preamble, the body of two parts, and a conclusion. The introduction states that the document declared the "causes" that made it necessary for the American colonies to leave the British Empire. The first section of the body gives evidence of the "long train of abuses and usurpations" heaped upon the colonies by King George III, and the second part of the body stated that the colonists had appealed in vain to their "British brethren" for a redress of their grievances. It concludes: "These United Colonies are, and of Right ought to be Free and Independent States; that they are Absolved from all Allegiance to the British Crown, and that all political connection between them and the State of Great Britain, is and ought to be totally dissolved."

In the past, we as believers lived under the authority and power of the god of this world. As we look back on our past life, we see a "long train of abuses and usurpations" by Satan. In Christ Jesus, we have been set free from Satan's power to live a new life in Christ. However, our battle with Satan has not ended. Satan seeks to bring each believer under his power and authority again. As Paul declares, there must be a daily renouncing of any allegiance to Satan and any connection with the things of Satan must be totally dissolved. In other words, we must not give place to the devil in any fashion or form. Today, remind Satan that you have been set free and you are no longer under his power.

July 9

Psalm 62:8, "Trust in him at all times; ye people, pour out your heart before him: God is a refuge for us. Selah."

ON THIS DAY in 1982, Michael Fagan climbed a fence into the grounds of Buckingham Palace and eventually made his way to the Queen's bedroom. Fagan, a thirty-one year old unemployed painter and decorator, shinned up a drainpipe to climb through an open window. He wandered the palace unchallenged for fifteen minutes before entering the Queen's bedroom. The Queen pressed an alarm bell, which failed to get a response. Twice she used her bedside phone to call security, but no one came. Fagan sat on her bed and told her all of his family problems. The Queen responded with small talk. When Fagan asked for a cigarette, she left the room promising to find one for him. Outside she found a chambermaid to whom she explained the problem, and soon security arrived to take Fagan away. It was later learned that Fagan had penetrated the palace five weeks earlier during a state visit by President and Mrs. Reagan.

As believers, we have the privilege of telling the King of Kings about our troubles, and we don't even have to climb a fence or shinny up a drainpipe to do so. All we have to do is to cry out to Him and He will be there. The Psalmist speaks of pouring our hearts out to God. Are you experiencing a time of difficulty in your life? Are the burdens of life pressing and distressing? Do you need someone to tell your troubles to? If so, then today pour out your hearts to the Lord. You need not worry that someone will escort you away. He will listen as long as you need to talk. The door to His palace is open and you are always welcome.

July 10

Genesis 1:27, "So God created man in his own image, in the image of God created he him; male and female created he them."

ON THIS DAY in 1925, the Scopes "Monkey" Trial in Dayton, Tennessee began. John T. Scopes, a teacher at Dayton's Central High School, had been charged with teaching "a certain theory or theories which deny the story of the divine creation of man taught in the Bible and teach instead that man descended from a lower form of animals." Leading the prosecution was the venerable William Jennings Bryan, and the renowned Chicago attorney Clarence Darrow led the defense. Scopes was found guilty, left Central High, and sought to shun publicity the rest of his life. In a rare interview in 1960, a reporter asked him why there was a continued battle for academic freedom. He replied, "Well, people just don't change that quickly."

Through out time, the teachings of the Bible have been attacked and put on trial. The story of creation has not been without its share of critics and adversaries. Where did man come from? Is he the result of an evolutionary process that occurred over thousands and millions of years or is he the result of divine creation? How you answer that depends entirely on whether you believe every word of God's Word. As for me, I may have had a few ancestors hung by the neck, but I don't think I had any hung by the tail. Christians embrace what God says in His Word, even the Bible's version of the creation of man. While others argue about how things happen, today, give thanks that God's Word is absolutely true. As for me, I will never change my mind about that.

July 11

1 Corinthians 15:34, "Awake to righteousness, and sin not; for some have not the knowledge of God: I speak this to your shame."

On This Day in 1929, spectators cheered as nine boys and six firemen burned to death in a fire. Each year, the firemen of Gillingham in Kent, England constructed a makeshift house for a firefighting demonstration at the annual Gillingham Park fete. Each year, a few local boys were selected from many aspirants to take part in the demonstration. The nine boys and six firemen climbed to the third floor of the house. The plan was to light a smoke fire on the first floor, rescue the party, and then set the empty house on fire to demonstrate the use of fire hoses. By mistake, the real fire was lit first. The spectators thought the bodies they saw burning were dummies. They cheered and clapped while firemen on the outside fought to put out the fire, which they knew was a catastrophe.

One of the sharpest rebukes Paul gave the church at Corinth was concerning those who took lightly the salvation of those around them who were lost. His words called for them to wake up and realize that people around them were perishing and needed to be saved. It is so easy to get wrapped up in our own little world and forget that others need what we have experienced in Christ. Each day we enjoy the blessings of being eternally saved while multitudes around are lost and perishing. Today, ask God to give you an awareness of those who are not saved and to give you a concern for their salvation. Hell is real! Don't ever forget that.

Colossians 2:14, "Blotting out the handwriting of ordinances that was against us, which was contrary to us, and took it out of the way, nailing it to his cross;"

ON THIS DAY in 1960, the first Etch A Sketch® toys were produced. In the late 1950's, Arthur Granjean invented in his garage what he called "L'Ecran Magique". He took his drawing toy to the International Toy Fair in Nuremberg, Germany. The Ohio Art Company saw it but had no interest in it. They saw it a second time and decided to take a chance on it. Renaming it the Etch A Sketch®, it became the most popular drawing toy in the business. Very little has changed over the years –the bright red frame, silver-gray drawing surface, and width of nine and one-half inches. The screen's reverse side is coated with a mixture of aluminum powder and plastic beads. Two knobs move a stylus that scrapes the screen leaving the line you see. All one has to do to remove the picture drawn on the screen is just shake it and start over.

There are many who wish they could take their past and just give it a shake so it would all be erased. Unfortunately, we cannot do that, but through the cross our record has been erased. In Paul's day, ink was much different. It did not bite into the paper as today and could be wiped off allowing the paper to be reused. When Jesus died on the cross, he blotted out the handwriting of ordinances that was against us. There was our record which contained every sin we had committed but at the cross, Jesus blotted out or wiped away that record. Today, give thanks that the blood of Jesus has cleansed the record of all our sins. In God's eyes, we have a clean screen.

July 13

1 Peter 4:6, "For this cause was the gospel preached also to them that are dead, that they might be judged according to men in the flesh, but live according to God in the spirit."

On This Day in 1985, pop superstars united to feed the world. Crowds filled London's Wembley Stadium for a star-studded Live-Aid concert to raise money for the famine victims of Ethiopia. The event ran for a full sixteen hours and was broadcasted to 152 countries. It is estimated that almost two billion viewers tuned in. The Prince and Princess of Wales attended the start of the concert. The Live-Aid project was the brain-child of Bob Geldot, lead singer of the Irish band *The Boontown Rats*. The concert adhered to its strict schedule with a red light to inform the performers it was time to leave the stage. The entire show ran only over a mere two minutes.

While humanitarian aid is a great cause, the body of Christ has an even greater cause. It is a cause that brings the Bread of Life to the hungry souls of those who are perishing without Christ. It is a cause that ought to unite every believer. It is a cause that should inspire our financial giving and personal involvement. The preaching of the gospel is a greater cause than providing humanitarian aid; for if we only feed them with the bread of this world, they may gain the benefit of a full stomach but remain with an empty soul. Humanitarian aid may be a means for the believer, but it should not be the end. The preaching of the Gospel is our priority. Are you doing your part financially and personally to see that others receive the Bread of Life? Today, rally around this great cause. If rock singers can work to feed the hungry, we can work to bring the Bread of Life.

July 14

Proverbs 22:6, "Train up a child in the way he should go: and when he is old, he will not depart from it."

ON THIS DAY in 1946, Dr. Benjamin Spock's "The Common Sense of Baby and Child Care" was first published. Following WWII, his book became the bible for parents, selling more than fifty million copies in paperback and translated into more than thirty languages. The claim has been made that his book was America's second best selling book after the Bible. His idea of child rearing was based on affection and respect as opposed to physical punishment. Because of the ideas he advocated, he was branded as "the father of permissiveness" and was blamed for the radical behavior of the youth in the 60's. Spock joined those youths in the protests again nuclear technology and the Vietnam War, leading Vice President Spiro Agnew to accuse him of corrupting the youth of America.

If you really want to know how to rear children, why settle for the book that came in second place? The Bible is the best book for parents to learn how to rear children. Its author knows everything and does not deal in theories but in time tested and proven facts. Toward the end of his life, Dr. Spock shifted to a more moralistic approach saying that parents should give their children strong values. He told the Associated Press in 1992, the year the sixth edition of his "Baby and Child Care" came out, "I've come to the realization that a lot of our problems are because of a dearth of spiritual values." In other words, the book that outsold his was really the best source for instructions on how to rear children. Today, let God's Word be your guide book in all things, even in how to rear children. All who follows its principles have found that they really work!

July 15

1 Samuel 17:4, "And there went out a champion out of the camp of the Philistines, named Goliath, of Gath, whose height was six cubits and a span."

ON THIS DAY in 1940, Robert Wadlow, the world's tallest man died. Known to everyone as the "Gentle Giant," Robert was born in Alton, Illinois, as a completely normal baby weighing eight and one-half pounds. However, due to an overactive pituitary gland, by the time he was a year old, he weighed twice the normal forty-four pounds. By the age of nine, he had grown to six feet two inches; by sixteen, seven feet ten inches and nearly 400 pounds. He died at the age of twenty-two from an infection caused by a brace on his ankle. His extreme height caused a lowered sensitivity in his legs, so he did not realize that the brace had caused a sore until it became infected. When he died at the age of twenty-two, he was eight feet eleven inches and weighed 439 pounds.

David found himself facing not a "Gentle Giant" but one who mocked and taunted the armies of Israel. According to the Bible, his height was a little over nine feet tall. In his hand he carried a spear, with a staff likened to a weaver's beam. The presence of this Philistine giant created widespread fear throughout the children of Israel. But David, just a young shepherd boy, saw him not as one to fear but as one to be conquered. With nothing but a sling and five stones, David boldly confronted the giant with the words, *"I come to thee in the name of the Lord of hosts, the God of the armies of Israel, whom thou hast defied"* (1 Sam. 17:45). As they say, you know the rest of the story. Today, do you face some giant in your life? Face that giant in the name of the Lord. There is no giant too big for God to bring down, even your giant. We may be no match for the giants of life, but then again we don't have to be.

July 16

1 Thessalonias 1:10, "And to wait for his Son from heaven, whom he raised from the dead, even Jesus, which delivered us from the wrath to come."

ON THIS DAY in 1976, Viola Walker's ten month vigil waiting for the return of Christ and the end of the world came to an end. In September of 1975, sixty-seven year old Mrs. Walker of Grannes, Arkansas told her relatives that she had received a message from God that the Second Coming and the end of the world was drawing near. Twenty-one of her relatives joined her in a vigil to wait for Christ's return in a three-bedroom house. They took their children out of school and quit paying their bills. Their vigil was interrupted ten months later when Deputy Marshals came to their house to evict them, because the bank had foreclosed on the mortgage of the house they were staying in.

There are many promises in the Bible to assure us of Christ's return. We are told to watch for His return (Matt. 24:42), to look for His coming (Phil. 3:20), to long for His coming (2 Pet. 3:12), and as our verse for the day declares, wait for His coming. Waiting for His return does not mean that we should isolate ourselves in a house but live each day in light of His return. Knowing that He is coming, we should live in such a way as to not be ashamed when He returns (1 John 2:28). To wait for His coming is to serve Him and seek to get as many ready for His coming as possible. Waiting for the Lord does not encourage inactivity but activity. Today, let the thought of His return fill your heart. Oh, yes, I would recommend that you pay your bills while you wait.

July 17

Ephesians 5:6, "Let no man deceive you with vain words: for because of these things cometh the wrath of God upon the children of disobedience."

On This Day in 1938, Douglas Corrigan earned the nickname "Wrong Way" Corrigan. An unemployed airplane mechanic and pilot, Corrigan had dreamed of flying across the Atlantic. After flying from Los Angeles to New York, he was denied permission from the Civil Aviation Authority to fly across the Atlantic from New York to Ireland. He was turned down on the grounds that his plane, called an "old rust bucket", was in poor condition. Corrigan seemed to accept the ruling but when he took off from New York, he banked sharply to the east and twenty-eight hours and thirteen minutes later landed at Dublin's Baldonnel Field. He said to the Irish authorities, "Oh my God! In the darkness I must have followed the wrong end of the compass needle." He always stuck to his story that he flew to Ireland by accident, even after he was made an honorary member of the "Liars Club of America." The American government suspended his license for five days and when he arrived back in the United States, he was greeted as a hero. More than a million people lined New York's Broadway for a ticker tape parade to honor the man who had flown the wrong way.

Disobedience may have made Douglas Corrigan a hero and earned the applause of the people, but disobedience is never honored, condoned, or celebrated by God. The scripture is very plain when it states that disobedience always results in God's displeasure and even discipline. Today, go the "right way" and not the "wrong way." To go the wrong way may cost you more than a five-day suspension.

Psalm 119:161, "Princes have persecuted me without a cause: but my heart standeth in awe of thy word."

ON THIS DAY in 64 A.D., the Great Fire of Rome began. Two-thirds of the city was left in ruins. It is not certain who started the fire, but many felt that Nero was the incendiary who took advantage of the fire's destruction to indulge his aesthetic tastes in the reconstruction of the city. His first task after the fire was the construction of a huge elegant palace. Nero saw himself losing favor with the public and blamed the fire on the Christians, which led to their persecution. For a man who had his own mother put to death for criticizing his mistress, divorced and killed his wife Octavia, married his mistress and kicked her to death, married another woman after executing her husband, the Christians were a way to shift the blame from himself. Eventually, the Senate declared Nero a public enemy. He could not bear the thought of being hunted down, so he had his servant stab him. His last words were, "What an artist I died."

You could say that the Christians were guilty of starting a fire but not setting fire to the city of Rome. Christians have often been the target of unjustified criticism and persecution. The history of the church is stained with the blood of an untold number who were fed to the lions, torn asunder, and burned at the stake for no other reason than just being a Christian. Maybe you have found yourself the target of someone's vicious attacks without a cause. The Psalmist found that during such times, God's Word was his strength and stay. When he was at his lowest, he found that God's Word kept him at his strongest. Today, let God's Word give you the strength you need to face what you are facing, even persecution.

July 19

1 John 2:27, "But the anointing which ye have received of him abideth in you, and ye need not that any man teach you: but as the same anointing teacheth you of all things, and is truth, and is no lie, and even as it hath taught you, ye shall abide in him."

On This Day in 1799, the Rosetta Stone was discovered near the Nile River. Carved in 196 B.C., the stone was found by French soldiers who were rebuilding a fort near the village of Rosetta (whence its name). The odd shaped, black basalt stone became an important key to understanding Egyptian hieroglyphics. The writing on the stone was in two languages (Egyptian and Greek) using three scripts (hieroglyphics, demotic, and Greek). After many years of studying the stone and other examples of Egyptian writing, in 1882, Jean-Francois Champollion was able to decipher the hieroglyphics. The stone had been written by a group of priests in Egypt to honor the Egyptian pharaoh. It listed all the things he had done that were good for the priests and the people of Egypt. The Rosetta stone had been written in three scripts so that the priests, government officials, and rulers of Egypt could read what it said.

When it comes to understanding the Bible, each believer has an indwelling teacher who gives interpretation to what God says. John tells us that we do not necessarily need anyone to be our teacher, but that the Holy Spirit is the One who teaches us. He is not saying that man cannot teach us God's Word or that we should not learn from others, but that man is not the ultimate source for understanding what God says in His Word. Today, do you need someone to teach you what God is saying? Why not ask the author? He is living in you. He is your own personal Bible professor!

July 20

Revelation 4:2, "And immediately I was in the spirit: and, behold, a throne was set in heaven, and one sat on the throne."

ON THIS DAY in 1969, Neil Armstrong and Edwin Aldrin Jr., became the first men to step on the moon. At 4:17:43 p.m. Armstrong reported, "Tranquility base here. The Eagle has landed." At 10:56:20 p.m., Armstrong's foot stepped on the moon's surface. Once they landed, Aldrin and Armstrong radioed earth and gave descriptions of what they saw: "There is a level plain cratered with a fairly large number of craters of the five to fifty variety. And some ridges, small, twenty feet to thirty feet, I would guess. And literally thousands of little ones and two foot craters around the area..." Although Armstrong seemed calm, his heart rate was beating at 156 beats per minute, twice its usual rate.

Can you imagine John's excitement when he got his first glimpse of heaven? Can you imagine our excitement when we get our first glimpse of our heavenly home? I have often wondered what those first few moments will be like? Will I just stand there in amazement or will I suddenly burst forth in praise to God? It is hard to imagine what those first moments will be like. Will our loved ones be the first persons we will see? Will our new mansion be the first thing that we view or will it be the Lord Jesus, who made it all possible? We can only imagine now, but there will come a day when we will step onto that heavenly land for the first time. What a day that will be! Today, spend a little time thinking about your heavenly home. Even now, my heart begins beating a little faster as I think about it.

July 21

Job 33:9, "I am clean without transgression, I am innocent; neither is there iniquity in me."

ON THIS DAY in 1906, Frenchman Alfred Dreyfus was declared innocent of espionage charges. In 1894, papers discovered in a wastebasket in the office of a German military attaché made it appear that a French military officer was providing secret information to the German government. Dreyfus came under suspicion, and the armies declared that his handwriting was similar to that on the papers. Dreyfus, a captain of Jewish descent in the French army, despite his protestations of innocence, was imprisoned on Devil's Island where he would serve for ten years. He seemed destined to die in disgrace but an unlikely defender came to his aid. Lieutenant Colonel Georges Picquart, an unapologetic anti-Semite, after examining the evidence, concluded that the guilty officer was a Major named Walsin Esterhazy. However, he found that the army was more concerned about preserving its image than rectifying its error. It was not until 1899 that the president of France pardoned Dreyfus and not until 1906 that he was exonerated of the charges.

Job found himself accused of things for which he was not guilty. He declared his innocence, yet it did not silence his accusers. Yet, as they say, when the smoke cleared, the truth came out and Job was exonerated of the charges. I am of the opinion that when believers find themselves the victim of false accusations, the Lord in time will bring the truth into light. God forbid that such a thing would ever happen to you, but if it does, always remember the Lord knows the truth. Today, if you are the victim of someone's lies, take your case to the Judge of the Universe. He has a way of making the truth known. He is always a defender of the righteous.

July 22

1 Corinthians 15:52, "In a moment, in the twinkling of an eye, at the last trump: for the trumpet shall sound, and the dead shall be raised incorruptible, and we shall be changed."

On This Day in 1933, Wiley H. Post ended the first solo flight around the world. Earlier in 1931, Post and Harold Gatty had flown around the world in eight days, fifteen hours and fifty-one minutes that broke the record of twenty-one days set in 1929 by the airship "Graf Zepplin." In an airplane named the "Winne Mae," a single engine Lockheed Vega equipped with a Sperry automatic pilot, a radio direction finder, and other new devices, Post covered 15,596 miles in seven days, eighteen hours, and forty-nine minutes. His accomplishment was considered the most remarkable display of flying endurance of the decade.

I doubt that I will ever have the opportunity of flying around the world, but a flight that I certainly will take is one out of this world. Paul describes this flight when he spoke of the last trump. The last trump was a Roman military term which described the signal given to an army that it was time to pull out and march. One of these days, the believer will hear the trump of God and it will be time to take our flight to our heavenly home. If you have been saved, then you have been given a ticket for this flight. I have made a few overseas flights and I confess that I have dreaded each one. Sitting in a small seat with barely enough room for several hours never gets me excited. But when I take this flight, I will board, depart, and arrive at my destination in the twinkling of an eye. Now that my friend, is the way to fly! Today, rejoice that you are booked for a trip out of this world. We may go solo, but there is a possibility that all of us could fly out together. Either way, it's a flight to look forward to.

July 23

Mark 12:37, "David therefore himself calleth him Lord; and whence is he then his son? And the common people heard him gladly."

On This Day in 1903, the Ford Motor Company sold its first motorcar. The Model A cost $850 and could reach a speed of 30 mph. In August of 1908, the first Model T rolled out of the factory costing $900 keeping with Henry Ford's dream to make a popular vehicle that the common person could afford. Ford was able to keep the cost of his cars down by using a new technique of mass production. The complex job of building a car was broken down in a succession of simple operations. He later introduced a moving assembly line, in which cars were being produced so fast that the cars were only available in black because black enamel was the only paint that would dry fast enough.

The common people found in the Lord Jesus someone who was greatly interested in them and therefore heard Him gladly. Jesus reached out to every man, regardless of their position in life or the condition of their lives. He made himself available to the common man, as well as to the rulers and wealthy. His offer of salvation was extended to every man. No one was excluded. He was called the friend of sinners, who were the worst of the worst and the lowliest of the lowly. As Henry Ford created "a motor car for the great multitude," Jesus provides salvation for every man. Today, gives thanks that Christ made salvation available to every man, even the common man. Many of us could not have been saved if He had not.

July 24

Hebrews 4:13, "Neither is there any creature that is not manifest in his sight: but all things are naked and opened unto the eyes of him with whom we have to do."

ON THIS DAY in 1974, in the *United States v. Nixon*, the Supreme Court ruled against President Richard Nixon's claim of "executive privilege." After a grand jury returned indictments against seven of President Nixon's closest aides in the Watergate affair, the special prosecutor and the defendants sought audio tapes of conversations recorded by Nixon in the Oval Office of the White House. Nixon asserted that he was immune from the subpoena, claiming "executive privilege," which is the right to withhold information from other government branches to preserve confidential communications within the executive branch to secure the national interest. The court ruled that the president's "executive privilege" did not include "the fundamental demands of due process of law in the fair administration of justice," and therefore, the President must obey the subpoena. Nixon resigned shortly after the release of the tapes.

The believer enjoys many privileges granted to him by his salvation. However, salvation does not grant the privilege of hiding or covering sin. Our salvation demands the uncovering of all sin and the confession of that sin. The writer of Hebrews declares that the Supreme Court of Heaven has ruled that all things are open to the eyes of God. God sees everything and knows everything. There is nothing we can hide from Him, therefore, we should never attempt to cover or hide our sins. Today, remember that Heaven has ruled that all sin must be dealt with in our lives. No one has "executive privilege" when it comes to sin.

July 25

Genesis 2:7, "And the Lord God formed man of the dust of the ground, and breathed into his nostrils the breath of life; and man became a living soul."

ON *THIS* DAY in 1978, the first "test-tube baby," was born. The method of In-vitro (IVF) was first employed successfully by gynecologist Dr. Patrick Steptoe and Cambridge University physiologist Dr. Robert Edwards at Oldham in Lancashire, England. In-vitro fertilization is a technique for fertilization of sperm and egg outside the human body. It actually takes place in a glass petri dish, from which "in-vitro" (in glass) is derived, rather than a test-tube. The first "test-tube baby" was a girl, Louise Brown.

The origin of life is often disputed and different theories exist. An example is the theory of chemical evolution of the 1970's which advocated the thought that life arose from a chemical reaction that took place from what is described as a kind of "primordial soup." There are those who believe that we are descendants of certain animals. When we come to God's Word, we find that God is the creator of life. After creating the first man, God breathed life into man and only then did he become a living soul. Regardless of how birth is brought about, God cannot be divorced from the process. He alone gives life. Man may be able to take sperm and egg and fuse them together to bring about a birth, yet God must give life. Life must always be acknowledged as a gift of God. Life is a miracle anyway you look at it, whether the result of IVF or natural processes. In either case, God alone must be given the credit. Today, see your life as God's gift and give thanks for the greater form of life—eternal life. They both come from Him.

July 26

Revelation 19:6, "And I heard as it were the voice of a great multitude, and as the voice of many waters, and as the voice of mighty thunderings, saying, Alleluia: for the Lord God omnipotent reigneth."

ON THIS DAY in 1887, the first book in Esperanto was published. Esperanto is a language invented by Polish Dr. L.L. Zamenhof, which is intended to facilitate communication among people from different countries. It is a language that does not belong to any specific country or people but belongs equally to everybody who speaks it, acting as a bridge between cultures. It has a simple, regular, and extremely flexible structure and a vocabulary of international character. According to studies, it is up to ten times easier to learn. There even exists a "Pasporta Servo" which lists speakers of Esperanto in more than seventy countries.

One of the scenes John saw in heaven was that of a great multitude, whose voice was as the sound of many waters. He heard them all worshipping and giving praise to the Lord God Omnipotent as they lifted their voices in saying "Alleluia." The multitude that he saw consisted of people from all nationalities and dialects, but when he heard them, he understood what they were saying. It would appear that they all spoke the same language. In all honesty, I have never heard anyone speak Esperanto (You are probably saying, "I've never even heard of it"). Dr. Zamenhof's multilingual language doesn't seem to have really caught on all that well, but one day God will solve the language barriers and all saints will have one common language by which they will praise and worship Him throughout all of eternity. Today, praise Him in English. It will not hurt to get a little practice in before we praise Him in heaven's universal language.

July 27

1 Corinthians 9:27, "But I keep under my body, and bring it into subjection: lest that by any means, when I have preached to others, I myself should be a castaway."

ON THIS DAY in 1984, Peter Rose broke Ty Cobb's record for the most singles in a career, hitting his 3,503rd base hit. The accomplishment all but guaranteed his induction into baseball's Hall of Fame. But then in 1989, former federal prosecutor John Dowd was hired to look into allegations that Rose had been betting on sports, including baseball. Investigations revealed that Rose was betting about $15,000 per day with bookies, including baseball. Baseball Commissioner Giamatti set a hearing for the matter and it was ruled, "Peter Edward Rose is hereby declared ineligible in accordance with Major League Rule 21, and placed on the Ineligible List." In 1990, the Hall of Fame added a clause to its eligibility rules, which stated that any player who had been placed on Baseball's ineligible list could not be considered as a candidate.

I remember watching the game when Rose broke Cobb's longstanding record. When Rose broke down on first base and began to weep, for a sports fan, it was hard not to weep with him. It was a special moment in baseball. Yet, that historic moment will always be overshadowed by his mistakes and ultimate expulsion from baseball. Paul's great fear was that he would do something that would disqualify him from being an effective servant for God. How tragic it would be to serve God for years and then destroy your testimony and ability to be an effective witness for God. Today, guard your life with great care. Heaven's Hall of Fame awaits the faithful servant. Don't jeopardize your induction.

July 28

Colossians 1:12, "Giving thanks unto the Father, which hath made us meet to be partakers of the inheritance of the saints in light:"

ON THIS DAY in 1868, Congress ratified and adopted the Fourteenth Amendment into the U.S. Constitution. The amendment resolved pre-Civil War questions of African-American citizenship by stating, "all persons born or naturalized in the United States...are citizens of the United States and of the state in which they reside." The Fourteenth Amendment ensured African-Americans citizenship and the privileges and rights of all citizens and granted all these citizens the "equal protection of the laws."

As believers, we are citizens of a heavenly kingdom. Our citizenship grants each believer the privileges and rights to enjoy all that their citizenship provides for them. All that Christ has made available to the believer can be enjoyed and experienced by each citizen, regardless of their race or standing in life. There is no segregation in God's kingdom and no restrictions. It is ours to enjoy! However, many believers do not take advantage of their privileges or exercise their rights as a citizen of God's kingdom. There is so much that is offered but in many cases, so little is appropriated. Do you want to have a peace that passes all understanding? It is one of the privileges for being a child of God. Do you need strength to face each day? There is heavenly strength available, and it is yours for the asking. Do you need your needs supplied? The vault of heaven is open for you to make a withdrawal. Today, be a partaker of what is your privilege and right to enjoy. As a citizen of God's kingdom, His heavenly constitution grants you the right to be a partaker of all that is offered.

July 29

Matthew 22:10, "So those servants went out into the highways, and gathered together all as many as they found, both bad and good: and the wedding was furnished with guests."

On This Day in 1981, Lady Diana Spencer and Prince Charles were married. An estimated television audience of 750 million watched what has been called the wedding of the century. More than 160 heads of state attended the service at St. Paul's Cathedral. Supported by his brothers Andrew and Edward, their vows were exchanged in the presence of 2,500 guests. During the ceremony, the couple showed their nervousness by fluffing their lines. Diana's wedding gown, which had been a closely guarded secret, was made of ivory silk, designed by the Emanuels. Archbishop Runcie began the wedding ceremony with the words, "Here is the stuff of which fairy tales are made." As they left, a hand-scrawled sign hung on the back of a seventy year old, gilded horse-drawn carriage that read, "Just Married."

The wedding of the royal couple may have been the wedding of the century, but the Bible speaks of the wedding of the ages. One of the great events that will follow the Lord's return for His children will be what is called the Marriage of the Lamb (Rev. 19:7). You may not have had the privilege of attending the wedding of the century, but you have received an invitation to the wedding of ages and you don't even have to be a head of state or a friend of the royal family. Even greater is the fact that every believer is actually the bride in this wedding. Our wedding gown will be the righteousness imparted by Jesus Christ (Rev. 19:8). Today, do a little wedding planning. Our wedding day will be here before we know it, and it is not a fairy tale.

July 30

Hebrews 12:1, "Wherefore seeing we also are compassed about with so great a cloud of witnesses, let us lay aside every weight, and the sin which doth so easily beset us, and let us run with patience the race that is set before us."

ON THIS DAY in 1908, Italian runner Dorado Pietri finished first in the Olympic marathon but was denied the gold medal. Pietri entered the new White Stadium in London in the lead for the final lap. It was visible that he was suffering from dehydration and cramps. He collapsed four times, but cheered on by the crowds, he managed to stagger to his feet, crossing the line first. Yet, he was disqualified for accepting the assistance of track officials over the last few yards. The gold medal went to American John Hayes, who covered the 26 miles and 385 yards in 2 hours, 55 minutes, and 19 seconds.

The writer of Hebrews speaks of the Christian life as running in a race. He also describes the great cloud of witnesses who observe the Christian in his race. Like fans filling the stands, they cheer the Christian on in his race. There are different opinions as to who these witnesses are. Some believe that they represent those who are in heaven at the present, having already run their race. Regardless of who they are, as runners in the heavenly race, we are being cheered on to the finish line. The objective in the race is not to see who finishes first, but to finish. Today, set your eyes on the finish line and listen for the cheers of those who are cheering you on. There will be times when we will need assistance, but don't worry. No believer has ever been stripped of a reward for being helped by others. In fact, there will be a reward for those who help others finish the race.

July 31

Hebrews 10:22, "Let us draw near with a true heart in full assurance of faith, having our hearts sprinkled from an evil conscience, and our bodies washed with pure water."

ON THIS DAY in 1910, a demonstration of the wireless across the Atlantic led to the capture of a murderer. The dismembered body of an American, Dr. David Crippen's wife, Bella, had been found in London. Crippen and his mistress had boarded the liner *Montrose* sailing for Quebec. Captain Henry Kendall became suspicious of the couple after reading newspaper reports of the search for the pair and sent radio signals about the passengers to London. Chief Inspector Walter Dew of Scotland Yard then crossed the Atlantic aboard the faster *Laurentic* and boarded the *Montrose*. When approached and arrested, Crippen said:, "Thank God, it's all over. The suspense has been too great. I could not stand it any longer."

The Bible has much to say about the conscience. It speaks of a good conscience, a pure conscience, and a defiled conscience to name a few. The writer of Hebrews speaks of an evil conscience. The evil conscience is one troubled with guilt. Someone has described the conscience as a red light that goes off in our hearts when we do wrong. God has put in all of us a red light that begins to flash when we sin. In some cases, that red light can be very bright and disturbing. An evil conscience can be a very heavy burden to bear. The answer to a troubled conscience is the confession of sin. Today, is there a red light that has been flashing in your heart? Confess your sins and the blood of the Lord Jesus can turn that red light off (Heb. 9:14). A good conscience is a much better companion than an evil one.

August 1

John 10:10, "The thief cometh not, but for to steal, and to kill, and to destroy: I am come that they might have life, and that they might have it more abundantly."

ON THIS DAY in 1966, Joseph Whitman climbed to the observation deck of the University of Texas at Austin and opened fire on the people below. Police stormed the tower, and an officer shot to death the twenty-five year-old architectural student and ex-Marine. In the predawn hours Whitman wrote a note which read, "I am prepared to die. After my death, I wish an autopsy on me to be performed to see if there is any mental disorder." Later that morning he stabbed and shot his mother to death and returning home, fatally stabbed his wife. Ultimately, sixteen people died during Whitman's twelve hour killing spree. An autopsy on Whitman revealed that he had been suffering from a brain tumor. Before leaving his home for the tower he wrote a bitter letter against his abusive father which closed with the words, "Life is not worth living."

Jesus declared that one of the purposes in His coming was to give men life. One of the blessings we enjoy as believers is that we have eternal life. Yet, Jesus also declared that He came to give us more than eternal life. He came that we might have an abundant life. The abundant life of which Jesus spoke is a blessed quality. In simple words, Jesus was telling us that He would make life worth living. The life that a person finds in the Lord Jesus is one which brings a joy and peace this world knows nothing about. Today, give thanks that one day you met the Lord Jesus and He gave you a new life—eternal and abundant. The life that one finds in Christ makes life worth living.

August 2

1 Samuel 20:3, "And David sware moreover, and said, Thy father certainly knoweth that I have found grace in thine eyes; and he saith, Let not Jonathan know this, lest he be grieved: but truly as the Lord liveth, and as thy soul liveth, there is but a step between me and death."

On This Day in 1876, "Wild Bill" Hickok was killed by Jack McCall. James Butler Hickok earned the nickname "Wild Bill" for his daring style of living and fighting while serving in the Union army. After the war, he served as a U.S. Marshall in the Western territories. His presence in Deadwood, South Dakota was not appreciated by the town's criminal element, so they hired McCall to murder him. During a poker game in Carl Mann's Saloon No. 10, McCall shot Hickok point blank in the back of the head. Hickok died instantly, toppling over backwards with his cards still in his hand—a pair of aces and a pair of eights. Since then that combination of cards has always been known as the "Dead Man's Hand."

There will come a day when each of us will be dealt a "Dead Man's Hand." When that hand will be dealt is uncertain. David was well aware that there was but a step between him and death, and for each of us the next breath could be our last. The certainty of death and the uncertainty of when it will come makes being ready an urgent matter. To live one minute without being saved is like playing poker with your soul. It is a gamble with eternity. Death is not a subject that we like to talk about all that often, but what a comfort it is to know that when death comes, we will be ready. Today, if you are not ready, trust Christ as your Saviour at this moment. The next hand may be the "Dead Man's Hand." If you are ready, let me rejoice with you.

August 3

Psalm 27:13, "I had fainted, unless I had believed to see the goodness of the Lord in the land of the living."

On This Day in 1492, Christopher Columbus sailed from Spain in search of a new route to the Indies. With three small ships, the *Santa Maria*, the *Pinta* and the *Niña*, a dream of many years had come true. After a short stop at the Canary Islands, he sailed due west. On October 7 he changed his course to the southwest. Three days later, October 10, his men threatened him with mutiny, but he convinced them to sail three more days, and if land had not been sighted, they would change course. It was on the morning of the third day that the land he christened San Salvador was sighted.

As you work toward some particular goal and seek to bring to fulfillment the dreams in your heart, it is not uncommon to become discouraged. When you have worked, given, prayed and sacrificed to see a certain thing come to pass, and yet it seems you are no closer to the goal than when you started, it is hard not to get discouraged. It makes you wonder if anything is ever going to happen. What should be our course? Believe in the goodness of the Lord. It was the Psalmist's confidence in the Lord that kept him from fainting. Just keep sailing! What if Columbus had turned back? Someone in time would have accomplished what he did, but it would not have been him, and he would have missed the thrill of a dream coming true. Today, keep striving for the fulfillment of your dream. Keep working and never stop believing. Those who keep after their dreams are the ones who experience the thrill of victory. You may not see land today, tomorrow, or even in the next year. But then again, you may be only three days from reaching your goal.

August 4

Jeremiah 45:5, "And seekest thou great things for thyself? seek them not: for, behold, I will bring evil upon all flesh, saith the Lord: but thy life will I give unto thee for a prey in all places whither thou goest."

ON THIS DAY in 1972, Arthur Bremer was sentenced to fifty-three years for his assassination attempt on the life of presidential candidate George W. Wallace. Bremer had shot Wallace at a political rally less than three months earlier. His reason? In 1972, Bremer had begun keeping a diary which revealed his dream of getting attention through assassination. His first entry: "Now I start my diary of my personal plot to kill by pistol either Richard Nixon or George Wallace." There was no political motive, just a desire, "to do SOMETHING BOLD AND DRAMATIC, FORCEFUL & DYNAMIC, A STATEMENT of my manhood for the world to see." As Bremer debated the merits of his target, Nixon was more appealing, but Wallace was more accessible. On May 15, 1972 at a campaign stop in Laurel, Maryland, Bremer fired five times at Wallace at close range. Wallace was left paralyzed from the assassination attempt.

Although most people never go to the extreme, as did Arthur Bremer, the goal and pursuit in life for many is to make a name for themselves or to be seen as someone or something special. There is nothing wrong in wanting to do something bold, dramatic, forceful and dynamic. I challenge you to do so. Yet, such goals should not to be so that the world can see how great you are. The ultimate goal is to glorify God and do great things for Him. If fame is the result, so be it. If not, God is glorified. Today, seek not great things for yourself, but for God. The only greatness we should seek is in His eyes.

August 5

1 Kings 19:4, "But he himself went a day's journey into the wilderness, and came and sat down under a juniper tree: and he requested for himself that he might die; and said, It is enough; now, O Lord, take away my life; for I am not better than my fathers."

On This Day in 1962, the West Los Angeles police station received a telephone call: "Marilyn Monroe is dead; she committed suicide." Shortly thereafter, police found her covered with a sheet lying face down on her bed. On her bedside table, among various bottles of pills and medications, was an empty bottle of Nembutal sleeping pills. Monroe, for some time had been seeing a psychiatrist to help her cope with the pressures of being a superstar and had been taking drugs to cope with insomnia and nerves. She had been recently fired from the filming of "Something's Got To Give," by 20th Century Fox. After an autopsy, the coroner's verdict was one of "probable suicide."

Depression is not a stranger to many people. Even the great man of God, Elijah, found himself deeply depressed. He was so depressed that he wanted to die. Sir Winston Churchill spoke of depression as a black dog that followed him. Some never seem to have a problem with depression; whereas, others constantly battle with it. Unfortunately, some like Marilyn Monroe seek a way out by taking their life. How do we deal with depression? The answer is not in taking one's life but by turning to the Life—the Lord Jesus (John 14:6) In Him we can cope with life and all it brings. Today, remember that in our lowest moments He is there. Like Elijah, we can find in Him what we need to cope with what we are going through.

August 6

Proverbs 13:4, "The soul of the sluggard desireth, and hath nothing: but the soul of the diligent shall be made fat."

On This Day in 1926, nineteen year-old Gertrude Ederle became the first woman to swim the English Channel. Starting in the morning at Cape Gris-Nez, France she reached Kingsdown fourteen hours and thirty-one minutes later becoming the sixth swimmer to cross the channel. Lloyd's of London gave 7-1 odds that she would not be able to cross the channel. During the last few hours of her swim, she had to fight a rough sea, the tide running strongly against her and a stinging spray hitting her in the face. Yet she stubbornly pursued her goal. Twice her trainer, aboard a tugboat which accompanied her, suggested she give up her quest, but she would not give up. Her father had promised her a car if she swam the channel, and on one occasion she told him, "Pop, I will have that roadster." She not only was the first woman to swim the channel, but did so one hour and fifty-two minutes faster than any man had done up to that time.

The wise man Solomon spoke of the "diligent". The word was sometimes used to speak of a trench that had been dug. Solomon was describing someone, as we might say, that had "dug in." He was speaking of one who was determined to reach his goal or stick to the task that was before him. It is descriptive of a person who will not quit. Solomon tells us that the diligent person shall be made "fat". He was not speaking of gaining weight physically but enjoying a growth and large measure of God's blessings. Would you like to become spiritually fat? Spiritual fatness is the reward of those who do not give up. Today, in spite of the difficulty, don't give up. Let's all become fat Christians.

August 7

Acts 4:36, "And Joses, who by the apostles was surnamed Barnabas, (which is, being interpreted, The son of consolation,) a Levite, and of the country of Cyprus,"

ON THIS DAY in 1877, U.S. astronomer Aspah Hall discovered Deimos, the outermost and smallest of Mars' two moons. Hall is credited with discovering both moons of Mars, Deimos ("DEE mos") and Phobos. Deimos is also the smallest known moon in the solar system. The night before Hall made his discovery, he was discouraged and ready to give up his search of the Mars satellites. But his wife, Chloe Angeline Stickney, who was also instrumental in his discoveries, insisted that he keep looking. He continued searching the next night due to her encouragement and made his discovery.

An important person in Paul's life was a man by the name of Barnabas. The name Barnabus means "son of consolation" or "encouragement" or "encourager". When Paul was first saved there were some that were a bit skeptical of him, but Barnabas took him under his wing and stood in his defense. It is not surprising that when Paul set out on his first missionary journey, he took with him Barnabas. Behind the many great things Paul did for God was Barnabas, the man who encouraged him in the beginning. There needs to be a little of Barnabas in all of us. There are enough things and people to discourage us. What we all need from time to time is someone who will encourage them. I'm sure there have been times when someone was an encouragement to you. We all would have quit at times if it had not been for those Barnabases in our life. Today, be an encouragement to someone.

August 8

Revelation 19:16, "And he hath on his vesture and on his thigh a name written, KING OF KINGS, AND LORD OF LORDS."

ON THIS DAY in 1866, the first queen visited the United States. When Queen Emma, the dowager Queen of Hawaii walked from the ship *Java* in New York City and her foot touched the wharf, she became the first queen to ever set foot on U.S. soil. Sleek carriages carried the queen and her retinue to a luxurious suite that had been reserved for her. R.S. Chilton, sent from Washington D.C. by Secretary of State William Seward, presented her with an official letter of welcome. Queen Emma traveled from New York to Washington for a meeting with President Johnson in the White House. During her visit, she cast her spell everywhere she went and on everyone she met, captivating all with her refinement and "eyes dark, large, and lustrous." The New York Times stated, "Tributes of the kind have rarely been paid to monarchs or their consorts so deserving of it."

Some day soon this earth is going to experience a visit from a royal visitor. The King of kings and Lord of lords will return to this earth in all His glory, power and majesty. When He comes, He will set up His glorious kingdom on the earth and reign in all His splendor. He will not be rejected and crucified as He was the first time, but will be worshiped and adored as He deserves. When He returns He will not be alone. His retinue will accompany Him. John saw those following Him, "*...clothed in fine linen, white and clean*" (Rev.19:14). All those who have accepted and acknowledged Him as King of kings will be with Him. Today, rejoice that you will be a part of His retinue.

August 9

1 John 2:28, "And now, little children, abide in him; that, when he shall appear, we may have confidence, and not be ashamed before him at his coming."

On This Day in 1974, President Richard Nixon officially ended his term as the thirty-seventh president of the United States. Having resigned the previous evening due to his involvement in the Watergate scandal, Nixon and his family walked from the White House across the lawn where a helicopter was waiting to carry them to their home in San Clemente, California. Just before he entered the helicopter, Nixon smiled farewell and raised his arms, and as he had done so many times before, spread his first two fingers in a victory or peace salute. Yet, it was not an hour of victory for the president but an hour of shame. Facing certain impeachment, he was the first president to resign from office.

John describes an even worse hour of shame than that of a president having to resign over some scandal. John speaks of the Lord's return and the shame some will have when they stand before the Lord. The word "ashamed" that John uses speaks of disgrace and great feelings of shame. The admonition is given to "abide in Him" that we be not ashamed at His coming. What does it mean to abide in Him? It is to live in unbroken fellowship with God. It is to live for God and live a life that is pleasing to Him every moment of our lives. We often describe the return of Jesus Christ as a glorious hour for the believer, but if we are not living for Him, it will be an embarrassing moment. Today, remember He is coming again. After all He has done for us by His grace, we certainly don't want to stand before Him in disgrace.

August 10

Psalm 147:3, "He healeth the broken in heart, and bindeth up their wounds."

ON *THIS* DAY in 1897, a young chemist working at Bayer in Germany made a discovery which gave us the world's most popular pain reliever. Felix Hoffman had been seeking a pain-relieving medication for his father's rheumatism, and the Bayer chemist discovered a stable form of acetylsalicylic acid, the active ingredient in aspirin. Acetylsalicylic acid (ASA) is the commercially synthesized form of the compound salicin that is found in the white willow tree. Bayer trademarked "Aspirin" in Germany on March 6, 1899. The name comes from "a" for "acetyl" and "spir" from "spirea," a plant offering a natural source of salicin, and "in," a common suffix for medications. Hoffman found that the drug not only helped ease his father's pain and inflammation, but when it was marketed it quickly became the world's most popular pain reliever. Today in the United States, as many as 29 billion tablets are consumed each year.

While aspirin may help ease the normal aches and pains of our body, it lacks the ability to ease the pain of a broken heart. There is no medicine known to man that can ease the pain of a broken heart. However, there is One who can ease the pain of a broken heart and even heal the heart that has been broken by the experiences of life. The Psalmist declares, *"The Lord is nigh unto them that are of a broken heart; and saveth such as be of a contrite spirit"* (Psa. 34:18). The Psalmist is saying that when our hearts are broken by things that happen in life the Great Physician always comes to our aid. He even makes house calls. Furthermore, He heals our broken hearts. Today, rejoice that the creator of all pain relievers is your personal Physician.

August 11

Exodus 13:3, "And Moses said unto the people, Remember this day, in which ye came out from Egypt, out of the house of bondage; for by strength of hand the Lord brought you out from this place: there shall no leavened bread be eaten."

ON THIS DAY in 1934, the first civilian prisoners were taken to the Federal Prison Alcatraz. A twenty-two acre rock island located one and one-half miles offshore in San Francisco Bay, Alcatraz served as a prison for military prisoners since 1859. In the early 1930's Alcatraz was fortified to become a high-security federal penitentiary designed to hold the most dangerous prisoners in the U.S. penal system. The first group of civilian prisoners was transferred from McNeil Island Prison in Washington in August 1934. Later that month a second group arrived, among them Al Capone. In September, George "Machine Gun" Kelly was placed in Alcatraz. Over the next three decades, more than 1,500 men would do time in "The Rock". Although many attempted to escape, no prisoner is known to have been successful.

As the children of Israel were preparing to leave Egypt in which they had been in bondage for 400 years, Moses told them to "*remember this day.*" It was to be a day that would forever be special to the children of Israel, for it was the day God delivered them from their bondage. As believers, the day God delivered us from the bondage of sin and Satan will always be a special day in our lives. Before the day of our salvation we were prisoners in Satan's Alcatraz. In ourselves there was no hope of escape, but Jesus came to our prison cell and set us free. Today, think back to the day when Jesus delivered you from the bondage of sin and Satan. Don't ever forget that day. It was the greatest day of your life.

August 12

Matthew 24:40, "Then shall two be in the field; the one shall be taken, and the other left."

On This Day in 1915, the First-Fifth Norfolks marched into a mysterious cloud and vanished. The First-Fifth Norfolks, consisting of 250 men, was a regiment of Britain's 163rd Brigade. The event took place during the Gallipoli campaign of WWI. The 163rd was ordered to advance on Turkish positions. The First-Eighth Hampshires and the First-Fifth Suffolks were pinned down and unable to move. The Norfolks advanced to a wooded area where, as described by witnesses, an odd shaped, dense cloud hovered close to the ground. The Norfolk soldiers marched into the cloud and witnesses claimed that as soon as the last soldier had disappeared into the cloud, the cloud rose up and moved away—against the wind. All 250 men disappeared, and the mystery has never been fully solved.

One of these days millions will suddenly disappear. As Jesus described, two will be in the field and suddenly one will vanish and the other will be left. Like the 250 soldiers of the First-Fifth Norfolks, they will disappear in the clouds. One day Jesus will return and every believer will suddenly vanish. As Paul declares in 1 Thessalonians 4:17, *"Then we which are alive and remain shall be caught up together with them in the clouds, to meet the Lord in the air: and so shall we ever be with the Lord."* I can imagine the headlines of the newspapers the next day: "Millions Missing." Newscasts will report stories from around the world of people suddenly vanishing. Today, rejoice that you will be among those that are missing. Look up at the clouds today. Who knows, this might be our cloud.

August 13

Ephesians 2:18, "For through him we both have access by one Spirit unto the Father."

On This Day in 1961, the Berlin Wall was erected. It was constructed with astounding speed from prefabricated blocks of concrete. In the night hours frightened East Berliners peaked from their windows as a military convoy of jeeps, trucks and buses crammed with steel-helmeted East German soldiers rolled through the streets. At each main intersection a platoon peeled off and ground to a halt. Stone blocks and rolls of barbed wire were unloaded off cargo trucks. When dawn came, a wall divided East Berlin from the West. The wall that became the symbol of the cold war was the first step in sealing the border. It was the Communist's answer to the more than 2,000 refugees leaving the east everyday. More than 50,000 East Berliners who worked in West Berlin were suddenly cut off from earning a paycheck. Armed guards patrolled the wall and gates. Special permits were needed to pass through the gates.

As believers we have access to the Father. When we need to come to God there is no armed guard to block our entrance. We do not need special permits. We do not have to fear being turned away. We have access to the Father twenty-four hours a day. When our hearts are heavy with the cares of life we can go to the Father to find grace and strength. When we need wisdom and direction we can come to the Father. Whatever our need or reason, we have immediate access to God. For twenty-eight years the Berlin Wall stood barring access for many in East Germany before it was torn down. Jesus has torn down the wall that separated men from God. Today, you have access to the Father. Why not take advantage of this wonderful privilege.

August 14

Isaiah 40:11, "He shall feed his flock like a shepherd: he shall gather the lambs with his arm, and carry them in his bosom, and shall gently lead those that are with young."

ON THIS DAY in 1859, the most famous of Niagara Falls daredevils performed his most difficult stunt. Jean Francois Gravelot, better known as "The Great Blondin," amazed audiences time and time again with his crossing of the Falls. He first came to Niagara Falls in 1858 and became obsessed with crossing the Falls on a tightrope. He first crossed the Falls on June 30, 1859 and would complete the crossing eight more times during the year. One of his acts involved pushing a wheelbarrow along as he crossed. His most difficult crossing was when he carried his manager, Harry Colcord, on his back. His final crossing was in September 1860, but none were more daring or famous than when he carried Harry across.

One of the pictures of the relationship believers have with the Lord is that of a shepherd and his sheep. As believers, we are the sheep of His pasture (Psa. 100:3), and He is our Good Shepherd (John 10:11), our Great Shepherd (Heb. 13:20) and our Chief Shepherd (1 Pet. 5:4). Because of our Shepherd we have no want (Psa. 23:1). He cares for us and watches over us as a shepherd does his sheep. He feeds His sheep like a shepherd, and even more comforting is that when we need to be carried He will carry us like a shepherd carries a lamb pulled close to his bosom. When we have to cross the raging rivers of life, our Shepherd will carry us. When we have difficult terrain to cross, He will pull us close and carry us. Today, if you need carrying, let your Shepherd carry you. He will get you across the river!

August 15

Revelation 5:11, "And I beheld, and I heard the voice of many angels round about the throne and the beasts and the elders: and the number of them was ten thousand times ten thousand, and thousands of thousands;"

ON THIS DAY in 1969, the Woodstock Music and Art festival began at Yasgur's farm in Bethel, New York. Often referred to as "three days of peace and music," the three-day festival drew nearly 500,000 people. It is taunted as one of the most celebrated rock and roll concerts of all time and starred thirty top entertainers. The festival began Friday afternoon at 5:07 p.m. and continued until mid-morning Monday, August 18. Due to the larger than expected crowd that attended, the festival closed the New York Thruway and created one the nation's worst traffic jams. Woodstock has become symbolic of the hippie movement of the 60's and an adjective of youthful hedonism and 60's excess. Woodstock has been described as "a countercultural mini-nation in which minds were open, drugs were all but legal and love was free."

John saw a huge gathering in heaven which superseded any that history has ever known. Instead of a "giant party" in which drugs flowed freely and any expression of sin was acceptable, he saw a crowd of which many had been saved from such a life. Instead of one of the largest outdoor stages ever built, he saw a throne. Instead of entertainers "rocking" through the hours, he heard those in attendance singing a new song and crying, "Worthy is the Lamb!" Instead of a huge gathering that glorified sin, this future event is a gathering that will glorify the One who saves from sin. Today, if you look closely you can see yourself among the crowd. This is one gathering that I am looking forward to attending.

August 16

Job 22:27, "Thou shalt make thy prayer unto him, and he shall hear thee, and thou shalt pay thy vows."

On This Day in 1858, U.S. President James Buchanan and Queen Victoria spoke to one another across the Atlantic to inaugurate the first transatlantic telegraph line. In 1854 American merchant Cyrus West Field conceived the idea of the telegraph cable and secured a charter to lay a line across the Atlantic. Obtaining the aid of British and American naval ships he made four unsuccessful attempts to lay the line. In July 1858, they began the fifth attempt, and by August 5, nearly 2,000 miles of cable had been successfully laid across the Atlantic often at a depth of more than two miles. On the inauguration of the transatlantic telegraph President Buchanan and Queen Victoria exchanged greetings and complimentary messages to one another. However, the cable proved weak and the current insufficient, and by September the telegraph line had ceased working. After the Civil War, Field succeeded in laying the first permanent telegraph line across the Atlantic.

Would you like to talk to the King? How would you enjoy the privilege of speaking to the King anytime you so desired? Well, you do have that privilege. Through prayer the believer has a direct line to the King of kings and Lord of lords. You never get a busy signal, answering machine or voice mail, and He is always at home. You can talk to the King as long as you want and as often as you want. In fact, He encourages you to call Him anytime you want and even at all hours of the night. Prayer is one of the great privileges of the believer, and through prayer we have access to God. Today, why don't you give the King a call? It's a free call.

Psalm 19:10, "More to be desired are they than gold, yea, than much fine gold: sweeter also than honey and the honey-comb."

ON THIS DAY in 1896, gold was found at Rabbit Creek, setting off the Klondike Gold Rush. Three men, Yukon natives Skookum Jim, Tagish Charlie and their American friend, George Carmack, were prospecting in Rabbit Creek, a tributary of the Klondike River in Canada. They discovered the bright yellow ore and quickly staked their claim, renaming the creek "Bonanza". Word of the "Bonanza" discovery spread fast, and soon thousands descended upon Dawson, a hastily built town at the point between the Yukon and Klondike Rivers. Steamships were swamped with requests, outfitters ran out of supplies, as more than 100,000 stampeded to the Yukon in search for gold. The great Klondike Gold Rush was on its way. As one wrote: "Like soldiers marching to the insistent beating of a drum, they set off with pounding hearts, mouthing pat slogans, and often enough believing them... ."

The history of gold rushes are all stories of those who left their homes, businesses, and families to strike it rich, some never to return again. Yet the believer has something more precious and valuable than gold, and that is God's Word. The Psalmist declares that it is of such value that it is to be desired more than even fine gold. He also states say, *"Therefore I love thy commandments above gold; yea, above fine gold"* (Psa. 119:27) and would even goes as far as to say, *"The law of thy mouth is better unto me than thousands of gold and silver"*(Psa. 119:72). Today, spend time reading God's Word. You may not have a lot of this world's gold, but you have something that is far greater in value.

August 18

1 Tim. 3:16, "And without controversy great is the mystery of godliness: God was manifest in the flesh, justified in the Spirit, seen of angels, preached unto the Gentiles, believed on in the world, received up into glory."

ON THIS DAY in 1587, the first child to be born of English parents in the New World was born. Just days after a group of colonists arrived on Roanoke Island off the North Carolina coast, a little girl named Virginia was born to Ananias and Eleanor Dare, the daughter of Governor John White. What followed remained one of the greatest unsolved mysteries in American history. When Governor White returned to England for supplies, Virginia was less than one month old. A secret code had been worked out that should they have to leave Roanoke Island, they were to carve their new location on a conspicuous tree or post. If the move had to be made because of danger, they were to carve the letters or a distress signal in the form of a Maltese cross. Three years to the month later, White returned to find the word "Croatoan" without any cross or other sign of distress. The colonists were never found or heard from again.

The Bible often speaks of the mysteries such as our text for the day speaks of the mystery of Godliness. In the case of Bible mysteries, they are not descriptive of unsolved disappearances or strange happenings which no one has an explanation for. A mystery in the Bible is a truth that is revealed which formerly had not been revealed. When it comes to the mystery of Godliness, a cross does indicate what happened. God became man, died for the sins of man and afterward was received into glory. Today, rejoice that we have a clear message as to what God has done for us, and that is no mystery.

August 19

Ephesians 6:16, "Above all, taking the shield of faith, wherewith ye shall be able to quench all the fiery darts of the wicked."

On This Day in 1812, the U.S. Navy frigate *Constitution* earned her nickname *Old Ironsides*. During the War of 1812 the *Constitution* captured no less than a dozen British ships and the success of the ship against the mighty British Navy was a tremendous moral booster for the young American navy. While the forty-four-gun frigate was engaged in battle with the *HMS Guerriere* off the coast Nova Scotia, British cannonballs appeared to bounce off her thick wooden sides. An unidentified sailor exclaimed, "Huzzah, her sides are made of iron." The inability of the eighteen pound British cannonballs to penetrate the sides of the *Constitution* was due to the fact that her hull comprised of three layers of live oak (one of the most durable woods in the world) that was twenty-five inches thick at the waterline.

Daily the world, the flesh, and the devil bombard the believer. These spiritual enemies hurl at us everything they can to get us to yield to temptation and fall prey to Satan. These enemies of the Christian life have but one objective—to sink us. Yet, clothed in the Armour of God the fiery darts of Satan do not harm us. The believer is given a shield of faith to deflect all that is "fired" at us. Because we are in a spiritual warfare it is important that the believer be clothed in the spiritual Armour that has been given to us by God. To face the enemy without the Armour of God is a sure recipe for defeat. Today put on the Armour of God. Let the enemy be heard to say, "Huzzah, there's a Christian made of iron."

August 20

Psalm 19:1, "The heavens declare the glory of God; and the firmament sheweth his handywork."

On This Day in 1975, *Viking* 1 was launched from Cape Canaveral, Florida on a mission to Mars. On June 19, nearly ten months later, the spacecraft entered into an orbit around Mars. On July 20 the *Viking 1* lander separated from the orbiter and touched down on the Chryse Planitia region, becoming the first spacecraft to successfully land on Mars. In September, *Viking 2*, launched three weeks after *Viking I*, entered into orbit around Mars to assist in imaging the surface of the planet. The two landers sent back over 1,400 images of the planet's surface.

For a moment let's do a little math. The distance from earth to Mars is 35 million miles. If my calculations are correct, if it took *Viking 1* 308 days to reach Mars, it would have traveled close to 4,734 miles per hour. Now when you stop and think of something traveling approximately seventy-nine miles per second and yet it takes 308 days to reach its destination you get the impression that the universe is amazingly large. When the Psalmist considered the heavens he burst forth in praise declaring, "*O Lord our Lord, how excellent is thy name in all the earth! who hast set thy glory above the heavens*" (Psa. 8:1). He saw the heavens as that which declared the glory of God and was an example of His handiwork. When we think about this universe and its majesty and scope, we are made to appreciate the greatness of our God and even more so when we realize that, "*By the word of the Lord were the heavens made…* (Psa. 33:6). Today, let God's glory and greatness fill your heart. The God that created this universe just happens to be your heavenly Father.

August 21

Nehemiah 4:8, "And conspired all of them together to come and to fight against Jerusalem, and to hinder it."

ON THIS DAY in 1959, the present design of the United States Flag was established by executive order of President Eisenhower. The design called for the arrangement of the stars in nine rows, staggered horizontally, and eleven rows of stars, staggered vertically. Where did the design come from? A seventeen year-old high school junior, Bob Heft, was in need of a class project. He came up with an idea for the flag, but his teacher turned down the proposal. He went ahead with the project, receiving a B minus. Heft's teacher promised to give him a better grade if he could get the U.S. Congress to accept his idea. He did and they did. Since Heft's flag was made public, he has been in all fifty states and thirty-seven foreign countries, traveling more than 100,000 miles a year as a speaker and has been the guest of nine presidents at the White House.

There will always be those who will try to discourage you when you want to do something for God. There are always "wet blankets" who try to put out the fire in our hearts. Some will say it can't be done, and others will do all they can to stop us. There were those in Nehemiah's day who gave his project a B minus and sought to hinder its completion. Yet, Nehemiah stayed at his task, responding to his critics, "*I am doing a great work, so that I cannot come down*" (Neh. 6:3). You are in a great work; don't let the doubters discourage you or hinder you from doing what God has put in your heart. The next time you see the flag, remember a teenager who did not abandon his project. Today, keep on keeping on. You may be surprised at what happens.

August 22

Revelation 19:12, "His eyes were as a flame of fire, and on his head were many crowns; and he had a name written, that no man knew, but he himself."

On This Day in 1485, King Richard III was defeated and killed at the battle of Bosworth Field. At dawn, on a field near the South Leicestershire town of Market Bosworth, King Richard III of the house of York and the Earl of Richmond, Henry Tudor of the house of Lancaster, faced each other in what would be the last battle in the thirty year War of Roses between the houses of York and Lancaster. Thirteen battles had been fought and over 100,000 lives had been lost. The battle lasted only two hours, but during the course of fighting, King Richard was unhorsed and killed in a bog. A weary, but victorious Henry Tudor gathered his forces together and set his standard on a small rise now called Crown Hill. As he thanked and congratulated his men, Sir Reginald Bray appeared with the golden crown Richard had been wearing in battle. It had been found by a soldier in a thorn bush near the spot where he fell. The crown was handed to Lord Thomas Stanley who placed it on Tudor's head, declaring, "Henry VII, King of England."

Many a king has risen only to lose his crown to another, but there is one King who will never lose His crown. John saw the Lord Jesus returning to earth with his heavenly armies, and on His head were many crowns. In the battle that followed, all the nations of the earth are gathered to make war against Him, yet when the battle is over the Lord Jesus emerges as the King of kings and Lord of lords still possessing His crowns. Today, bow at the feet of the King who has never lost a battle and will never lose His crown. Lift your hands in worship and declare, "The Lord Jesus Christ, the King of the Ages."

August 23

Numbers 23:10, "Who can count the dust of Jacob, and the number of the fourth part of Israel? Let me die the death of the righteous, and let my last end be like his!"

ON THIS DAY in 1977, Elvis Presley was buried at his Graceland Mansion in Memphis, Tennessee. Best known as the king of rock and roll, Presley was found dead at his home August 16th. His funeral sparked off scenes of fanatical hero-worship as more than 80,000 fans arrived to pay their last respects. Crash barriers had to be erected around his mansion to keep the crowds back. Dozens fainted from either the heat or the pressure of the crowd. Two fans were killed when a drunken driver ran his car into the crowd. More than 30,000 filed into the house to see the singer lying in state. Thousands more lined Elvis Presley Boulevard to watch the funeral procession of white Cadillac's. The grave was decked out with wreaths in the shape of hound dogs and guitars. His death was officially blamed on an irregular heartbeat which many speculate was drug related.

When death comes, and it will come to us all, what will matter is not the size of our funeral or if it draws national attention. What is important is not even how we die. What will be important is whether or not we are saved. All the fame and wealth of the world will mean nothing. What will matter is our relationship to God. Balaam's request was to die as the righteous and his end to be as the righteous. John Wesley once said of the Methodists, "Our people die well." If we know Christ, we are righteous in Him and because we are righteous in Him we should live a righteous life. Today, ask God to help you live the way you want to die. Since we know that death is certain, why not make plans to die as the righteous man. That's the only way to live and die.

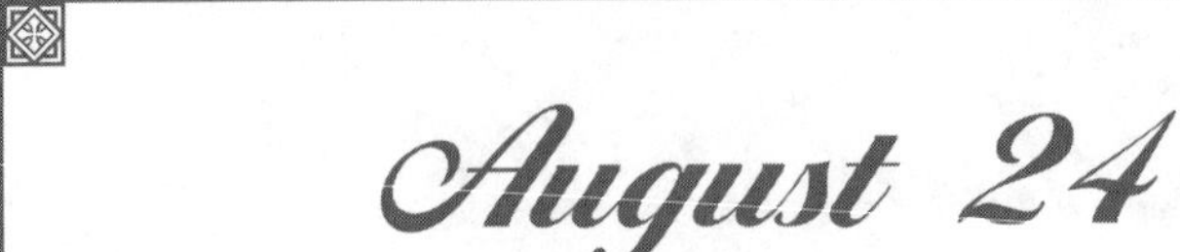

August 24

Hebrews 11:36-37, "And others had trial of cruel mockings and scourgings, yea, moreover of bonds and imprisonment: They were stoned, they were sawn asunder, were tempted, were slain with the sword: they wandered about in sheepskins and goatskins; being destitute, afflicted, tormented;"

ON THIS DAY in 1572, King Charles IX of France ordered what is known as the Saint Bartholomew's Day Massacre. Under the influence of his mother, Charles ordered the assassination of Huguenot Protestant leaders in Paris, which resulted in the massacre of more than 70,000 Huguenots all across France. Catholic Parisians began a general massacre of the Huguenots. After hundreds of men, women, and children were slaughtered, Charles ordered the killing to be halted, but his order went unheeded as the massacres spread. Mass slaughters continued into October. An estimated 3,000 Huguenots were killed in Paris alone.

Hebrews chapter 11 is one of those chapters that thrills the heart as you read of wonderful things that were accomplished through faith in God. The faith of Noah, Abraham, and Moses ignite our faith and makes us want to believe God. Yet, not every example in the chapter describes great things accomplished by faith. There were others—others whose faith cost them dearly. They were the "and others" who paid the ultimate cost for their faith in God. I think it does us good to once in a while stop and realize that the history of our faith is stained by the blood of many saints who gave their lives for the cause of Christ and their faith. Today, take a few minutes to think about those whose faith cost them their lives and let their devotion to Jesus Christ inspire you to greater faith and devotion to Jesus Christ.

August 25

1 Corinthians 3:15, "If any man's work shall be burned, he shall suffer loss: but he himself shall be saved; yet so as by fire."

On This Day in 1814, the White House was burned by the British. Six days earlier, a British invading army landed at Chesapeake Bay and marched unopposed to the capital city. With only 500 militiamen to defend the city against 4,000 infantrymen, the militiamen had little chance. The British marched into the city setting fire to the White House leaving it a charred hulk; the fire also gutted the House of Representatives and Library of Congress along with many other buildings. President Madison was forced to flee; his wife Dolly, rescued a life-size portrait of George Washington and the original Declaration of Independence.

Paul spoke of a day when every believer will stand before God and give an account for their life and service. Each believer's life will be reviewed and passed through the fires of the Judgment Seat of Christ. The motives of our service and quality of the life we lived will be scrutinized. Sadly, Paul tells us that the works of some believers will not be acceptable. Their works will be burned by the fires of the Judgment Seat and will not survive. Yet, Paul tells us that they will be saved, yet so as by fire. The issue of the Judgment Seat is not to determine whether one is saved. It is our works that is the issue. To be saved, yet live a life without serving God is to be saved so as by fire. Today, live for God and serve Him. There will be a day when you will be glad you did. I don't want to survive the fires of the Judgment Seat with just my spiritual "Declaration of Independence." How about you?

August 26

Exodus 21:6, "Then his master shall bring him unto the judges; he shall also bring him to the door, or unto the door post; and his master shall bore his ear through with an aul; and he shall serve him for ever."

On This Day in 1839, the Cuban schooner *Amistad* was seized off the coast of Long Island, New York. On June 28, the *Amistad* sailed from Cuba carrying fifty-three slaves recently captured in Africa, bound for a sugar plantation at Puerto Principe. Three days later, one of the slaves known as Cinque, freed himself and the other slaves and planned a mutiny. Early in the morning of July 2, in the midst of a storm, the slaves rose up against their captors, and killed the captain of the *Amistad* and a crew member. Two other crew members were either thrown overboard or escaped. The two Cubans who had purchased the slaves were captured and Cinque ordered them to sail the schooner back to Africa. During the day the two men complied but at night they would turn the vessel in a northerly direction, toward U.S. waters. After almost two months at sea, the so-called "black schooner" was spotted and seized by the *U.S.S. Washington.*

In the case of the fifty-three slaves aboard the *Armistad* one readily understands their desire for freedom and the steps they took to regain their freedom. Yet, in the Old Testament we find an interesting situation in which a slave chose to remain a slave even after being given his freedom. A hole bored through his ear was a mark that he had chosen to serve his master for the rest of his life. As believers our hearts ought to bear the mark that indicates that we have chosen to serve the Lord Jesus for the rest of our life. Today, tell your Heavenly master you want your ear bored.

August 27

Psalm 124:4, "Then the waters had overwhelmed us, the stream had gone over our soul."

On This Day in 1958, a ticker-tape parade was held in New York for the crew of nuclear submarine *Nautilus* for making history's first undersea voyage across the North Pole. The *Nautilus* began its historic journey on July 23 at Pearl Harbor, Hawaii, and cruised north through the Bering Strait. It went under the polar ice cap at Point Barrow, Alaska, and remained submerged thereafter, sending its periscope up only once to check its bearings. The *Nautilus* passed beneath the polar ice pack at the North Pole at 11:45 a.m. on August 3rd. Its trip across the polar region took four days and ended at Iceland.

The Psalmist describes the circumstances of his life as being overwhelmed or submerged beneath the waters. Yet, he found that when overwhelmed by the troubled waters of life that in the Lord he found a Divine environment that sustained life. The historic journey of the *Nautilus* was possible because the vessel provided an environment to sustain life in circumstances in which man could not normally exist—under water. You may have heard someone say, "I don't know how he or she keeps going on." The Psalmist declares that if it had not been for the Lord he would not have been able to make it through the overwhelming circumstances he was facing (Psa. 124:1-2). Believers may find themselves in circumstances that are overwhelming, but in the Lord they find the help and strength to survive. Many a believer has found himself beneath the waters of a troubled sea yet emerged victorious. Today, give thanks that the Lord enables us to face whatever life may bring. Even when we are under the water, we can make it.

Ephesians 5:18, "And be not drunk with wine, wherein is excess; but be filled with the Spirit."

ON THIS DAY in 1859, the first oil wells in America began to yield oil. For over 300 years oil was known about in America. It seeped from the ground and was used as a medicine to cure blindness, rheumatism, coughs, colds, sprains, and even baldness. In early days it was skimmed from creeks in its crudest form and was found to be valuable for lighting even though it gave off a smelly odor. In 1833 the value of oil as an industrial lubricant was realized, and a major case for oil exploration was created. Edwin Drake, a former railroad conductor began using techniques used in drilling salt wells, and boring down sixty-nine feet was producing twenty-five barrels of oil per day from the Allegheny Valley in Pennsylvania.

Oil in the Bible is a symbol of the Holy Spirit. Paul's command was that the believer was to be filled with the Holy Spirit. To be filled with the Holy Spirit is more than some kind of emotional or religious experience. It is to be controlled by the Spirit. To be filled with the Spirit, the believer must completely yield his or her life to God and allow the Holy Spirit to have complete and total control of their life to carry out God's purposes for their life. In our day and time, so much is dependent on oil. A shortage of oil can almost shut down the nation. Oil has become a crucial part of our daily lives. But even more important is the need for spiritual oil or to be filled with the Spirit. It is impossible to live the Christian life or be effective for God without being filled by the Spirit. Today, ask God to fill you with His Spirit. Don't settle for a can or two. We need more than a blessing here and there. We need a well! Be ye filled with the Spirit!

August 29

Galatians 6:2, "Bear ye one another's burdens, and so fulfill the law of Christ."

ON THIS DAY in 1893, Whitcomb L. Judson patented the zipper. Called, at the time of the patent a "hookless fastener," Judson who was always experimenting with many gadgets came up with a slider fastener that could be opened or closed with one hand. When the B.F. Goodrich Company decided to market galoshes with hookless fasteners the product became popular, and by the 1920's was being used in clothing and a score of other items. Because the galoshes could be fastened with the zip of a hand they became known as "zippers". Judson's "zipper" came about because a friend who had a stiff back could not bend over and tie his shoes and asked for his help.

Thoughtfulness for others is a characteristic that should be found in every believer. Paul's command is that we are to bear (to lift) one another's burdens. Paul writes to the Corinthians that we should "*care one for another*" (1 Cor.12:25) and to the Thessalonians that we are "*taught of God to love one another*" (1 Thess.4:9). Jesus is our great example, "*who went about doing good, and healing all that were oppressed of the devil; for God was with him*" (Acts 10:38). The people "*came to him from every quarter*" (Mark 1:45), for they saw and found in Him one who cared for them and would reach out and lift their many burdens. This world is full of people who carry burdens and need someone who will love them, care for them, and help lift the burdens they bear. Today, maybe there is someone you know who has a "stiff back" who you could be a friend to and help.

August 30

Galatians 6:10, "As we have therefore opportunity, let us do good unto all men, especially unto them who are of the household of faith."

ON THIS DAY in 1983, U.S. Air Force Lieutenant Colonel Guion S. Bluford became the first African-American to travel into space. Born in Philadelphia, Pennsylvania, in 1978, Bluford became one of thirty-five people accepted from more than 10,000 applicants to NASA's astronaut program. At 2 a.m. as the eighth launching of the *Challenger* took place, more than 250 black educators and professionals gathered in Houston, Texas and watched Bluford's historic venture into space. On the second day of the flight, President Ronald Reagan called the *Challenger* crew and said to Bluford, "You are paving the way for many others and making it plain that we are in an era of brotherhood here in our land." Describing his place in African-American history, Bluford declared, "From a black perspective, my flight on the shuttle represented another step forward. Opportunities do exist for black youngsters if they work hard and strive to take advantage of opportunities."

Paul described how we as believers should take advantage of our opportunities to do good things for others. We live in a very selfish and self-centered day when it seems that people think only in terms of what others can do for them. As believers we should be characterized by selflessness and our motto "others". As Paul says, "*Look not every man on his own things, but every man also on the things of others*" (Phil. 2:4). Today, watch for an opportunity to do something good for someone else. When those opportunities come along strive to take advantage of those opportunities. Ask God to give you such an opportunity.

August 31

Luke 24:1, "Now upon the first day of the week, very early in the morning, they came unto the sepulcher, bringing the spices which they had prepared, and certain others with them."

ON THIS DAY in 1997, the world was stunned to learn of the death of Princess Diana. In the early morning hours Diana, Princess of Wales, Dodi Fayed and their chauffeur were killed in a car accident in Paris. It is believed that the crash was partly due to speeding as they sought to elude the paparazzi that were chasing them. Because Princess Diana was immensely popular internationally, expressions of sympathy began to pour in from around the world. Thousands began to bring flowers to her London home of Kensington Palace and to Buckingham Palace. People stood in line for up to twelve hours to sign a condolence book at St. James Palace. Shops, pubs, banks and sporting events were cancelled the day of her funeral in her honor. Prime Minister Tony Blair said of the Princess: "She touched the lives of so many others in Britain and throughout the world with joy and comfort." She was only thirty-six.

When the Lord Jesus died there were only a handful that mourned and came with expressions of their grief. His tomb was not surrounded with bouquets of flowers. There were no expressions of grief or sympathy from the leaders and rulers of the day. For the most part, they were glad He was dead. When He was placed in a borrowed tomb, no shops or businesses were closed in His honor. Things for the most part went on as usual. Yet, no one has touched more lives than He did. The thoughts of Princess Diana's death still fill our hearts with sorrow, but we are thankful that Jesus died. Today, rejoice that Jesus died and rose again. No one has touched our life as He has.

September 1

1 Peter 5:8, "Be sober, be vigilant; because your adversary the devil, as a roaring lion, walketh about, seeking whom he may devour."

ON THIS DAY in 1939, Hitler's armies invaded Poland, launching WWII. At the pre-established moment of 4:45 a.m. one and one-half million German troops, led by 2,700 panzers (tanks) and bombers of the German *Luftwaffe* (air force), lashed out along the 1,750-mile Polish border. The dawn surprise invasion marked a bold new mode of warfare: the *blitzekreig*, or lightning attack. The night before Hitler commenced his surprise attack, twelve prisoners in a German concentration camp dressed in Polish army uniforms, were killed and their bodies dumped near the border. Hitler made the claim that these "Polish casualties" had died trying to invade Germany. The century's deadliest war started on lies and murder.

The great enemy of the Christian life is the devil. He stalks the believer like a lion searching for its prey. Like a hungry lion, he lies in wait for an opportunity to attack the believer. Paul's instruction, "*Neither give place to the devil*" (Eph. 4:27) is given because Paul knew that if we give the devil a chance he will leap on the believer as a roaring lion to devour and destroy us. We must be watchful and always on guard for his surprise attacks. He could invade our borders at anytime. You can be certain it is in his plans and given the chance he will sweep in with lightning speed. Today, watch for the enemy advances. Do not give the devil an opportunity to make you his next victim. He will lie and do anything he can to defeat you. Don't ever forget he is the devil and he always lives up to his name.

September 2

Isaiah 40:31, "But they that wait upon the Lord shall renew their strength; they shall mount up with wings as eagles; they shall run, and not be weary; and they shall walk, and not faint."

ON THIS DAY in 1910, Blanche Scott became the first woman to fly a plane. The notion of a woman flying a plane was considered ludicrous, but Scott was determined to fly. She first approached Glenn H. Curtiss, a developer and manufacturer of aircraft, but he turned her down. She got her chance when the manager of Curtiss's traveling air show envisioned people paying money to watch "a woman freak pilot" risk her life. He convinced Curtiss to let her fly. Scott began training at an airfield in Hammondsport, N.Y. For the first three days the closest she came to flying was "grass cutting", short runs along the airstrip. Curtiss had her throttle blocked to make sure she never left the ground. But then on September 2, Scott began another grass-cutting drill and suddenly her plane lifted off the ground and leveled off at forty feet. In that moment she had become the first woman to fly an airplane.

All of God's people can be flyers. Isaiah speaks of those who wait upon the Lord. Waiting can be a very difficult thing. Many are like the lady who prayed, "Lord, I need patience and I need it now." There are times when we must wait upon the Lord. What does it mean to wait on the Lord? It is to put everything in His hands and allow Him to work in His own time and way. What is the reward for waiting? We have a destiny in the sky for we shall mount up with wings of eagles. Today, leave everything in His hands. It's the only way to get to fly.

September 3

Deuteronomy 6:7, "And thou shalt teach them diligently unto thy children, and shalt talk of them when thou sittest in thine house, and when thou walkest by the way, and when thou liest down, and when thou risest up."

On This Day in 1991, Wanda Holloway of Channelview, Texas was convicted of trying to hire a hit man to kill the mother of her daughter's cheerleading rival in high school. According to the story Holloway, the organist at a local Baptist church, hired her ex-brother-in-law to kill Verna Heath, the mother of Amber Heath, thinking that Amber would be so distraught that she would drop out of cheerleading and her daughter, Shanna, would replace her on the squad. Her ex-brother-in-law told police that she toyed with the idea of killing both mother and daughter, but couldn't afford the $7,500 fee. The verdict was thrown out when it was discovered that a juror was on probation. In 1996 Mrs. Holloway pleaded no contest and received a ten year prison term. She was released after serving six months in prison.

As Moses gave the children of Israel instructions about their life in the land God was going to give them, one of the things he admonished them about was the teaching of their children. Their method of teaching was to be by both talk and walk. The parents were to tell their children what the statutes of God were, and furthermore, model those teachings before them. There was to be a walk with their talk. I don't think trying to have the neighbor murdered next door so their children can make the "Tabernacle Worship Team" would meet the standard Moses gave to parents. Teaching children is a great responsibility for a parent. A godly example is the greatest method of teaching a parent can use. Today let your walk match your talk.

September 4

2 Timothy 4:10, "For Demas hath forsaken me, having loved this present world, and is departed unto Thessalonica; Crescens to Galatia, Titus unto Dalmatia."

ON THIS DAY in 1957, the Ford Motor Company introduced the Edsel. Realizing that there was a void in the selections of mid-sized automobiles, the Ford Motor Company instituted plans for an entirely new car division and an entirely new car—the Edsel. Advertising said, "Once you've seen it, you'll never forget it. Once you've owned it, you'll never want to change." Referred to as the "E" car (for Experimental) the name "Edsel" was chosen after reviewing a list of nearly 8,000 suggestions. By the time the first Edsel hit the showroom the country was in a recession. The car also suffered from parts that did not fit together correctly. The Edsel was more costly than comparable cars making the car a flop. After three years and just 110,847 Edsel's later, Ford Motor Company discontinued the Edsel, and the name will always be synonymous with failure.

There is a name in the Bible that will always be associated with failure—Demas. There is not much that we know about him, but what little we do know has forever made his name synonymous with failure. As Paul closed his second letter to Timothy he made a passing remark about how Demas had forsaken him, having loved this present world. Did he ever get back into God's work? No one knows, but from henceforth he was branded as a quitter and a failure. What do people think of when they think of you? Are you thought of as someone who loves the Lord and is faithful to God? Today, ask God to help you to be known as anything but an Edsel.

September 5

1 Thessalonians 5:12, "And we beseech you, brethren, to know them which labour among you, and are over you in the Lord, and admonish you."

ON THIS DAY in 1882, Labor Day was first celebrated. Matthew Maguire proposed the holiday in 1882 while serving as secretary of the Central Labor Union in New York. Some 10,000 men participated in a Labor Day parade to honor the workingman. In 1884, the first Monday in September was selected as the holiday and the Central Labor Union urged similar organizations in other cities to follow the example of New York. Oregon became the first state to make Labor Day an official holiday. On June 28, 1894, Congress passed an act making the first Monday in September a legal holiday.

God's laborers anticipate and await a future reward and recognition of their labor. There will be an eternal "Labor Day" when God will honor those who have served Him. Yet, God wants us to be respectful of His servants in this life. Those who have been placed over us in the Lord and labor among us to admonish us in the things of God are not to be without our recognition and respect. The pastor that preaches to us week after week, ministers to us in time of personal need, is due our love and honor. They do not serve to win our love and respect, and most would serve God and us if never recognized and honored by anyone. Yet, they are worthy of our love, honor, and respect. Today, give thanks for those God has placed over you in the Lord. Maybe a call, card, or letter would be an encouragement to your pastor. God will reward them one day, but it would be in order for us to get in on that rewarding down here.

September 6

Psalm 122:6, "Pray for the peace of Jerusalem: they shall prosper that love thee."

ON THIS DAY in 1941, it was announced that it was a crime for Jews in Germany to appear in public without a yellow Star of David sewn to their clothing. The order, published in the *Legal Gazette*, was extended to all Jews "who have completed their sixth year." The order also stated that Jews were not allowed to leave their areas of residence without getting permission from the police. Shortly thereafter, posters with the yellow Star of David and the words, "When you see this sign…" written over the symbol were put up to remind the public to avoid and even abuse Jews. The order was one of the early acts of Hitler's "final solution" to the "Jewish problem" that led to the extermination of over six million Jews.

We read in Deuteronomy 7:6, "*For thou art an holy people unto the Lord thy God: the Lord thy God hath chosen thee to be a special people unto himself, above all people that are upon the face of the earth.*" The Jewish people were chosen by God to be His people for a special purpose in God's eternal plan. It was through the Jewish people that God gave us a Saviour. Even as God's chosen people, their history has been marked by persecution and hatred by different races and nations. Hitler's effort to rid Europe of the Jews is an example of Jewish persecution and a people who have often been the target of hate. Even today, the unrest and turmoil in the Middle East, stems from the hatred of the Jewish people. Today, pray for the Jewish people. Pray that Jewish people will come to the understanding that the Messiah they wait for has already come. With David may we pray for the peace of Jerusalem.

September 7

Colossians 3:10, "And have put on the new man, which is renewed in knowledge after the image of him that created him:"

ON THIS DAY in 1813, the nickname "Uncle Sam" was first used as a symbolic reference to the United States in an editorial in the Troy Post of New York. During the war of 1812, Sam Wilson was a meat packer living and working in Troy, New York. Each barrel of meat shipped to the soldiers was stamped US. The soldiers equated their supplied meat rations with Uncle Sam Wilson. The story grew to mythical proportions resulting in a image of Sam Wilson as the white bearded, red, white and blue clad symbol of America. The Sam Wilson image as "Uncle Sam" became one of the most recognized national symbols. In 1961, the U.S. Congress adopted the following resolution: "Resolved by the Senate and the House of Representatives that the Congress salutes 'Uncle Sam' Wilson of Troy, New York, as the progenitor of America's National symbol of 'Uncle Sam'."

Paul speaks of the believer as being in the "*image of him that created him.*" When God created man it was declared, "*So God created man in his own image, in the image of God created he him; male and female created he them*" (Gen. 1:27). When Paul speaks of the believer as being in God's image he declares that believers are representatives of the Lord. Just as "Uncle Sam" has become a national symbol of the United States, the believer is to be a representative of the One who in creation gave them life and in salvation gave them new life. As a new person in Christ Jesus, we are to live a life which bears resemblance to the one who saved us. Today, let your life be an image of the Lord Jesus.

September 8

Psalm 107:30, "Then are they glad because they be quiet; so he bringeth them unto their desired haven."

ON THIS DAY in 1827, Williams Forsyth staged the first tourist stunt at Niagara Falls. Forsyth bought an old condemned lake schooner named *Michigan* and advertised that he would send the schooner over the Falls with a cargo of ferocious animals. To further add to the stunt, the schooner was decorated to look like a pirate ship with human shaped dummies tied to her deck. The ferocious animals ended up being a buffalo, two small bears, two raccoons, a dog and a goose. As a crowd of approximately 10,000 watched, the *Michigan* was released into currents and drifted toward the falls. The advertisement read, "Should the vessel take her course though the deepest of the rapids, it is confidently believed that she will reach the Horse Shoe unbroken… ." As it reached the rapids, its hull was torn open and the schooner began filling with water before plunging over the edge.

A very popular analogy of believers has been that of a ship—the "Old Ship of Zion." For the believer, we are guaranteed and assured that it will reach its desired harbor. Its hull has often been battered by many a stormy sea. Its sails have been torn by the winds of life, but we as its passengers never have to fear that it will not get us home. Jesus is our Captain and He is on board. Most of Forsyth's ferocious animals were lost, but the Old Ship of Zion has never lost a passenger. Everyone that has stepped on board has been given a heavenly promise they will reach their destination. Today, give thanks that you are a passenger aboard a ship that will never sink. We are assured of heaven as if we were already there. Aren't you glad you are aboard!

September 9

Genesis 50:17, "So shall ye say unto Joseph, Forgive, I pray thee now, the trespass of thy brethren, and their sin; for they did unto thee evil: and now, we pray thee, forgive the trespass of the servants of the God of thy father. And Joseph wept when they spake unto him."

ON THIS DAY in 1942, the continental United States was bombed from the air for the first and only time. During WWII, in a Japanese strategy to induce U.S. leaders to withdraw part or all of the U.S. Navy from the Western Pacific, thereby reducing pressure on Japan's navy, Nobuo Fujita launched his seaplane from a surfaced Japanese Imperial Navy submarine off the coast of Oregon. Fujita's plane was armed with incendiary bombs that he dropped near Brookings, Oregon for the purpose of starting a forest fire. A few days later, he launched his second raid. Both raids were unsuccessful. In 1962, the people of Brookings invited Fujita and his family to the town as a gesture of goodwill and made him an honorary citizen.

Have you ever had someone do you wrong? Have you been the target of someone's unprovoked and unjustified anger? If so, what has been your response? If you are like many, the last thing you want to do is to show forgiveness and kindness. Yet, that is precisely the response the Lord expects of us. Joseph is a good example of forgiving those who had done him wrong. When his brothers came to him and asked forgiveness, instead of venting his wrath, he showed love and forgiveness. Forgiveness is not always the natural thing to do, but it is the Christian step to take. Today, search your heart for any unforgiveness that exists in your heart. Maybe it is time to extend a welcome to those who did you wrong.

September 10

Numbers 32:7, "And wherefore discourage ye the heart of the children of Israel from going over into the land which the Lord hath given them?"

ON THIS DAY in 1948, "Axis Sally" was indicted in Washington, D.C. for treason. During WWII, American born Mildred Gillars made propaganda broadcasts for the Nazi's through a program known as "Home Sweet Home." Her program aired between 8 p.m. and 2 a.m. daily and was heard all over Europe, the Mediterranean, North Africa and the U.S. Although she referred to herself as "Midge at the mike," GI's dubbed her Axis Sally. In an effort to discourage the allied forces she would say such things as: "Your wives and girlfriends are probably home in a nice warm building, dancing with some other men. You're over here in the cold," or "There was a big push up North; you might as well give up. The war's over, the Germans captured 50,000 Americans." After the war she was convicted of treason and served twelve years in a U.S. prison.

The tribes of Gad and Reuben wanted to stay on the side of Jordan opposite the land of Canaan. Moses considered their request an act that would discourage the other tribes from possessing the land. They had wandered 40 years in the desert because of others that had previously discouraged them. Moses did not want anything else to discourage them from possessing what God had given them. Satan is always seeking to discourage the believer. He has many methods, even his "Axis Sallie's," to try and get us to lose heart. Today, don't let Satan get you discouraged. When he tries to discourage you, change the station. Listen to the God on the throne and His Home Sweet Home program.

September 11

Psalm 37:25, "I have been young, and now am old; yet have I not seen the righteous forsaken, nor his seed begging bread."

ON THIS DAY in 1841, all of President John Tyler's cabinet, except Secretary of State Daniel Webster, resigned to protest Tyler's veto of the banking bill. Tyler was the first president to be elevated to the office of President by the death of his predecessor, the first president to be widowed and remarried while in office, and the first president that the House of Representatives brought an impeachment resolution against. The resignation of his cabinet followed Tyler's veto of a bill by Henry Clay to establish a National Bank with branches in several states. Congress passed a similar bill and he vetoed it. When he later vetoed a tariff bill, a resolution for his impeachment was introduced in the House of Representatives, claiming he had misused his veto power, but the resolution failed. Dubbed "His Accidency" by his detractors for the way he assumed office, he became known as a president without a party.

There have been times when others have forsaken a believer for the decision they made and the stand they took on a certain matter, but one thing a believer is assured of is that the Lord will never forsake them. As David reflected back over his life, he rejoiced in the fact that in both youth and old age the Lord had been with him and at no point had He forsaken him. Paul testified that in the hour that he was forsaken by others, *"Notwithstanding the Lord stood with me"* (2 Tim. 4:17). Today, rejoice that the Lord will never forsake you even when others call for your impeachment. He is always there when you need Him.

September 12

Matthew 7:22, "Many will say to me in that day, Lord, Lord, have we not prophesied in thy name? and in thy name have cast out devils? and in thy name done many wonderful works?"

ON *THIS* DAY in 1878, the obelisk known as Cleopatra's Needle was erected in London. Pharoah Thotmes III first erected this obelisk of pink granite standing 68 feet high and weighing 180 tons, in 1500 B.C. in front of the great temple of Heliopolis in Egypt. Mohammed Ali, Viceroy of Egypt, presented it to Britain in 1819 in recognition of Nelson's victory over the French fleet at the battle of the Nile in 1798. It was not brought to London until 1878. Erected opposite the Embankment Gardens, it sits on a pedestal that encloses various objects such as a full set of British Empire coins, Bibles in various languages, a railway guide, an almanac, and copies of various newspapers. It is one of a pair and it's companion is located in New York's Central Park. Interestingly, the obelisk had nothing to do with Cleopatra but was christened with the nickname by Londoners.

Jesus spoke of those who claim that they have done many wonderful things in His name such as prophesying and casting out devils, yet in reality have no connection or relationship with Him whatsoever. Just because something or someone goes by the name "Christian" does not necessarily mean that it is Christian. Being a Christian has nothing to do with what a person does but with what Christ has done. Today, ask yourself if you are trusting in Jesus and Jesus alone as your Saviour or are you trusting in what you have done? It is one thing to call yourself a Christian and actually be one. A real Christian is more than a name. It is a relationship.

September 13

Psalm 37:23, "The steps of a good man are ordered by the Lord: and he delighteth in his way."

On This Day in 1899, Henry M. Bliss became the first known automobile fatality. According to the National Highway Transportation and Safety Association, in 1999 there were 37,140 fatal crashes in the United States. Of that number, there were 25,257 drivers, 10,521 passengers, ninety-seven unknown occupants and 5,842 non-motorists for a total of 41,717 fatalities in automobile accidents. In the case of Mr. Bliss, he stepped off a streetcar at Central Park West and 74th Street and was hit by a car driven by Arthur Smith. Bliss was rushed to the hospital but died a short time later. Arthur Smith was arrested, but not held.

Ironically, I had just written the above paragraph when I received a call to tell me that Grace Cleaver, a very special lady in our church, had been killed in an automobile accident a few hours earlier. She had been on her way to our mid-week service. When I sat back down at my computer I was still numb from the news I had just received. Grace was the kind of person who would do anything you asked of her. She had a big heart for people and was one of the best workers in our church. I found that big word "why" rising in my heart. I must confess that we don't always know why such tragedies happen. Yet I think of something Warren Wiersbe said, "In the believer's life there are no accidents, only appointments." The believer lives with the assurance that their steps, and as someone has said, "even stops", are ordered by the Lord. Today rest in the promise that God makes no mistakes, and that with Him there are no accidents, only divine appointments. We may not know why, but we are assured there is always a divine reason.

September 14

Revelation 19:6, "And I heard as it were the voice of a great multitude, and as the voice of many waters, and as the voice of mighty thunderings, saying, Alleluia: for the Lord God omnipotent reigneth."

ON THIS DAY in 1741, George Frederick Handel completed his *Messiah*. Considered Handel's most highly esteemed and popular work, the *Messiah* has become one of the most renowned pieces of English sacred music. In 1741, during a low spot in Handel's career, Charles Jennens convinced him to compose an oratorio based on a compilation of Scriptures Jennens' had recently arranged. Handel began work on the oratorio on August 24 and 24 days later, September 14, completed his work. It was performed for the first time in Dublin, Ireland, on April 13, 1742. The *Messiah* is divided into three parts, representing the birth, death and resurrection of Christ. The most recognized part of the *Messiah* is the "Hallelujah Chorus" which declares, "The Lord God omnipotent reigneth, Hallelujah, hallelujah, hallelujah...King of kings, hallelujah, hallelujah, hallelujah, Lord of Lords..."

I still remember the first time I heard the *Messiah*. It was during my first semester in Bible College. I must confess, for the most part, not having an appreciation for certain kinds of music that I should have had, I was not all that excited. But then the choir began the "Hallelujah Chorus." As we used to say back home, business picked up in my heart. If I had not been where I was, I think I would have shouted out loud. Blessed be His name, He does reign! Today, lift your voice in praise to the Lord God omnipotent that reigneth. He is on His throne and will reign throughout eternity. Hallelujah!

September 15

Ephesians 2:3, "Among whom also we all had our conversation in times past in the lusts of our flesh, fulfilling the desires of the flesh and of the mind; and were by nature the children of wrath, even as others."

On This Day in 1949, the *Lone Ranger* premiered on ABC to become the longest-running Western series in television history. The *Lone Ranger* began as a local radio show in 1933 and quickly was being broadcast nationwide. The masked man and his companion, Tonto, appeared in 221 made-for-TV episodes. The opening episode told the story of how the *Lone Ranger* got his name and mission in life. He was one of a posse of six Texas Rangers that was lured into an ambush in which five were slaughtered. John Reid was left for dead, but was found and nursed back to health by an Indian named Tonto. The lone ranger (hence his name) sought to avenge the death of his comrades. Tonto vowed to stay with him giving us the familiar words, "You kemo sabe," meaning "faithful friend." Reid buried his past at the grave of the five rangers, donned a mask, and set out to avenge wrongs throughout the Old West.

Praise God our past has been buried in the depths of the sea and we don't even have to wear a mask! As believers we point back to an empty grave to celebrate the new life we have been given and the death of our past life. For many of us, we look back and remember the sinful lives we lived, but thank God the past is gone and we have a new life and new mission. Today, rejoice that your past has been put away through the death and resurrection of Jesus Christ.

September 16

Isaiah 55:7, "Let the wicked forsake his way, and the unrighteous man his thoughts: and let him return unto the Lord, and he will have mercy upon him; and to our God, for he will abundantly pardon."

ON *THIS* DAY in 1974, President Gerald Ford pardoned Richard Nixon. Although mounting evidence indicated that former President Nixon may have engaged in criminal acts in the Watergate scandal, President Ford granted a full and unconditional pardon to his predecessor. On the same day he granted immunity to Vietnam-era draft evaders. Ford said that Nixon had already "paid the unprecedented penalty of relinquishing" the presidency. His reasoning was that that the act would spare Nixon and the nation additional grief. Reaction varied from agreeing with the president to seeing it as an act of disservice to justice.

The simple truth of the matter is that each of us deserves justice. We all are guilty. We all have sinned. In the eyes of the world some are worse sinners than others, yet none can claim innocence. Yet, instead of getting what we deserve, we find mercy and receive a pardon for our sins. We should have gone to hell, but through the Lord Jesus Christ we were pardoned and given heaven instead. To be pardoned by God simply means that God has forgiven us. There is no sin God will not forgive and no sinner God will not pardon. All that He asks is that we come to Him and ask for His forgiveness. All of our sins have been removed from our record. Today, give thanks that one day you received a pardon and that God has forgiven you of all sins.

September 17

Ephesians 5:30, "For we are members of his body, of his flesh, and of his bones."

On This Day in 1953, the first successful separation of Siamese twins was performed. Siamese twins are formed from a single fertilized ovum that divides imperfectly. A complete division produces identical twins. The name Siamese twins (sometimes called conjoined twins) is derived from the famous twins Eng and Chang, born in Siam (now Thailand). They were exhibited in Barnum's Circus for many years before settling in Wilkesboro, North Carolina where they purchased a retail store, later took up farming, married, and raised a family. The first successful separation of conjoined twins was on twins who were joined at the base of the spine and shared the lower intestinal tract.

The Bible describes how at our new birth we are joined with Christ in a union that is inseparable. As Paul declares, we become members of His body, of His flesh, and of His bones. As believers, we enjoy a union and oneness with Christ by which we share His very life. It is this relationship and union with Christ that is the secret of living the Christian life. The Christian life is more than trying our best to be all that we should be. Our best efforts always end in frustration and failure. The secret is the life of Christ in us. By our union with Him, we draw from His life and by His life, we are able to be and do all that we should as believers. Do you find yourself struggling to be all that God would have you to be? If so, let Christ be your wisdom, redemption, righteousness, and sanctification (1 Cor. 1:31). Today, draw from the inseparable union you have with Christ. That union is your source for Christian living.

September 18

1 Thessalonians 5:3, "For when they shall say, Peace and safety; then sudden destruction cometh upon them, as travail upon a woman with child; and they shall not escape."

ON THIS DAY in 1978, Israel's Prime Minister Begin and Egypt's President Sadat announced that they had reached a peace agreement. For thirteen days, the two leaders had met at Camp David in the United States with President Carter shuttling between the two often hostile delegations to reach a peace agreement. Sadat and Begin signed two separate documents. The *Framework for Peace in the Middle East* called for more negotiations to determine the future of the West Bank and the Gaza Strip. Carter acknowledged that the accords were only the beginning and that, "There are still great difficulties that remain." Sadat praised Carter and Begin congratulated him for "a great victory," and added, "He worked harder than our forefathers did in Egypt building the pyramids."

While hailed as a great victory, the years that followed have been less than peaceful in the Middle East. In my personal opinion, there will never be lasting peace in the Middle East until the Prince of Peace rules and reigns upon the earth. Paul describes the period before the Lord returns as a time when men will speak of peace and safety. Just about every day, we hear something on the news about peace (or the lack of peace) in the Middle East. The talks and hope of peace around the world, especially the Middle East, only remind us that the hour of our Lord's return is getting close. Today, turn your eyes to the skies. All this talk about peace and safety makes me wonder if He will not come today.

September 19

1 Corinthians 1:10, "Now I beseech you, brethren, by the name of our Lord Jesus Christ, that ye all speak the same thing, and that there be no divisions among you; but that ye be perfectly joined together in the same mind and in the same judgment.

ON THIS DAY in 1902, panic broke out at the Shiloh Baptist Church in Birmingham, Alabama, leading to the death of 115 people. More than 2,000 people crowded into the Shiloh Baptist Church to hear Booker T. Washington. Someone shouted, "fight" and it was misunderstood as "fire." The congregation stampeded for the stairs which led from the auditorium to the doors on a lower level. Those who reached them first were pushed from behind and fell. Others fell on top of them until the entrance was completely blocked by a pile of screaming humanity ten feet high. Efforts by Washington and church leaders were in vain. People were trampled and suffocated to death. It all began over an altercation over an unoccupied seat.

If you have never had the unfortunate experience of church problems and altercations between members, then you have been blessed. Many believers live with the scars of a bitter church split or harbor in their hearts the hurt of seeing a church divided over some internal conflict. Families have been strained, and friendships of many years have been severed over church problems. The testimony of many churches has been injured over a church problem, a problem that could have begun over a little thing such as who occupies a seat. Today, pray for your Church. Ask God to bless the church and protect it from strife and division. Going to church to worship is much more enjoyable than a church fight.

September 20

Genesis 35:7, "And he built there an altar, and called the place El-beth-el: because there God appeared unto him, when he fled from the face of his brother."

ON THIS DAY in 1258, the Salisbury Cathedral of England, considered one of the finest medieval cathedrals in Britain, was consecrated. Construction began in 1220. Its spire (404 ft), added a generation later, makes it the tallest medieval structure in the world. The cloister (the largest in England) and the Chapter House, with its stone-carved frieze of Old Testament Bible stories, were added in 1280. In the Chapter House you can find one of only four original Magna Carta dating back to 1215. Built to reflect the glory of God in glass and stone, it is one of the best-preserved cathedral's in England. More than 750,000 visitors pass through it each year.

During my visits to England and throughout the United Kingdom, the architecture and grandeur of their cathedrals and churches have always fascinated me. They stand as majestic reminders of hundreds of years of British history. However, I am reminded that a beautiful and majestic building without God is nothing more than glass and stone. Our scripture verse for the day tells of Jacob erecting an altar and calling the place El-bethel. "Bethel" means "House of God." "El" is a name of God and when you combine the two (El-beth-el), it means the "God of the House of God." We may call a building the house of God but if the presence of God is not there, it is nothing but a building. We can have buildings that cost millions of dollars, but if God's presence is not there, we will have nothing more than a gathering of people. I would rather have a shack with God than a cathedral without Him. Today, pray that God will always be in His house. His presence is what makes a building a church.

September 21

Revelation 1:18, "I am he that liveth, and was dead; and, behold, I am alive for evermore, Amen; and have the keys of hell and of death."

ON THIS DAY in 1897, eight year-old Virginia O'Hanlon wrote the *New York Sun* asking: "I am eight years old. Some of my friends say there is no Santa Claus. Papa says, 'If you see it in *The Sun*, its so.' Please tell me the truth. Is there a Santa Claus?" Editor Frank Church's reply became one of the most memorable editorials in newspaper history: "Yes, Virginia, there is a Santa Claus. He exists as certainly as love and generosity and devotion exist...Alas! How dreary would be the world if there were no Santa Claus! It would be as dreary as if there were no Virginia's...Nobody sees Santa Claus, but that is no sign that there is no Santa Claus. The most real things in the world are those that neither children nor men can see...No Santa Claus? Thank God! He lives and lives forever. A thousand years from now, Virginia, nay 10 times 10,000 years from now, he will continue to make glad the heart of childhood."

Let me give you my editorial for the day. Is there a living Saviour? Yes, my dear friend, Jesus is alive! He arose from the dead on the morning of the third day, and he lives and will live forever. A million, million years from now, He will still be living and the multitudes of heaven will be lifting their hearts and voices in praise and worship of the living and reigning Lord. How dreary life would be today if He were not alive. He lives and lives within the heart of every believer, filling the heart with cheer. Yes, my friend, Jesus is alive! Today, rejoice that a living Saviour is more than a story. He is a blessed reality and that, my friend, is the real truth!

September 22

James 5:20, "Let him know, that he which converteth the sinner from the error of his way shall save a soul from death, and shall hide a multitude of sins."

On This Day in 1975, Oliver W. Sipple thwarted an assassination attempt on the life of President Gerald Ford. Sipple was part of a crowd of about 3,000 who had gathered outside the Saint Francis Hotel in San Francisco to see the president. As Ford was coming out of the hotel, Sipple noticed that the woman next to him had pulled out a .38 caliber pistol and was aiming it at the president. Sipple lunged at the woman, Sara Jane Moore, just as she pulled the trigger. He hit her arm slightly, just enough to deflect her aim and cause her shot to miss the president. Had it not been for Sipple's action, the bullet would have struck the president in the head.

As believers, we are in the business of saving lives. Of course, when I speak of saving lives, I do not mean keeping someone from assassinating the president or someone else. As James describes, we are to be witnesses for Christ and seek the conversion of those who are lost and, in so doing, save their souls. Each day, we meet people who are unsaved and in danger of dying in their lost condition. Telling others about Christ and seeking their salvation is the greatest work that anyone could ever do. You could call it a life-saving work. Does someone come to your mind at this moment who needs to be saved? Is there someone you have opportunity to tell about Christ, yet you have failed to seize that opportunity? Today, ask God to let you tell someone about Christ. It may be the means of saving his soul.

September 23

Joshua 10:26, "And afterward Joshua smote them, and slew them, and hanged them on five trees: and they were hanging upon the trees until the evening."

ON THAT DAY in 1916, an elephant was hanged in Erwin, Tennessee for killing a man. The Sparks Circus was stationed in Kingsport, Tennessee when Mary, a circus elephant, yanked Walter Eldridge, an inexperienced trainer, off her back and stepped on his head killing him. A Kingsport resident came running and fired five shots into Mary but she did not die. The next day, the circus moved to Erwin where authorities decreed that Mary should die on the gallows. A chain was slung around her neck while she was hoisted into the air by a derrick. The chain broke. A second chain held and Mary died instantly. She was buried in a grave dug by a steam shovel.

As Joshua conquered Canaan, one of his actions was the hanging of five kings who had hid themselves in a cave. These five kings had formed an alliance to defeat the Gibeonites and Joshua. These kings represent the enemies of the Christian life that seek our destruction. Joshua demonstrates the principle that the believer must put to death the things that hide away in our hearts and life that can destroy our effectiveness and testimony. Those kings which hide in our heart can be bitterness, jealousy, hatred, unforgiveness, pride, and a score of other things. They must be hanged—put to death. To allow such things to dwell in our heart is to only invite hurt and harm to our effectiveness as a believer and rob us of God's blessings. Today, look in your heart and see if there is a king hiding there. If you find one, hang it.

September 24

Proverbs 15:18, "A wrathful man stirreth up strife: but he that is slow to anger appeaseth strife."

ON THIS DAY in 1969, the trial of the "Chicago Eight" began. Tom Hayden, leader of the Students for a Democratic Society, David Dellinger, chairman of the National Mobilization against the War, Jerry Rubin, leader of the Youth International Party, Bobby Seale, co-founder of the Black Panther Party for Self-Defense, and four others were charged with inciting the riots that occurred during the 1968 Democratic Convention in Chicago. They had staged demonstrations to protest the Vietnam War and its support by Vice President Hubert Humphrey, the Democratic presidential candidate. The four days of the convention were the most violent in U.S. history as police and national guardsman clashed with antiwar protesters. On February 18, 1970, five of the eight were found guilty of crossing a state line with intent to incite riots and were sentenced to five years in prison. In 1972, an appeals court overturned the convictions.

Solomon speaks of an angry and vindictive person as one who stirs up strife. In a similar fashion, he declares in Proverbs 10:12, "*Hatred stirreth up strifes: but love covereth all sins,*" and in Proverbs 29:22, "*An angry man stirreth up strife, and a furious man aboundeth in transgression.*" A person with a heart full of anger and bitterness is often the cause of much strife. Many church problems can be traced to someone who was angry and displeased with something that had happened. They have no hesitancy to incite division and create strife. On the other hand, a person with a heart of love seeks harmony and promotes unity. Today, ask God to help you to always be a uniter, not a divider.

September 25

1 Corinthians 8:6, "But to us there is but one God, the Father, of whom are all things, and we in him; and one Lord Jesus Christ, by whom are all things, and we by him."

ON THIS DAY in 1851, the followers of Hong Xiuquan in China announced that he had been chosen by God to be the heavenly king of their movement, the Tiaiping tienkuo or heavenly kingdom of great peace. Hong, a schoolteacher-mystic influenced by Protestant Christian tracts, believed that he was the younger brother of Jesus Christ. Passionately dedicated to his beliefs, he appealed to all types, poor miners and peasants as well as landlords and scholars. Converts flocked to join the Taipings, as they called themselves. The Tiapings proclaimed, "Our heavenly king has received the Divine commission to exterminate the Manchus, to exterminate all idolaters generally, and to possess the empire as its true sovereign."

While God gives us spiritual leaders to lead us and provide godly examples, the believer has only one God appointed Lord and King. There is only one Lord and that is the Lord Jesus Christ. There are those who greatly influence our lives for God, and we owe them a tremendous debt for their dedication to God and the example and leadership they have given us. But we must never forget that man, any man, at his best is but a sinner saved by God's grace. All men have received a Divine commission, but none has been commissioned to be a heavenly king on earth and to set up a heavenly kingdom. Those who make such a claim are nothing less than false prophets and deceivers. Only Jesus Christ is Lord. Today, let no one or anything take the place in your heart that Christ alone should have. He only is Lord!

September 26

Proverbs 20:9, "Who can say, I have made my heart clean, I am pure from my sin?"

ON THIS DAY in 1796, the "Independent Chronicle" of Boston published George Washington's Farewell Address. Probably Washington's best-known speech, it was never delivered orally by Washington but was published and then read to the House of Representatives. In the speech, he gave the reasons why he would not seek a third term. The advice he gave in the document has continued to exercise a profound influence on the policy of the United States. At the end of his Farewell Address, Washington said, "Though, in reviewing the incidents of my administration, I am unconscious of intentional error—I am nevertheless too sensible of my defects not to think it probable that I may have committed many errors..."

Washington was aware that no man could make the claim that he was pure from sin and error. I wish that we as believers could make such a claim. Knowing that sin breaks our fellowship with God and, most of all, grieves the heart of God, it would be great if we were pure from sin. Yet, we all fail the Lord each day of our lives. One of the reasons why we should look forward to life in our glorified bodies is that we will no longer sin. Oh, that will be a wonderful day when we no longer have a problem with our flesh, temptation, and our old human nature. However, our failures should not be intentional. With Washington we ought to be able to say, "I am unconscious of intentional error." Our sin should not be the result of a careless and unguarded life. Today, ask God to help you be as pure from sin as possible in this life. Until the day when we are sinless, seek to sin less. It would be a good way to say goodbye to this old world.

September 27

Mark 11:2-3, "And saith unto them, Go your way into the village over against you: and as soon as ye be entered into it, ye shall find a colt tied, whereon never man sat; loose him, and bring him. And if any man say unto you, Why do ye this? say ye that the Lord hath need of him; and straightway he will send him hither."

ON THIS DAY in 1938, the RMS *Queen Elizabeth* was launched. Built in honor of Queen Elizabeth, the ship was the largest passenger liner built to that date. However, before she would serve her days as a lavish passenger liner, she was called into a more important service. When WWII broke out, the ship was commissioned and hastily fitted for wartime service. Until the war's end, the *Queen Elizabeth* was used as a transport vessel for the Allies, carrying troops and supplies around the world. During her war service, she carried over 811,000 soldiers and sailed over 500,000 miles. She was released from war duty in March of 1946 and underwent an extensive refit. In October of the same year, she left on her maiden voyage and began a twenty year career of transatlantic crossings.

As the Lord Jesus neared the city of Jerusalem, He sent His disciples to get a colt on which He would ride into the city. He gave them directions where to find the colt and instructions to tell the owners that the Lord had need of it. There was the normal service of the colt, but the Lord commissioned it into a greater service. As believers, we have been commissioned into our Lord's service. We all have our plans, goals, and ambitions, but we have also received a call to serve in a greater role. We have been called to serve the Lord and fulfill His will in our life. Today, if you haven't already done so, surrender to God's will for your life. It is a call to greater service.

September 28

Proverbs 24:28, "Be not a witness against thy neighbour without cause; and deceive not with thy lips."

ON THIS DAY in 1980, a story appeared in the *Washington Post* about the tragic ghetto life of Jimmy, an eight-year-old heroin addict. Reported by Janet Cooke, the story drew immediate attention by police and social workers. They searched for the boy but were unable to find him. Cooke refused to reveal any information about the boy, claiming that it would put the boy and herself in danger. The Post submitted the story for consideration by the Pulitzer Prize Committee. When the story won, Cooke was asked to supply biographical information to the committee. The resume she provided was so full of errors that it cast doubt on the truth of the story. When questioned, Cooke finally admitted that the story was a hoax. The next day she publicly apologized and resigned.

Solomon speaks of deceiving others by the things we say and tell. The word "deceive" carries the idea of enticing and flattering. It would describe someone whose desire to be accepted, popular, or make himself look better to others leads him to tell stories that are untrue. It would also be descriptive of someone taking a true story and adding things to it to make it sound better or make him look better. Call such deception with your lips anything you want to, but it is nothing more than lying and God makes it very clear how He feels about lying (Prov. 6:16-17). Whatever the motive or reason, lies are never condoned by God. Today, remember a lie may make you look good at first, but it's how you look after the truth is known that you should consider.

September 29

Colossians 1:28, "Whom we preach, warning every man, and teaching every man in all wisdom; that we may present every man perfect in Christ Jesus:"

On This Day in 1982, McNeil Consumer Products, a subsidiary of Johnson & Johnson, issued a recall on all Tylenol capsules because seven people on Chicago's West side died from taking Extra-Strength Tylenol. Authorities determined that the Tylenol capsules had been laced with cyanide. Someone had tampered with Tylenol bottles by putting anywhere from five to ten cyanide laced capsules in the bottles and then putting them back on the shelf. As soon as the connection was made, the nation was warned. Police drove through Chicago announcing the warning over loudspeakers, while all three national television networks reported about the deaths and the contaminated drugs. The Food and Drug Administration advised consumers to avoid the Tylenol capsules. The recall included approximately thirty-one million bottles of Tylenol with a retail value of more than $100 million. The person or persons responsible were never caught.

One Apostle Paul's passions was to warn others about the need of being saved. Paul knew that hell was real and the only way that men could avoid an eternity in hell was by accepting Christ as their Saviour. Paul viewed the matter of preaching the gospel and telling others about Christ as urgent. People were perishing without Christ and they needed to be warned that without Christ, they would spend eternity in hell. As believers, we are to warn others. If we have to go up and down the streets in our neighborhoods, we must warn others. Today, tell someone about Jesus. Tell them Jesus can save them from an eternity in hell.

September 30

John 1:45, "Philip findeth Nathanael, and saith unto him, We have found him, of whom Moses in the law, and the prophets, did write, Jesus of Nazareth, the son of Joseph."

ON THIS DAY in 1928, Scottish biologist Alexander Fleming discovered penicillin. As an army medic during the war, Fleming became aware of the rampant wound infections that took the life of many soldiers, rather than their underlying injuries. After the war, he returned to London and a fortunate accident in his cluttered laboratory at St. Mary's Hospital led to his discovery. After mistakenly leaving a dish of Staphylococcus bacterial culture uncovered, he noticed that a green fungus had formed on the surface, destroying the sections of bacteria with which it came into contact. His accidental discovery became one of the most significant medical discoveries of the century. Fleming attributed the discovery to his untidiness, remarking that it could never have occurred in the pristine laboratories run by some of his colleagues.

Philip made a wonderful discovery in his life. It was such a wonderful discovery that he had to tell others about it. He ran straight to Nathaniel and told him about his discovery. It was a life-changing discovery. He had met the Lord Jesus and his life would never be the same again. Have you made this wonderful discovery? Have you met the Lord Jesus? If you have, then you understand the excitement of Philip. Maybe you know someone who needs to be told of what Jesus can do for him. Today, share with someone your wonderful discovery. What you have found is the "medicine" that many need. It is too great of a discovery to keep to ourselves.

October 1

2 Peter 2:9, "The Lord knoweth how to deliver the godly out of temptations, and to reserve the unjust unto the day of judgment to be punished:"

ON *THIS* DAY in 1946, the International War Crimes tribunal sentenced Nazi war criminals to death. The atrocities of the Nazi's during WWII are almost beyond human imagination and description. Over six million Jews died as a result of Hitler's Nazi regime. During the Nuremberg Trials, high-ranking officials of the Nazi's were tried for their war crimes against humanity. The result was twelve high-ranking Nazi officials were sentenced to death, and seven others were given terms ranging from ten years to life. Three were acquitted. Two weeks after being sentenced, ten of the twelve were hanged. Of the remaining two, Hermann Goering, founder of the Gestapo and chief of the German air force committed suicide on the eve of his execution, and Chancellor Martin Bormann, who was judged in absentia, was suspected to be dead.

There will come a day when the court of heaven will be called into session and every person from the beginning of time who has not accepted the Lord Jesus as Saviour will go on trial. On that "Day of Judgment" the "unjust" will stand before God and their sin will be reviewed and sentenced. In each case, the sentence will be life in hell without the possibility of parole. However, there is a way that this "Day of Judgment" can be avoided and a person's sins forgiven. The "blood of Jesus Christ, God's Son cleanseth from all sin" and "delivered us from the wrath to come" (1 John 1:7 & 1 Thess. 1:10). Today, if you are saved, rejoice that your case has already been judged and that you have been forgiven of all your sins.

October 2

Romans 1:16, "For I am not ashamed of the gospel of Christ: for it is the power of God unto salvation to every one that believeth; to the Jew first, and also to the Greek."

ON *THIS* DAY in 1836, Charles Darwin returned to Falmouth, England, ending a five year surveying expedition of the southern Atlantic and Pacific oceans. He described the cannibals who lived in the South Sea Islands as primitive creatures and was convinced that nothing on earth could possibly lift them to a higher level. He thought he had indeed found a lower stratum of humanity which would fit his theory of evolution. However, he returned thirty-four years later to the same islands, and to his amazement he discovered churches, schools, and homes occupied by some of those former cannibals. In fact, many of them wore clothes and frequently gathered to sing hymns. The reason was soon learned: Missionary John G. Paton had been there preaching the gospel of Jesus Christ! Darwin was so moved by their transformation that he made a generous contribution to the London Missionary Society.

Paul speaks of the Gospel of Jesus Christ as the power of God unto salvation. The power of the Gospel is such that no man or people are so low or so primitive that it cannot bring about a marvelous transformation. Some of us were among the lowest of the low, yet the Gospel brought a total change in how we lived. There is no one too hard, too sinful, or too depraved that the Gospel of Jesus Christ cannot produce a wonderful transformation. I'm sure some thought we were hopeless cases. Today, rejoice in the saving power of the Gospel of Jesus Christ. We are all a testimony of its power.

October 3

Psalm 133:1, "Behold, how good and how pleasant it is for brethren to dwell together in unity!"

ON THIS DAY in 1990, East and West Germany were united as one nation. The rebirth of a united nation was ushered in at the stroke of midnight. As fireworks filled the sky the Freedom Bell at Berlin's Schöneberg City Hall rang with a triumphant peal. A roar went up from thousands of cheering, weeping people who hugged each other with joy and waved a sea of black, red, and gold flags. For forty-five years their Germany had been divided, but now they were united and free as one nation. Known as the Federal Republic of Germany with a population of 78.5 million, their constitution, currency, flag, and national anthem are those of what was under West Germany.

The Psalmist speaks of the beauty and blessing of unity among the people of God. When the Psalmist speaks of unity he is describing more than union. Someone has said that you can tie the tails of two tomcats together and throw them over the clothesline, and you have union but you do not have unity. Unity is when people are united and working together as a unit. One of the problems Paul dealt with when he wrote to the Corinthian church was the divisions and schisms that existed among them. They were in union because of their relationship to Christ but they were not in unity. Christ, has brought us into union with one another, but we are also to be united and working as a unit. Today, pray for unity in your church and in the family of God. It is a blessed experience when there is unity and when you find a people united and working together as a unit to glorify God and reach others for Christ.

October 4

Luke 4:4, "And Jesus answered him, saying, It is written, That man shall not live by bread alone, but by every word of God."

ON THIS DAY in 1535, the first complete English translation of the Bible was printed. John Wycliffe is credited for the first whole English translation of the Bible (1384). The English preacher and theologian desired to "put the Bible into the hands of the common people." John Gutenberg printed the first Bible. It was a copy of the Vulgate and was printed in Latin. William Tyndale's (an English reformer and martyr) English translation became the basis for the King James Bible. His translation created an appetite for the Bible in English. While he was imprisoned in Belgium, Miles Coverdale published the first complete Bible in English, a translation that relied mostly upon Tyndale's English version.

One of the most prized gifts the believer has received from God is His Word in printed form. Each time we pick up our Bible we ought to give thanks to God that we have His Word in printed form and in our own language. When we think of how, in ages past, the common people did not have the privilege of having a personal copy of God's Word, should make us even more grateful for our Bibles. During the reformation people would gather to hear someone read the Bible, for they did not have the privilege of having a personal copy of God's Word. The blessing of being able to read God's Word at anytime by any person is a privilege that should never be taken for granted. Today, when you read your Bible, hold it lovingly in your hands and read it with a heart of gratitude.

October 5

1 John 2:6, "He that saith he abideth in him ought himself also so to walk, even as he walked."

On This Day in 1974, American David Kunst completed his walk around the world. It took Kunst four years and twenty-one pairs of shoes to complete the 14,450-mile journey across four continents. George Shilling claimed to have accomplished the feat nearly 100 years earlier, but it was never verified. According to the Guinness Book of World Records, Arthur Blessitt holds the record for the greatest distance walked and most countries visited. Beginning his walk on December 25, 1969, Blessitt has walked over 34,184 miles visiting 367 countries on all seven continents. The interesting feature of Blessitt's record walk is that he has carried a cross twelve feet long, six feet wide weighing forty pounds. Wherever he goes he preaches the gospel. At age sixty, he continues to walk up to twenty miles per day. His wife Denise has been with him since 1990. Blessitt said that one night Jesus told him to take a cross that was hanging on the wall and walk.

God has much to say to the believer about walking. God speaks to us, not about a walk that takes us around the world carrying a cross but of a walk and life that is reflective of the life of the Lord Jesus while He was on this earth. John says, the believer is to walk as Jesus walked. Paul's instruction to the believers at Thessalonica is: *"Furthermore then we beseech you, brethren, and exhort you by the Lord Jesus, that as ye have received of us how ye ought to walk and to please God..."* (1 Thess. 4:1). Today, ask God to let your walk be pleasing to Him. You may not carry a cross, but your walk should reflect the Christ of the cross.

October 6

2 Corinthians 4:4, *"In whom the god of this world hath blinded the minds of them which believe not, lest the light of the glorious gospel of Christ, who is the image of God, should shine unto them."*

ON THIS DAY in 1014, the blinded army of the Bulgarians returned from battle. For thirteen years the Byzantine emperor, Basil had sought to vanquish Samuel's Bulgarian empire. He led a campaign of unprecedented terror in which massacre became the norm. On the banks of the river Strymon, after Basil's forces had surrounded and defeated the Bulgarians, 15,000 men were blinded on his orders. One man in every 100 was left one eye to guide his pathetic comrades on their long march home to Samuel. To celebrate his victory and horrible aftermath, Basil was given the title of Bulgaroctonus—slayer of the Bulgars. As the pathetic regiments made their way home, their ruler, Czar Samuel, was so shocked that he died, apparently of apoplexy.

Paul tells us that Satan, the god of this world, blinds those who are unsaved. He blinds to prevent those who are lost from coming to a saving knowledge of Jesus Christ. Satan does not want the unsaved to understand the gospel. He wants them to remain under his control and ultimately to die lost. He does not want them to see that Jesus Christ can give them a new and eternal life. As believers, we can rejoice that one day we met the Lord Jesus who gave sight to our spiritually blinded eyes. As John Newton states in his great hymn "Amazing Grace", "I once was blind, but now I see." Today, rejoice that Jesus Christ has opened your eyes to His wonderful saving grace and that you are no longer blinded by the god of this world.

October 7

John 13:35, "By this shall all men know that ye are my disciples, if ye have love one to another."

On This Day in 1952, Joseph Woodland and Bernard Silver were issued a patent for the "bar code". Silver was a graduate student at Drexel Institute of Technology in Philadelphia. A local food chain store owner had made an inquiry to the institute about a method of automatically reading product information at checkout. Silver joined with Woodland and came up with a method of identifying patterns known as the bar code. The Bar code was first used commercially in 1966, and in 1973 a Universal Product Code (U.P.C.) was created. The first U.P.C. scanner was installed at a Marsh's supermarket in Troy, Ohio. The first product scanned with a bar code was a pack of Wrigley's gum.

The bar code in simple language is a method of identifying a product. God has several identifying methods by which His people are identified. Jesus spoke of loving one another and declared that disciples of Jesus Christ are identified by a type of "spiritual barcode". When people "scan" our lives are we identified as a disciples of the Lord Jesus? Paul's prayer for the Thessalonians is, *"And the Lord make you to increase and abound in love one toward another, and toward all men, even as we do toward you"* (1 Thess.3:12). The action of our love is not to be restricted to those we know but to all men. Furthermore to love another is a command: *"This is my commandment, That ye love one another, as I have loved you"* (John 15:12). Today pray that God will put His love in your heart for all men. Pray that your "bar code" reads, "This is a disciple of the Lord Jesus Christ." It's a great way to be known.

October 8

1 Samuel 16:7, "But the Lord said unto Samuel, Look not on his countenance, or on the height of his stature; because I have refused him: for the Lord seeth not as man seeth; for man looketh on the outward appearance, but the Lord looketh on the heart."

ON *THIS* DAY in 1906, the permanent wave was introduced. German born Karl Ludwig, a London hair stylist introduced his Nessler Permanent Waving at his salon on Oxford Street. At first there were few customers. They had to wear brass curlers weighing over a pound each, and the process took over six hours. At a cost of fifty-five dollars, only the rich could afford his new hair treatment. During WWI he came to the United States to avoid being turned in as an enemy alien. Shortly thereafter, exhibition dancer Irene Castle introduced "bobbed" hair, and permanent waving became a craze that swept America.

The Lord reminded Samuel that the proper to way to judge a person is not by the outward appearance but by what is in the heart. Now there is nothing wrong with giving attention to our appearance. In all honesty, I have met a few whom I wished had given more attention to their appearance (Please forgive me for that comment). If people want to spend a few dollars to have their hair done, they get my okay. Yet that which deserves the most attention and care is the heart. When the Lord looks upon us it is not our appearance that interests Him but what He sees in the heart. Today, when you look in the mirror, also take a look at your heart. Nice hair is no substitute for a messy heart. Maybe the heart needs attending to as well as your hair. What the Lord sees is most important.

October 9

Acts 4:12, "Neither is there salvation in any other: for there is none other name under heaven given among men, whereby we must be saved."

On This Day in 1998, Ted Turner, declared in a speech that we can save ourselves. Turner, one of America's richest men, on several different occasions has made statements which vent his dislike of Christianity. In a 1990 speech to the American Humanist Association he stated "Christianity is a religion for losers." He ridicules the idea of hell and believes nature is God. Speaking at the meeting of the Society of Environmental Journalists in Chattanooga, Tennessee, he referred to different religions in which nature was God and then singled out Christianity as a religion that was not environmentally friendly. He said, "You will do a lot better at saving yourself than praying to someone to save you…I think the savior is right here. With our current technology, we can save ourselves."

With our current technology we may be able to save trees, lakes and streams, the rain forest and natural habitats, but we can never save ourselves. Our Saviour is not found in a program or plan, but in a person. In reality, many of us tried everything we could think of to save ourselves. We turned over a new leaf only in time to end up worse than we had been. We tried to stop this and that but slipped deeper into the grip of sin. The greatest day in our lives was when we quit trying to save ourselves and prayed to the Lord Jesus to save our souls. Today, rejoice that one day God helped you to realize that you could not save yourself and when you turned to Him he saved you. Oh, by the way, Christianity is not for losers. It is for those who have realized they need a Saviour.

October 10

Titus 2:10, "Not purloining, but shewing all good fidelity; that they may adorn the doctrine of God our Saviour in all things."

ON *THIS* DAY in 1971, the 140-year-old London Bridge was opened in Lake Havasu City, Arizona. In order to make way for a much-needed larger bridge and to keep from raising taxes, the city of London decided to sell the London Bridge which had been opened in 1831. Robert P. McCulloch, Sr., had purchased 16,630 acres of barren Arizona desert with plans to build a town and tourist destination. When he heard that the bridge was for sale, he thought, what better way to attract people than the celebrated London Bridge. He bought the bridge for $2.46 million. The bridge was carefully dismantled; each stone numbered (10,000 tons of granite blocks) and shipped to the U.S. It took over two years to reassemble the bridge and a total cost of $17.2 million, but land buyers flocked to obtain lots.

Paul spoke of adorning the doctrine of God our Saviour. The word "adorn" carries the idea of "decorating". Paul was speaking of living a life that gives the Gospel of Jesus Christ an attracting influence. As believers, we are to live in such a way that others are drawn to what we have in Christ. Unfortunately, some live lives that are a hindrance rather than a help in getting people to Christ. They profess to be Christians, but clothe the Gospel in the rags of this world, which weakens the influence of the Gospel. How is your life dressed? Is there something about your life that draws people to want to know what you have? Today, ask God to make your life an attractive influence for the Gospel. We want to attract as many people as we can.

October 11

Job 33:4, "The Spirit of God hath made me, and the breath of the Almighty hath given me life."

On This Day in 1972, the Supreme Court heard arguments for the second time on the right of a woman to have an abortion. Roe, a Texas resident, had sought to terminate her pregnancy by abortion. Texas law prohibited abortions except to save the pregnant woman's life. The case was first argued before the Supreme Court in December of 1971. After the second argument, the Court ruled in January of 1973 that a woman's right to an abortion fell within the right to privacy protected by the Fourteenth Amendment. The decision gave a woman total autonomy over the pregnancy during the first trimester and defined different levels of state interest for the second and third trimester. The laws of forty-six states were affected by the Court's ruling.

There is one important factor that the Court failed to recognize and realize. The right to life is not the decision of any man or woman. The right to life is God's decision. A person can make the decision to have or not have children. That is a personal matter and up to each individual. But the decision to terminate life is not in our hands. It matters not if it is in the first, second, or third trimester. God alone has total autonomy over life. Job declares that God is the source of life and He alone gave him life. Since God is the source of life, He alone is to make the decision whether one lives or dies. The battle of abortion rights is really one against God. It is a battle for the freedom to do what we want verses what He wants. Today, pray for those who are dedicated to preserving human life. Since God gave you life, allow His control over your life.

October 12

Mark 11:26, "But if ye do not forgive, neither will your Father which is in heaven forgive your trespasses."

ON THIS DAY in 1915, British nurse, Edith Cavell, was executed by a German firing squad. Cavell, the daughter of a Norfolk vicar, after the German occupation of Belgium, ran a nursing institute in the Belgian capital as a Red Cross hospital treating injured German and Allied soldiers as well. She became involved in an underground group to help Allied soldiers escape. She was arrested and placed in solitary confinement, charged with helping 130 British, French, and Belgian soldiers escape (the number was probably closer to 300). She made full confession of her involvement and was sentenced to death. Her last words were, "I realize that patriotism is not enough. I must have no hatred or bitterness toward anyone."

Forgiveness is a hard step for some people. They find that what people have done to them and said to them or about them is difficult to forgive. Yet, Jesus speaks of the need to forgive others. He describes personal forgiveness as depending on the one forgiving. In simple words, if we can't forgive someone for what they have done, God will not forgive us for what we have done. Why? Unforgiveness is a sin. God can only forgive sin that we confess and ask Him to purge from our heart. Yes, it is hard to forgive at times, but we must ask God to help us to forgive. There may be a part of us that will not want to forgive, but if we are willing to let God make us willing, we will find the ability to forgive. Today, if you struggle with forgiving someone, ask yourself if you want to be forgiven. God will forgive you, but it may depend on you forgiving as well.

October 13

John 14:2, "In my Father's house are many mansions: if it were not so, I would have told you. I go to prepare a place for you."

On This Day in 1792, the cornerstone was laid by George Washington for the President's House–later called the White House. President Washington and city planner Pierre L'Enfant, chose the site for the new residence at what is now 1600 Pennsylvania Avenue. Competition was held to find a builder for the President's House. Nine proposals were submitted, and Irish-born architect James Hoban's design was chosen. His design called for three stories with more than 100 rooms. Washington oversaw the construction but never lived in it. It was not until 1800, when the White House was nearly completed, that President John Adams became the first resident. During the presidency of Harry Truman, the interior of the White House, with the exception of the third floor was gutted and renovated. However, the exterior stonewalls are the original walls constructed two centuries ago.

As Jesus was preparing to return to heaven He spoke to His disciples about another house—the "Father's House". He described it as a unique house, for it would be a house that would contain more than rooms. It would be made of many houses (mansions). Jesus identified Himself as the architect and designer of its unique design and declared that it would be the permanent home of every believer. His promise is that when it is completed He will return for us so that we can take up residence in the Father's House. Today, rejoice that one day you will become a resident in the Father's House. The good news is that you won't have to move out four or eight years later.

October 14

2 Corinthians 4:8-9, "We are troubled on every side, yet not distressed; we are perplexed, but not in despair; [9] Persecuted, but not forsaken; cast down, but not destroyed."

ON *THIS* DAY in 1912, Theodore Roosevelt, while campaigning as a Bull Moose candidate for presidency, was shot, yet gave his speech before going to the hospital. James Schrank, standing just six feet from Roosevelt, pulled out a gun, raised his arm, aimed and fired. The bullet ripped through Roosevelt's heavy overcoat at breast pocket level. Inside the pocket was his fifty page speech folded in half in a wad of 100 pages thick and his metal eyeglass case in which were his glasses. The bullet passed through each and lodged in his chest just before reaching his lungs. The two items probably saved his life. Yet, instead of going for immediate treatment he insisted on giving his speech. He began his speech by saying, "I don't know whether you fully understand that I've just been shot, but it takes more than that to kill a Bull Moose."

Someone has said that the real test of a man's character is what it will take to stop him. Paul was a man who experienced much suffering and adversity in his life. Yet, he did not let all that he went through stop him. I can hear Paul saying, "It takes more than persecution to stop a Christian." How about you? Do you let problems stop you from serving God? Do you let the things that happen in your life defeat you? Do you let other people discourage you? Today, ask God to help you to be strong and faithful to His work. Why not say to all your problems, "It will take more than you to stop me from serving the Lord."

October 15

1 Corinthians 15:10, "But by the grace of God I am what I am: and his grace which was bestowed upon me was not in vain; but I laboured more abundantly than they all: yet not I, but the grace of God which was with me."

ON THIS DAY in 1860, Abraham Lincoln received a letter from eleven year old Grace Bedell, recommending that he grow a beard. Lincoln was seeking the nomination for President and was trailing William H. Seward in popular support. Young Grace of Westfield, N.Y., having listened to the political talk by her elders and having seen a picture of Lincoln, thought he would have a better chance if his appearance were better. She wrote Lincoln telling him that he would be more popular with the ladies, and thus influence more votes, if he would grow whiskers. She wrote, "All the ladies like whiskers and would tease their husbands to vote for you and then you would be President." Lincoln did grow a beard and during a campaign stop in Westfield he met Grace. As she was lifted up to meet the future president He said to her, "You see, my dear, I let these grow for you. Perhaps you made me President."

Lincoln's "whiskers" may have helped him to become President of the United States, but we as believers know that we are what we are because of God's grace. Like Paul, we know that the secret to the life we now live and enjoy is all because of God's amazing grace. We are saved by His grace and are His "workmanship" (Eph. 2:8-10). All that we do for God and anything that we become in His work, we have to say it is because of His grace. Today, give thanks for His grace. "Whiskers" or not, we are what we are by the grace of God.

October 16

Psalm 73:24, "Thou shalt guide me with thy counsel, and afterward receive me to glory."

ON THIS DAY in 1955, Esther Pauline Friedman, replaced Ruth Crowley as a columnist in twenty-six newspapers. Mrs. Crowley, a writer of advice to the lovelorn, had died in July. Her replacement has become the most widely syndicated columnist in the world with an estimated readership of 90 million and advice columns in more than 1,200 newspapers. The author of five books and many public services booklets on various subjects, a World Almanac Poll asserted that she was the most influential woman in the United States. She was appointed by President Jimmy Carter in 1980 to serve on the board of the National Cancer Institute for a six-year term, and in 1981, President Ronald Reagan appointed her to the board of the President's Commission on Drunk Driving, and in 1995, she was asked by the U.S. departments of Justice and Health and Human Services to serve on the Advisory Council on Violence Against Women. Her column is a popular arena for the exchange of ideas, opinions and information on virtually every topic from medical to ethical. You may be asking, "Who is Esther Pauline Friedman. I've never heard of her." You probably know her as Ann Landers.

I am always appreciative of those who give us good advice, but I have found the greatest person to get advice from is our Lord. His columns have been published in over 10,500 languages and dialects and contain advice that you can always trust (all 66 books, 1,189 chapters, 31,173 verses and 773,692 words). Today, do you need advice? Read God's Word! Whatever you need advice about, it has a word for you. It is the Book by which we judge all advice columns, even Ann Landers.

October 17

1 John 4:1, "Beloved, believe not every spirit, but try the spirits whether they are of God: because many false prophets are gone out into the world."

On This Day in 1960, fourteen people were arrested for perjury in the Quiz Show Scandal. During the 1950's, Americans were captivated with quiz game shows on television. One of the most popular was *Twenty-One, The $64,000 Question*. In 1955 approximately 3 million television sets and 47,560,000 viewers tuned in to watch the show where two people competed against each other from dual soundproof isolation booths. At first the show failed to attract a large audience until the show found a common, average-Joe-type man in Herb Stempel. The show supplied him with answers, and viewers watched to see a man they could identify with keep winning. Then along came Charles Van Doren, college professor, whom the show thought would make a more amiable contestant. After setting up a standoff which ended in several ties, Doren defeated Stempel. Feeling betrayed by the show, Stempel exposed the engineering behind the show, setting off what has become known as the Quiz Show Scandal.

John warns that some things (and even people) are not what they claim or appear to be. For that reason, he encourages the believer to try the spirits (put to the test) to make sure they are real. Satan is a master in deception, and often his methods include those who appear to be real. Just because someone says he or she is religious and quotes a few verses from the Bible, does not mean they are of God. Today, watch out for Satan's counterfeits. He knows how to set up a "show" to draw you in.

October 18

Psalm 1:1-2, "Blessed is the man that walketh not in the counsel of the ungodly, nor standeth in the way of sinners, nor sitteth in the seat of the scornful. [2] But his delight is in the law of the Lord; and in his law doth he meditate day and night."

On This Day in 1767, American colonial officials agreed to the Mason-Dixon Line as the border between Maryland and Pennsylvania. Often referred to as the border between the free states and the slave states in the first half of the 18th century or the border between the Union States and the Confederate States during the Civil War, the original Mason-Dixon Line was defined and restricted to the Pennsylvania and Maryland border which runs east-west and the part of the Maryland and Delaware border which runs north-south. Two British astronomers, Charles Mason and Jeremiah Dixon (hence the name), surveyed and determined the line between 1763 and 1767 in order to settle a dispute between the Calvert and Penn families. The boundary was recognized and accepted as the Pennsylvania and Maryland state lines.

The Psalmist described the line that is drawn between the godly and ungodly. The godly man recognizes the boundaries of a life that pleases God and draws the line in how he walks, stands, and sits. As believers we must live a life that is distinct and in contrast to those who do not know the Lord. We think differently, therefore we live by a different set of standards. We are sons of God, therefore our course of life is different, and we are associated with divine matters and our affections are set on things above. Today, draw the line in your life in how you live, what you do and even where you go. It is the "Godly-Ungodly Line."

October 19

Acts 17:6, "And when they found them not, they drew Jason and certain brethren unto the rulers of the city, crying, These that have turned the world upside down are come hither also."

ON THIS DAY in 1781, General Charles Cornwall, commander-in-chief of the British army surrendered to General George Washington at Yorktown. America had won their independence from Great Britain after five years of fighting. Cornwall could not bring himself to watch the surrender of his army, so he pleaded ill health and sent a subordinate officer to hand his sword to the American victors. American troops watched as British soldiers marched out of their encampment, their bright red coats contrasting vividly with the victors tattered clothing. One reported, "Their step was irregular and their ranks frequently broken." As the British soldiers threw their weapons on a pile, a band played a tune entitled *The World Turned Upside Down*.

In the few years following the death, resurrection and ascension of the Lord Jesus, a small band of followers, dedicated to proclaiming the message of a risen Lord, turned their world upside down. What a most unlikely group they were to change their world. They were simple people who were considered unlearned and ignorant by their contemporaries. Against great odds and a society that treated them with great scorn, their number swelled into the thousands. Their impact was so great that those who hated them most marveled at their deeds and declared that they had turned the world upside down. We live in an age when this world needs turning upside down. I guess we could say it needs turning right side up. Today, give yourself to God and ask Him to use you to make a difference in this world.

October 20

Philippians 2:9, "Wherefore God also hath highly exalted him, and given him a name which is above every name:"

ON THIS DAY in 1973, President Richard Nixon proclaimed Jim Thorpe the greatest athlete of the century. An American Indian, Thorpe represented the U.S. at the 1912 Olympics where he won a gold medal in the pentathlon and decathlon. During his career, he excelled not only at the amateur level but also at the professional level in three major sports—track and field, football, and baseball. The honor of being called the greatest athlete was not unusual for Thorpe. His performance in the 1912 Olympics held in Stockholm, Sweden, prompted King Gustav V of Sweden to say to him, "You, Sir, are the greatest athlete in the world." Joining President Nixon's designation, on May 27, 1999, the following resolution was submitted to the 106th Congress of the United States: "Resolved: That the United States House of Representatives designates James Francis Thorpe 'America's Athlete of the Century.'"

Who is the greatest in certain fields is often a matter of opinion. The deeds of some certainly set them apart in their profession and earn them the praise and admiration of their peers. Yet, when it comes to who is the greatest of the great, there is no debate or competition. The Lord Jesus stands alone in a class all to Himself. He has no rival, no competitor, and no equal. When it comes to designating who is the greatest, the Lord Jesus stands head and shoulders above them all. He has been given a name that is above every name. He is exalted above the greatest. Today, spend some time worshipping the greatest of the great. He is worthy of all our praise.

October 21

Psalm 44:18, "Our heart is not turned back, neither have our steps declined from thy way."

ON THIS DAY in 1931, America dipped its lights for a minute in honor of the man who gave us the electric light bulb. Thomas Alva Edison, perhaps the most prolific inventor in history, died at the age of eighty-four. During his extraordinary life and career he was credited with a huge catalog of nearly 1,300 inventions. To him the world owes not only the light bulb, but also the phonograph, tickertape machines and moving pictures, just to name a few. When asked about his abilities he declared, "Genius is one percent inspiration and ninety-nine percent perspiration." His 3,500 crammed notebooks gave testimony to an energy that was tireless. He once said, "To stop is to rust."

Have you ever gotten a little "rusty" as a believer? I think of Demas (2 Tim. 4:10). There was a time when he served God but this present world drew him away from God's work. It would appear that he had a bad case of rust. We all no doubt can think of someone who used to live for God and serve Him, but somewhere and for some reason they became rusty. Someone has said that they would rather burn out than rust out. When it comes to living for God and serving God there is no place to stop. As we live in light of the nearness of the return of Jesus, it certainly is not the time to stop. Oh, yes, we all get discouraged and even tired at times, but we can't stop. There is too much at stake to quit or even take a spiritual vacation. Today, renew your commitment to live for God and serve Him the rest of your life. With the Psalmist say, "My heart is not turned back and my steps have not and will not decline from thy ways." Anyway, who wants to be a rusty Christian?

October 22

1 Peter 2:21, "For even hereunto were ye called: because Christ also suffered for us, leaving us an example, that ye should follow his steps."

ON THIS DAY in 1938, the first Xerox copy was made. Chester Carlson was a patent lawyer who hated all the copy work that was required in reproducing detailed drawings and descriptions. He set out to make a machine where you could just "push a button and get a copy." For the next ten years on his own limited resources he worked on his machine in a tiny room behind a beauty parlor in New York. Then on October 22 he pushed the button on his machine, and the first copy was made, produced by electrically charged surface that was treated with resinous powder. The first copy simply read: 10-28-38 ASTORIA. It would be ten more years before Carlson would find a company to invest in and market the machine after at least twenty companies rejected the invention.

Peter spoke of the Lord Jesus as our example. The word "example" used described the process whereby a student would learn to write. A teacher would lightly draw the letters on a piece of paper and then the student would trace over the letters. As our example, we are to follow every line and curve of the life of the Lord Jesus. If I may put it this way, we are to be a copy of His life. We are to live after the Father's will as He did (Matt. 26:42). We are to hate sin and love righteousness as He did (Heb. 1:9). It is impossible for us to live perfect as He did, but to the best of our ability and by His help we are to be a living copy of His life. Today, ask God to help you to be as much like Jesus as possible. This world needs to see a good copy of the Lord Jesus.

October 23

Ecclesiastes 4:11, "Again, if two lie together, then they have heat: but how can one be warm alone?"

On This Day in 1946, the United Nations General Assembly convened in New York for the first time. Formally established the next day by fifty-one countries, today, membership totals 189 countries. According to the U.N. Charter, the U.N. has four purposes: to maintain international peace and security, to develop friendly relations among nations, to cooperate in solving international problems and in promoting respect for human rights, and to be a center for harmonizing the actions of nations. President Franklin D. Roosevelt devised the name "United Nations." All U.N. members are represented in the General Assembly which holds its annual regular session from September to December.

The importance of believers working together cannot be overstated. The wise man Solomon spoke of the benefits enjoyed when people work together and how those benefits are missed when there is not cooperation. The ultimate purpose of believers working together is two-fold—the glory of God and the salvation of the lost. The Church is a local example of believers coming together and working together. As a Church, members unite to worship God, build one another through teaching and service, and then reach out in their communities to win the lost to Christ. As each nation is an important part of the international effort of the U.N. to maintaining peace and security and developing relationships between nations, each believer is important to the Church in its united role of glorifying and serving God. Today, pray for your Church and the work of God around the world. We are all serving the same Lord and striving for the same goals.

October 24

Psalm 62:10, "Trust not in oppression, and become not vain in robbery: if riches increase, set not your heart upon them."

On This Day in 1929, the New York Stock Exchange crashed. In what has become known as "Black Thursday" the financial boom of the previous years was abruptly ended when prices on the Stock Exchange fell dramatically causing thousands to panic and sell their shares at virtually any price offered. In a period when investors were rushing to make large and quick profits, the market seemed unstoppable and invincible in the weeks before the crash. In a matter of hours, thousands of American's saw their life savings wiped out in the biggest catastrophe ever to hit the financial world.

Someone has said that there is nothing wrong with having things. What is wrong is when things have us. David, speaking to his people, reminded them not to trust in their riches, but in the Lord. As many found in 1929, all that you have worked for all your life can be wiped out in a matter of hours. However, what we have in the Lord is eternal. Regardless of what happens on Wall Street, He is our rock and refuge. David tell us that we can trust in Him at all times even when the "crashes" of life come (Psa. 62:8). If riches increase in your life, give God the credit and allow your wealth to increase your love for the Lord. Do not set your heart upon riches and make wealth and possessions the focus and priority of your life. Today, give thanks for what you have in the Lord Jesus. You possess something that is worth more than all the wealth of this world and you never need to fear a crash in heaven. It is eternal.

October 25

Nahum 1:9, "What do ye imagine against the Lord? he will make an utter end: affliction shall not rise up the second time."

ON THIS DAY in 1994, Susan Smith of Union, South Carolina, claimed that a carjacker had driven off with her two sons. Smith claimed that she was stopped at a red light when a man jumped into the passenger seat, forcing her to drive off at gun point, and that she at one point was able to escape, but here two children were still in the car. Her story was suspicious from the start, and a few days later she confessed to having ditched her car in the John D. Long Lake, drowning her two children who were in the backseat. In a handwritten confession she wrote: "I dropped to the lowest point when I allowed my children to go down the ramp into the water without me. I took off…screaming, What have I done? Why did you let this happen?'"

Susan Smith was correct when she asked, "What have I done," for she and no other was to blame for the death of her two children. But then she seemed to suggest that God was responsible when she asked, "Why did you let this happen?" Her words make me think of a preacher who was asked to leave his church because of moral indiscretions. His words to me were, "I don't know why God allowed this to happen?" God often gets the blame for things for which He is not guilty. The prophet Nahum spoke of those who think and conceive (imagine) things for which God is not responsible. We cannot blame God for the decisions we make and the consequences of those decisions. Today, remember that God gives you the freedom of choice. You choose what is right or what is wrong. If you choose what is wrong, don't blame God for what happens.

October 26

Genesis 13:8, "And Abram said unto Lot, Let there be no strife, I pray thee, between me and thee, and between my herdmen and thy herdmen; for we be brethren."

ON THIS DAY in 1881, the O.K. Corral of Tombstone, Arizona was the scene of the gunfight between the Earps and the Clantons. The tension that had been building between the two families came to a head in a thirty second shoot-out. The Earp brothers, Wyatt, Virgil, and Morgan, and "Doc" Holliday marched down the street to a lot next to Fly's Photography Studio where they met Ike and Billy Clanton, Frank and Tom McLaury and Billy Claiborne. A large crowd gathered at the street corner sensing something was about to happen. From that point on there is much debate, but there was sound of a gun being cocked, and the shooting started. Who fired the first shot is uncertain but thirty seconds later three of the Clanton bunch lay dead or dying. Virgil had been shot in the leg, Morgan in the back and "Doc" grazed on the hip.

Abraham realized that tension was building between his herdsmen and the herdsman of his nephew Lot. The strife between the two was beginning to cause tension between Abraham and Lot. In order to prevent an "O.K. Corral" scene between the two families, Abraham presented his nephew with the first choice of land. Abraham wanted to solve the problem that existed and settle the differences between the two. When we find ourselves at odds with others we always have the choice of either "fighting it out" or taking steps to bring about reconciliation. Reconciliation is always God's plan. Today, make harmony your constant goal. Never forget that everybody gets hurt in an "O.K. Corral."

October 27

John 4:35, "Say not ye, There are yet four months, and then cometh harvest? behold, I say unto you, Lift up your eyes, and look on the fields; for they are white already to harvest."

ON THIS DAY in 1994, the U.S. Justice Department announced that the U.S. prison population had topped one million for the first time in American history. The numbers have continued to rise as shown by a report by the Bureau of Justice Statistics in 1999 that revealed the numbers of prisoners in the U.S. state and federal prisons had reached a record of 1,302,019 inmates. That number combined with the 592,462 inmates in local jails, gives the United States a national incarceration rate of 627 inmates per 100,000 residents. The BJS report stated that thirty-three state prison systems are operating above designed capacity, averaging thirteen to twenty-two percent over capacity, with the federal prison system averaging at 127 per cent of capacity. The largest increase was among women. The United States is second only to Russia in the world for incarceration rates.

With a growing population, not only are state and federal prison numbers growing, but also the number of those who are in sin's prison. As the world's population grows day by day, so does the number of those who are lost and need to hear about the Lord Jesus. Jesus told His disciples that the fields were white unto harvest. The task of the Church of Jesus Christ to win others to Christ has never been greater and the task gets bigger with each passing day. The fields are indeed white unto harvest, and if ever there was a need for all of God's people to be witnesses, it is today. Today, tell someone about Jesus. The numbers are increasing and every believer is needed to reach the growing number that is lost.

October 28

1 Thessalonians 4:16, "For the Lord himself shall descend from heaven with a shout, with the voice of the archangel, and with the trump of God: and the dead in Christ shall rise first."

ON *THIS* DAY in 1992, the capital of South Korea virtually closed down waiting for the Rapture. Lee Jang-rim of South Korea's Dami Mission had predicted the Rapture. Over 1,000 people gathered at the mission's main temple on October 28 awaiting the midnight deadline. Because four of Lee's followers had committed suicide in preparation for the Rapture, streets were filled with 1,500 riot police and ambulances fearing mass suicides. More than 200 plain-clothes detectives surrounded the mission. Ten minutes after the deadline passed, a teenage boy stuck his head out a window and shouted, "Nothing's happened." By morning all the people had gone home.

Nothing may have happened on Lee's predicted day of the Rapture, but you can be certain that one day something will happen. At a time scheduled by the Father, the Lord Jesus himself will descend from heaven with a shout. The Lord Jesus will return just as He promised. When He returns, every believer will be raptured (caught up) and will meet the Lord in the air along with their loved ones who have died in the Lord. Jesus said, "*And if I go and prepare a place for you, I will come again, and receive you unto myself; that where I am, there ye may be also*" (John 14:3). That is a guaranteed promise. He will come again just as He promised. Today, give thanks that the Lord keeps His promises and that one-day "something will happen." We may not know the date, but we know He is coming.

October 29

Proverbs 4:23, "Keep thy heart with all diligence; for out of it are the issues of life."

On This Day in 1958, the first implantable pacemaker was inserted in the chest of a patient. Dr. Ake Senning of Stockholm inserted a pacemaker which had an external coil and internal receiver into Swedish cardiac patient Arne Larson. The purpose of the pacemaker is to correct abnormal heart rhythms. A pacemaker transmits an electric impulse to the heart, stimulating the organ to beat in a regular manner. The German company, Biotronik introduced the first programmed pacemaker in 1986.

Our hearts are about the size of our fists. The heart and fist grow about the same rate. It beats about seventy times a minute and more than 100,000 times in a single day. It pumps about five quarts of blood through its chambers every sixty seconds and is linked by 100,000 miles of pipelines to all parts of our body. The care of the heart is essential to sustaining life. Solomon was aware of the necessity of maintaining a good heart—your spiritual heart. He spoke of keeping the heart with all diligence. Why? For our spiritual life depends on a spiritually healthy heart. The Bible often speaks of spiritual heart conditions such as an evil heart, cold heart, etc. Just as we go to all measures to care for our physical heart, we should guard our spiritual heart with all diligence. Heart problems must never be taken lightly but need our immediate attention. A healthy Christian life depends on a healthy spiritual heart. Today, guard your heart. If there is a heart condition that needs attention, take it to the Great Physician. He is a heart specialist.

October 30

Matthew 6:33, "But seek ye first the kingdom of God, and his righteousness; and all these things shall be added unto you."

ON THIS DAY in 1938, Orson Welle's Mercury Theater terrorized the northeast United States with a radio dramatization of H.G. Well's *War of the Worlds*. As radio listeners sat glued to their radios, they heard news bulletins describing a Martian landing in Grovers Mill, N.J. and of creatures with tentacles as large as a bear, black eyes, and v-shaped mouths dripping with saliva. Between musical interludes the horrors mounted with police being turned into flaming torches by the Martian's flamethrowers. Though only a novel being dramatized over radio, many thought it was real. Thousands of Americans panicked filling the streets. People huddled and prayed in churches. Others fled for their lives.

I think of one high school girl from Pennsylvania, Helen Anthony, who said, "I was really hysterical. My two girl friends and I were crying and holding each other and everything seemed so unimportant in the face of death." May I say that it should not take something to terrorize us to make us realize that all the things that we think are important in life are not what is important. In view of eternity, what is important is knowing Christ as our Saviour and living for God. When this life is over all the things that we so often put first in our life will mean nothing. As it has been so well stated, "Only one life to live and twill soon be past. Only what's done for Christ will last." Today, seek ye first the kingdom of God. Remember, only what you do that has eternal value is really important.

October 31

Romans 3:25, "Whom God hath set forth to be a propitiation through faith in his blood, to declare his righteousness for the remission of sins that are past, through the forbearance of God;"

ON THIS DAY in 1517, Martin Luther nailed his ninety-five theses to the door of the Wittenburg Palace. Luther, an ordained priest and a district vicar of the Augustinianp order, was disturbed and in disagreement with the teachings and practices of the papal church, especially the selling of indulgences (a term in the Catholic Church signifying the freeing from the punishment of sin) to raise money for the church. In his ninety-five theses, he expressed his views on the doctrine of penance, the powers of the church, and the practices of indulgences. The first fifty-five theses primarily covered the doctrine of penance (a sacrament in which sins are confessed to a priest and forgiven by the priest). In essence, Luther proclaimed that the forgiveness of sin was obtained by faith and by the grace of God. The declarations of his theses were the result of his own personal experience in the failure of trying to obtain favor with God by his own efforts and accomplishments and realizing that God's Word declared that God's favor is not something won, but a gift of God's grace. His act paved the way for the Protestant reformation.

Oh blessed day it was when we were made to understand that salvation and the forgiveness of sins were not something we earn, but receive by faith. I had nothing to offer God and certainly had done nothing to earn His favor. Today, give thanks that God accepts sinners, not on the basis of what we have done, but on what Jesus has done. The thesis of every believer is that salvation is by grace through faith.

November 1

James 5:7, "Be patient therefore, brethren, unto the coming of the Lord. Behold, the husbandman waiteth for the precious fruit of the earth, and hath long patience for it, until he receive the early and latter rain."

ON THIS DAY in 1512, Michelangelo's paintings on the ceiling of the Sistine Chapel were revealed to the public for the first time. Considered Michelangelo's greatest project, the frescoes on the chapel ceiling show nine scenes from the Old Testament—three scenes of God creating the earth, the story of Adam and Eve, and Noah and the flood. twelve Old Testament prophets and classical prophetic women called sibyls surround each scene. He began painting the frescoes on the ceiling in 1508 and completed the work three years later in 1511. The paintings were done while lying on his back on a scaffolding high above the chapel floor.

For the most part, we are not very patient. We are often like the lady who prayed, "Lord, I need patience and I need it now!" When it comes to seeing things done, we want to see results immediately. Yet, oftentimes, the greatest works are those that require patience and endurance. James spoke of the patience of the farmer. The fields have been plowed and the seed has been sown, but the farmer knows that he cannot expect a harvest the next day. He knows that there is a period of weeks and even months before there will be a harvest. When it comes to the work of God, we all want to see results; but we must never forget that once we have sown the seed, results may not come until much later. The secret is sowing the seed. If we sow the seed, we can be assured that at sometime we will reap a harvest. Today, don't lose heart. Keep sowing the seed. The ceiling of the Sistine Chapel was not done over night.

November 2

1 Corinthians 15:57, "But thanks be to God, which giveth us the victory through our Lord Jesus Christ."

ON THIS DAY in 1948, President Harry Truman won a surprise re-election over Republican challenger Thomas E. Dewey. Republicans, confident of their return to the Oval Office for the first time in sixteen years, were already celebrating victory. Every public opinion poll conducted throughout 1948 had shown Truman losing. The outcome appeared so certain that the respected Gallup organization had quit collecting data ten days before the election. Defections and insurgencies within his own party seemed to have doomed any chance that may have existed. The *Chicago Daily Tribune* was so convinced that Dewey would win; the editors had rushed the issue with the headline "Dewey Defeats Truman" to newsstands prior to the close of voting. Only Truman believed that he had a chance. It came as a shock to all the political prognosticators when the fiery Missourian triumphed, winning a second term as President of the United States.

The believer is promised "victory." If you are like me, there have been times when I did not feel very "victorious" and wondered if there would be victory. However, victory is available and assured to the believer. The Lord Jesus is our source of victory and we are more than conquerors through Him (Rom. 8:37). Paul found that by the Lord Jesus he could always live in triumph (2 Cor. 2:14). By trusting in Christ and drawing from His life, we can be victorious over the world, the flesh, and the devil. Today, live in victory through the Lord Jesus. Look to Him for the ability to be victorious in every situation of life. Even when it looks like defeat, in Him we can be victorious.

November 3

Romans 12:5, "So we, being many, are one body in Christ, and every one members one of another."

On This Day in 1957, the first living creature to orbit the earth was launched into space by the Soviet Union. That first living creature was a two-year old female dog named Laika. The purpose of the Sputnik II mission was to study the effects of space travel on a live animal in order to prepare for humans in space. Laika's space journey was not without opposition. One animal rights group in the United Kingdom called for a moment of silence every day in honor of Laikia. A German newspaper wrote: "For a few days, black and white, democrats and communists, republicans and royalists in all countries, islands, and continents have one feeling, one language, one direction...our feeling of compassion for this little living being twirling helplessly over our heads."

It is amazing how a certain belief or cause can unite people, jumping all lines of race, nationality, and language. In a world of so many differences, one single cause, such as the concern for a dog in space, can bring all together in one united effort and demonstration of compassion. I think of a very special group that has been brought together by a very special cause—the family of God. The family of God is made up of people from all countries, islands, and continents. It is a family of many, yet one body. In this family, Jew and Gentile, black and white become brothers and sisters. It is a relationship that lasts more than a few days. It is a union that will last for eternity. Today, give thanks that you are a member of the family of God. Pray for your brothers and sisters in Christ. You have them all around the world.

November 4

John 20:7, "And the napkin, that was about his head, not lying with the linen clothes, but wrapped together in a place by itself."

ON THIS DAY in 1922, English archaeologist Howard Carter found the first signs of what proved to be the tomb of King Tutankhamen. Carter had a hunch that the tomb of Tutankhamen (commonly called King Tut) laid beneath the Valley of the Kings, although archaeologist believed all the areas with tombs had been found. Carter began his search in 1914 and for seven years his efforts bore no fruit. But then in November 1922 his persistence paid off as workers uncovered a series of steps leading down to a sealed door. On the 26th, he broke through a second sealed door and it was as Carter described, "the day of days, the most wonderful that I have ever lived through." Behind that second sealed door was the greatest collection of Egyptian antiquities ever discovered. It took the archeological team more than two months to clear and catalog the items that were discovered, and more was yet to be found.

What a contrast to the tomb the disciples walked into early that morning. All they found was a napkin that served as face cover and the linen that had been wrapped around the body of the Lord Jesus. There was no glitter of gold as they appeared inside, and no artifacts that would grab the attention of archeologist in the years to come. Yet, Peter and those disciples would say that their discovery was the, "day of days," the most wonderful that they would ever live through. What they did not find was the greatest discovery that has ever been made. Jesus was gone! He had risen from the dead! He was alive! Today, give thanks for a tomb in which nothing but a napkin and linen cloths were found.

November 5

Revelation 5:9, "And they sung a new song, saying, Thou art worthy to take the book, and to open the seals thereof: for thou wast slain, and hast redeemed us to God by thy blood out of every kindred, and tongue, and people, and nation;"

ON THIS DAY in 1605, a plot to blow up Britain's Parliament building was uncovered. Known as the "Gunpowder Plot," hours before King James I was to sit with the rest of the British government in a general parliamentary session, Guy Fawkes was found lurking in the cellar of the Parliament after an order was given to search the premises, and nearly two tons of gunpowder were found hidden within the cellar. It was determined that Fawkes was a participant in an English Catholic conspiracy to annihilate England's entire Protestant government. Fawkes was sentenced, along with other chief conspirators, to be hanged, drawn, and quartered in London. In remembrance of the Gunpowder Plot, each November 5th as dusk falls, people across Great Britain light bonfires, set off fireworks, and burn an effigy of Guy Fawkes, celebrating his failure to blow up Parliament.

John saw a glorious scene of celebration in heaven. However, the celebration was not over someone's failure to carry out their plan, but celebrating the victorious accomplishment of their plan. John saw and heard a great multitude celebrating the finished work of the Lord Jesus on the cross and His glorious accomplishment to provide redemption for all men. While some failures are worthy to be celebrated, we as believers celebrate the victory of the Lord Jesus. Through His death and the shedding of His blood, we are redeemed. Today, we celebrate the eternal plan of God which was accomplished.

November 6

Psalm 119:103, "How sweet are thy words unto my taste! yea, sweeter than honey to my mouth!"

ON THIS DAY in 1986, Edy's Ice Cream Company took out a $250,000 policy to protect the taste buds of John Harrison, ice cream taste-tester. In 1928, William Dreyer, ice cream maker, and Joseph Edy, candy maker, shook hands on a partnership to make the highest quality ice cream possible. Dreyer's ice cream expertise and Edy's skill in making candy proved to be a winning combination. They opened a small ice cream factory at 3315 Grand Avenue in Oakland, California, and their ice cream factory quickly became a gathering place for people to eat a sundae, pick up a five-layer ice cream cake, and other ice-cream products. One night, Dreyer was whipping up a batch of chocolate ice cream and decided to add nuts and marshmallows. It was 1929; the stock market had crashed and tough times were beginning to face people. Dreyer and Edy picked a name for the ice cream creation that would give folks something to smile about. "Rocky Road" became a blockbuster flavor and remains one of the best sellers of all time.

Before you lay down this book and head for the refrigerator, let me tell you about something that is better than a bowl of Rocky Road ice cream. It is sweet as honey to the mouth. I am speaking of God's wonderful Word. The Psalmist found that the sweetest thing he ever "tasted" was God's blessed words. He declares in Psalm 19:10, "*More to be desired are they than gold, yea, than much fine gold: sweeter also than honey and the honeycomb.*" Today, "taste" the wonderful Word of God. There is no sweeter taste! Taste all you want, for it is good for you.

November 7

Philippians 2:12, "Wherefore, my beloved, as ye have always obeyed, not as in my presence only, but now much more in my absence, work out your own salvation with fear and trembling."

On This Day in 1805, Captain Meriweather Lewis and Captain William Clark reached the Pacific Ocean. The 28-man (and one woman) expedition, called the "Corps of Discovery," journeyed 4,000 miles across unmapped plains, forests, mountains, and deserts during an 18-month mission to survey the newly purchased Louisiana territory. The explorers left St. Louis and journeyed up the Missouri River in six canoes and two longboats. They wintered in Dakota before crossing Montana. The woman—who carried her baby all the way—was a sixteen year old Shoshone Indian who was married to the expedition's interpreter. The last leg of the journey brought them down the dangerous rapids of the Clearwater and Snake River in canoes, which brought them to the Columbia River and the sea.

Paul speaks of working out our salvation. Notice carefully he did not say to work for your salvation. Salvation is by grace and not by works (Eph. 2:8). It is a matter of working *out* our salvation. He is speaking of experiencing what we already have. The verb "work" was a miner's word that described a miner going into a mine and getting all the valuable ore out of that mine. In Christ, there are many wonderful things to be experienced as a believer. Our salvation is a rich mine in which there is much to be worked out. There is much to be discovered and enjoyed. Today, put on your miner's helmet and begin to find out all that has been given to you in Christ. It's yours! All you need is to discover what belongs to you.

November 8

Mark 9:23, "Jesus said unto him, If thou canst believe, all things are possible to him that believeth."

ON THIS DAY in 1970, New Orleans Saints kicker Tom Dempsey kicked a record setting sixty-three yard field goal to win the game. With just eleven seconds left in the game, Errol Mann of the Detroit Lions had just kicked a field goal to put the Lions ahead 17-16. After the kickoff and a Billy Kilmer pass to the Saints forty-four yard line, Dempsey was sent in to kick with two seconds left on the clock. His attempt would be seven yards longer than the existing field goal record. Reporters had already started leaving the press box and heading for the locker rooms for interviews. A CBS reporter had already told Greg Landry, the quarterback for the Lions, that he wanted to interview him after the game. Practically no one thought Dempsey would make the field goal and considered the game over. The snap was made and Dempsey boomed his right foot through, scoring the winning field goal. Adding to the drama of the moment was the fact that Dempsey was wearing a special leather boot, because he was born without part of his right foot (his kicking foot).

So you think miracles never happen? I am not talking about record setting field goals either. Jesus says all things are possible to the one who believes. Do you need a miracle in your life? Miracles still happen and the one thing required is taking God at His Word and believing that His promises are true and that He can do the impossible. Maybe you are about ready to call the "game" lost and over. Knowing that nothing is too hard for the Lord, the "game" is never over. The Lord is able to do amazing things in our life, if we will but trust Him. Today, have faith in God and put your faith in Him. All things are possible to the believer who will trust Him.

Proverbs 10:7, "The memory of the just is blessed: but the name of the wicked shall rot."

ON THIS DAY in 1984, the "Three Servicemen" sculpture was unveiled in Washington, D.C. as an addition to the Vietnam Veterans Memorial. The Vietnam Wall was dedicated on November 13, 1982. Containing the names of 58,220 men and women who were killed or remain missing from the war, the memorial is a 500-foot, chevron shaped wall, that is composed of 140 tablets of polished black granite set into the earth. The names listed on the wall are in order in which men and women were killed or listed missing. The first name is Major Dale R. Buis and the last is Richard Vande Geer. More than two and one-half million visit the wall each year. Although the memorial was designed to make no political statement about the war, veterans were angered and hurt by its design, feeling that its placement below ground level hid it from view and that its color hinted at a feeling of shame. One veteran assailed the design as the "black gash of shame", while others attacked it as being "unheroic," "death-oriented," and "intentionally not meaningful." The "Three Servicemen," a seven foot bronze statue, was a compromise to the controversy.

Because of the great debt that we owe every man and woman who served and fought for our country, they deserve to be honored and remembered in a proper way. The memory of the just has a special place in our hearts. Solomon speaks of their memory as "blessed," meaning their memory has present benefits in our life. As we think of the dear saints of God who are no longer with us, their life inspires us to love and serve God as they did. Today, bless their memory and be blessed by their memory.

November 10

Matthew 5:24, "Leave there thy gift before the altar, and go thy way; first be reconciled to thy brother, and then come and offer thy gift."

ON THIS DAY in 1801, the state of Tennessee became the first state to outlaw dueling. Governor Archibald Roane signed an act passed by the Fourth General Assembly that outlawed the "evil practice of dueling." The practice of dueling, a prearranged fight with deadly weapons, usually swords or pistols, dates back thousands of years. In most cases, an offended party would present a challenge to fight which had to be accepted by the person challenged. Dishonor was often the reward for refusing the challenge. Ironically, one of Tennessee's leading politicians at the time was Andrew Jackson, who would become one of the nation's most notorious duelers. In 1806, he participated in his first duel, one of several duels Jackson is said to have participated in during his lifetime.

I can't help but wonder how Jackson voted on the issue of dueling? Unfortunately, members of the body of Christ find themselves at odds with one another. I am thankful that dueling is illegal, for I believe a few would have no doubt chosen it as a method to settle their differences. Yet, the believer is instructed to settle his or her difference in a much different way. Jesus says that the method of settling differences is by being reconciled with one another. Instead of guns and swords being used to settle differences, the altar is chosen. The settling of differences among believers starts in the heart and one's relationship to God, which leads to steps to bring about reconciliation. Today, make reconciliation the goal of every strained relationship. Having problems with someone? Go to the altar before you get out the guns.

November 11

2 Corinthians 10:3, "For though we walk in the flesh, we do not war after the flesh."

On This Day in 1918, Germany surrendered to the Allied forces, bringing WWI to an end. At 11 a.m., the 11th hour of the 11th day of the 11th month, Germany agreed to the demands placed upon them. They were to evacuate all territories occupied after August 14, 1914; to remove all military forces west of the Rhine; to release all Allied prisoners; to hand over 2,500 heavy guns, 25,000 machine guns, 1,700 airplanes, all its U-boats, 5,000 trucks, 5,000 locomotives, and 150,000 wagons. People filled streets to cheer and express relief as headlines proclaimed Allied victory. One newspaper announced that the "war to end all wars was over." The surrender occurred in a railway carriage in the forest of Compiègne.

The Bible speaks of the war that every believer is fighting. It is not a war fought in the flesh but a spiritual warfare. It is not a battle fought with guns, tanks, and earthly weapons (2 Cor. 10:4). It is not a battle where we are fighting Germans or any other nationality. It is a battle with the world, flesh, and the devil. It is a battle fought each day of our life, but thank God that one day this war will be over for the child of God. We will lay our spiritual sword and armour down and rejoice that the battle is over. As a soldier in God's army, we are assured of victory. The battle has already been won and it has already been announced that we are on the winning side. Today, remember that even though the victory has been won, there are daily battles that can be lost. We have not yet seen the end of the war to end all wars. We are more than conquerors. Let's live like it.

November 12

Revelation 6:13, "And the stars of heaven fell unto the earth, even as a fig tree casteth her untimely figs, when she is shaken of a mighty wind."

ON THIS DAY in 1799, Andrew Ellicott Douglass recorded the first known record of a meteor shower in North America. An astronomer from Vermont, he was aboard a ship off the Florida Keys when he witnessed the meteor shower. Douglass wrote in his journal that the "whole heaven appeared as if illuminated with sky rockets, flying in an infinity of directions, while I was in constant expectation of some of them falling on the vessel. They continued until they were put out by the light of the sun after day break." Douglass witnessed the Leonids meteor shower, which is an annual event that is greatly enhanced every three decades or so by the appearance of the comet Tempel-Tuttle.

The book of Revelation is a description of future events in both heaven and earth. The earthly scenes that are described are filled with happenings unlike any the world has ever known. In our text for the day, it describes the stars of heaven falling to the earth. Other strange phenomenom are depicted throughout the book that paint a picture of dark and tragic days for those who are on earth. Many of the events of the book describe a time when God's wrath will be poured out on the earth. Things will be so terrible that men will pray for death (6:16). On the other hand, the heavenly scenes are thrilling to the heart, for we find those who are saved with the Lord and enjoying all the wonderful things that lay ahead for the believer. Today, rejoice that when the stars fall from heaven, you will be with the "Bright and Morning Star" enjoying the glory of a new home and life.

November 13

1 John 5:11, "And this is the record, that God hath given to us eternal life, and this life is in his Son."

On This Day in 1871, missionary-explorer David Livingstone was found by Henry Morton Stanley. After it was feared that Livingstone had been dead for four years, New York Herald journalist Stanley found him alive at Ujiji in Central Africa. He found Livingstone frail and short of supplies. Mr. Stanley's greeting, "Mr. Livingstone, I presume," was the first words the fifty-eight year old explorer had heard spoken by a white man for five years. Dr. Livingstone said to Stanley, "You have brought me new life." Livingstone insisted on hearing about major events he had missed, such as the Franco-Prussian War, the opening of the Suez Canal, and the inauguration of the transatlantic telegraph.

There was a day when many of us were in a spiritually impoverished condition, but the Lord Jesus found us and gave us new life. The condition was worse for some more than others, but in every case the condition was serious. We were lost! We were dead spiritually! But thank God the Lord Jesus came to where we were and brought us new life. The sweetest words I had ever heard were, "*Whosoever shall call upon the name of the Lord shall be saved*" (Rom. 10:13). Do you remember when He spoke your name? Do you remember that blessed hour when He gave you a new life? The promise of the Lord is, "*That whosoever believeth in him should not perish, but have eternal life*" (John 3:15). Today, take a few moments to praise the Lord for the day when He came to where you were and brought you new life. Take a few moments to reflect on the condition He found you in. If you will do so, you can't help but praise Him.

November 14

Psalm 41:9, "Yea, mine own familiar friend, in whom I trusted, which did eat of my bread, hath lifted up his heel against me."

ON THIS DAY in 1943, President Franklin D. Roosevelt and all of America's top military brass were nearly killed by friendly fire. All were aboard the battleship *Iowa* en route to the Big Three Conference in Iran to meet Winston Churchhill and Joseph Stalin. To demonstrate to the president and his guests the defensive capabilities of the *Iowa*, a series of weather balloons to use as anti-aircraft targets were launched. On the nearby *William D. Porter*, Captain Wilfred Walker ordered his men to battle stations and the men began shooting down the balloons that the *Iowa* had missed. However, torpedoer Lawton Dawson neglected to disarm torpedo tube #3, and an actual torpedo was fired toward the Iowa. Immediately, the *William D. Porter* informed the *Iowa* what had happened, and the *Iowa* rapidly began evasive maneuvers. Fortunately, the torpedo exploded behind the ship's wake as the president sat in his wheelchair watching the approach of the torpedo. Upon docking, Captain Walker and his crew were arrested and Lawson was later court martialed. Thereafter, the *William D. Porter* was often hailed with the greeting, "Don't shoot, we're Republicans."

David found himself the target of attacks, but what was so devasting to him was that the attacks were coming from someone who had been a dear friend. It always hurts to be slandered and attacked, especially by someone you love. Yet David found that the Lord was a faithful friend. Today, rejoice that even though others may let you down, the Lord never will. He is a friend who will always remain a friend.

November 15

Zechariah 7:11, "But they refused to hearken, and pulled away the shoulder, and stopped their ears, that they should not hear."

ON THIS DAY in 1901, Miller Reese of New York first patented the hearing-aid. Alexander Graham Bell is considered the father of hearing aids, but he never patented his invention. Earlier, hearing aids consisted of small horns that wrapped around the ear or were hidden in the handle of a cane, but they only increased users hearing level ten to fifteen decibels. In the 1900's ,electrical hearing aids were developed, such as Reese's, which were large awkward boxes that were almost impossible to carry. It was not until the 1930's that wearable sized hearing aids were invented. They could correct hearing up to thirty to thirty-five decibels but had a separate battery pack. Smaller and more convenient, they were not without their problems. They were noisy and would turn off if the hearer bent over or sat down. The development of the transistor in 1952 was a major breakthrough in the development of hearing aids.

People with good hearing have been known to have a problem with hearing. The people of Zechariah's day is a good example. They refused to hear what God had to say and even went as far as stopping their ears so they could not hear. Do you have a hearing problem? A spiritual hearing problem? Have you turned your spiritual hearing aid down so that you can't hear what God is saying to you? The Psalmist declares, *"I will hear what God the Lord will speak..."* (Psa. 85:8). Today, join with the Psalmist and listen to what God may have to say to you. If you need to turn your spiritual hearing aid up, do so. God has great things to say to you.

November 16

Romans 3:19, "Now we know that what things soever the law saith, it saith to them who are under the law: that every mouth may be stopped, and all the world may become guilty before God."

ON THIS DAY in 1966, Dr. Sam Sheppard was acquitted in his second trial of the charges that he had murdered his wife. Inspiring the TV series and movie The Fugitive, Marilyn Sheppard was bludgeoned in her bed early on July 4, 1954. Dr. Sheppard claimed that he was sleeping downstairs at the time of the murder and awoke to his wife's cries. He ran to her help but was knocked out by a bushy-haired intruder. A jury convicted Sheppard of murder, and he spent nearly a decade in prison before the U.S. Supreme Court overturned the verdict. Sheppard was acquitted at a retrial and died four years later. Prosecutors maintained their belief that he was guilty but public opinion was divided. His son, Sam Reese Sheppard, has spent years trying to clear his fathers name for all time. In April of 2000, a jury rejected his claim that his father had been wrongfully imprisoned.

What really happened may never be certain, and whether Dr. Sheppard was guilty or not will probably be a matter of debate; but when it comes to our guilt before God, there is no question. The whole world is guilty before God and there is no denying the evidence. As we might say, "It is an open and shut case." The good news is that even though we are guilty, we can be forgiven. No matter the depths of our guilt before God, His grace goes even deeper and where "*sin did abound, grace did much more abound*" (Rom. 5:20). Today, give thanks to God that He has forgiven the guilty. There is no doubt about that.

November 17

Proverbs 28:13, "He that covereth his sins shall not prosper: but whoso confesseth and forsaketh them shall have mercy."

ON THIS DAY in 1973, President Richard Nixon denied any involvement in the Watergate scandal. Choosing Disney World as the place to tell the American people that its president was "not a crook", he claimed that he had no knowledge of or involvement in a cover-up of a break-in at the Democratic Headquarters. The scandal came to light after investigations by *Washington Post* reporters Bob Woodard and Carl Bernstein. Nixon continued to insist that he knew nothing about the burglary or cover-up. The investigation found the involvement of four top Nixon aids. Legal advisor John Dean, one of the four, later told a senate committee that Nixon had known all along. On August 9, 1974 Nixon resigned as president.

Solomon reminds us that we can do one of two things with our sin. We can try to cover our sins, but we will not prosper. Sin always robs the believer of God's blessings, and the covering of sin separates us from the good things God wants to give and do for us. We are only deceiving ourselves if we think we can cover sin and still be blessed of God. On the other hand, Solomon tells us that if we confess and forsake our sin, we will find mercy. Confession brings forgiveness and when sin has been forgiven, we can be blessed of God. Solomon does not deny the presence of sin in the believer's life. He is very much aware that we do fail the Lord. The issue is what will we do when we sin? Today, instead of covering sin, confess sin. Instead of denying sin, be honest with yourself and God. The blessings of the Lord will make you glad that you did.

November 18

Matthew 7:15, "Beware of false prophets, which come to you in sheep's clothing, but inwardly they are ravening wolves."

ON THIS DAY in 1977, the Rev. Jim Jones led his members to commit mass suicide. Jones founded the Indianapolis Peoples Temple Full Gospel Church in 1956. He received notoriety for claiming to have raised forty people from the dead. He eventually moved to California with 100 of his members and by the 1970's, his congregation had flourished to over 4,000. He left the U.S. to take charge of the Temple's operations in Jonestown, Guyana, after reports of financial misappropriations, sexual improprieties, beatings, and other serious crimes. His final act was to lead 914 people, including 276 children, to drink a fruit flavored, cyanide-spiked drink.

Jesus warned of those who have the appearance of being of God, yet in reality are false prophets. Jesus also warned of false Christs who would appear and deceive people through great signs and wonders (See Matt. 24:24). The devil is a deceiver, and he is a master of clothing the false in sheep's clothing. As believers, we must never judge what is true or false by what we see but by what we read. All things must be filtered through what God says in His Word. We must never accept something to be true just because it looks or sounds good. Furthermore, the Bible must never be interpreted by our experiences, but we must interpret our experiences by God's Word. Today, remember that God never leads anyone to take their life but to give their life to Him. That's the difference between the false and the real.

1 Corinthians 14:19, "Yet in the church I had rather speak five words with my understanding, that by my voice I might teach others also, than ten thousand words in an unknown tongue."

ON THIS DAY in 1863, President Abraham Lincoln delivered his Gettysburg Address. Asked to make "a few appropriate remarks," to honor the more than 20,000 Union soldiers who had died at Gettysburg, Lincoln gave a speech consisting of 266 words that is considered one of the finest speeches ever given by an American politician. However, at the time, his speech was not without its critics. An editorial by the *Chicago Times* said, "The cheek of every American must tingle with shame as he reads the silly, flat, and dishwatery utterances of the man who has to be pointed out to intelligent foreigners as the President of the United States." The *Patriot and Union* wrote that they hoped "they shall no more be repeated or thought of."

A short, simple speech, yes; but one that will be remembered as long as time shall stand. Oh, by the way, Lincoln was not the main speaker that day. The chosen orator was Edward Everett. He prepared an oration that was scholarly and eloquent enough to satisfy all the conventions of such an occasion. But I ask you, if you have any knowledge of what he said that day? Never even heard of him, you say? Paul, dealing with the confusion caused by the speaking of tongues in the Corinthian church, states that what was most important was speaking in a way which people understand and are helped. Today, remember that we can try to impress people with our big words and deeds, but if we want to be remembered, it is the simple things that touch people's lives that count.

November 20

Colossians 3:15, "And let the peace of God rule in your hearts, to the which also ye are called in one body; and be ye thankful."

On *This* Day in 1923, Garrett A. Morgan applied for and acquired a U.S. patent for his invention called the traffic signal. Morgan, an African-American born in Paris, Kentucky, devoted his life to inventing things that made the lives of other people safe and convenient. The Morgan traffic signal was a T-shaped pole unit that featured three positions: stop, go, and an all-directional stop position. This third position halted traffic in all directions to allow pedestrians to cross streets more safely. He sold the rights to his traffic signal to the General Electric Corporation for $40,000. In 1963, shortly before he died, the United States government awarded him a citation for his traffic signal.

God has put a stop and go signal in the heart of every believer. Paul spoke of the peace of God ruling in our hearts. The word "rule" is descriptive of an arbitrator. The peace of God in our heart will tell us if we are right or wrong. If we are right, God's peace will fill the heart. God's peace abiding in the heart is God's "go" signal. It tells us that our actions and direction are right. But if we are wrong, the peace of God will be interrupted in our heart. This interruption is God's "stop" signal in our heart. To ignore this signal is to only invite disaster. The moment we do something that interrupts the peace of God in our heart we should stop and correct our actions and direction. Today, let the peace of God be God's signal in your life telling you what is right and wrong. If the signal is green, go, but if it's red, stop. It is always dangerous to run a red light.

November 21

Proverbs 8:8, "All the words of my mouth are in righteousness; there is nothing froward or perverse in them."

ON THIS DAY in 1973, an eighteen and one-half minute gap was found in a subpoenaed Watergate tape. In July, a former White House aid had brought to the attention of the Senate committee investigating Watergate the existence of recordings of conversations of President Richard Nixon and his White House staff. The recordings were subpoenaed, and the Senate committee had to file suit against the president before he agreed to turn the tapes over to the committee. When the recordings arrived, several of the key tapes were missing, including an eighteen and one-half minute gap in one of the tapes that contained a conversation between Nixon and White House staff member H.R. Haldeman. Two months later, an expert testified before the House Judiciary Committee that the gap was caused by deliberate and repeated erasures.

Have you ever said something that you wish you could erase from your mind, other's mind, and from time? Oftentimes in a moment of anger, we have said things that once we cooled down, we deeply regretted saying. It may only take a second to say what we said, but it may require years to undo the harm our words cause. It would be great if we could erase some of things we have said. Since that is impossible, we should strive that in our words, as Solomon says, there is nothing froward (that which would hurt someone) and perverse (that which is distorted). Today, guard your words for once they are spoken, they cannot be "unsaid." Some things we say have a way of coming back to haunt us, therefore speak only words of "righteousness."

November 22

Proverbs 14:9, "Fools make a mock at sin: but among the righteous there is favour."

ON THIS DAY in 1978, eighteen year-old Charles A. Meriweather broke into a home in northwest Baltimore. Adding to his crime of breaking and entering was the rape of the woman who lived there. During his crime spree, he ransacked the house only to discover that she only had $11.50 in cash. He asked, "How do you pay your bills?" She replied, "By check." He ordered her to write him a check for thirty dollars, then changed his mind and ordered her to write the check for fifty dollars. She asked, "Who shall I make it out to?" "Charles A. Meriweather," said Charles A. Meriweather. Police picked him up a few hours later.

I would not classify Mr. Meriweather as one of the brightest criminals. Would you? People have been known to do many foolish things. Yet, the Bible tells us that anyone who takes sin lightly is behaving foolishly. The Bible is clear that we cannot get by with sin, yet some seem to think they are an exception. Sin may be mocked and taken lightly, but the results and consequences of sin cannot be escaped. You may hide your sin from man but not God. Understanding that there is always a price to pay for sin, we must never take sin in any form lightly, the consequences are at times very costly. To do so is to live foolishly. The wise man takes God seriously, even what He says about sin. Solomon says that with the righteous is favor. The blessings of God and the joy that one experiences living for the Lord far outweigh any pleasure one might find in sin. Today, live wisely. Don't act foolishly and take sin lightly.

November 23

Revelation 2:5, "Remember therefore from whence thou art fallen, and repent, and do the first works; or else I will come unto thee quickly, and will remove thy candlestick out of his place, except thou repent."

ON *THIS* DAY in 1978, Hans Mullikin completed a journey to the White House that took two and one-half years. Mullikin, a logger and sometimes Baptist minister, crawled the entire distance from his home in Marshall, Texas to the gates of the White House. Mullikin would crawl a certain distance on his knees, equipped with goalie kneepads donated by the Dallas Blackhawks hockey team, then jog back to his car and drive it up to his stopping point, repeating the process all over again. He returned home for the winters and worked to finance his expedition, and then pick back up in the spring where he had stopped off. What was his purpose? To "show America that we need to get on our knees and repent."

The Lord Jesus rebukes the church at Ephesus for leaving their first love and calls for their repentance and a return to their first works. The first love that Jesus speaks of has often been described as a honeymoon love. It is descriptive of a burning heart for Christ and the things of God. It has been said that oftentimes the older we get in the Lord, the colder we get. What is the cure for a cold heart? Repentance! Repentance is asking God to forgive the coldness that has crept into our hearts and asking Him to fill our hearts with a burning love for Christ. Today, if your heart has grown cold, fall on your knees and ask Him to rekindle that honeymoon love. Where you are right now will work. You don't have to crawl to the Whitehouse.

November 24

Psalm 37:37, "Mark the perfect man, and behold the upright: for the end of that man is peace."

ON THIS DAY in 1971, D.B. Cooper pulled off the world's only successful skyjacking. Cooper had boarded a Northwest Airlines Boeing 727 Portland, Oregon and about thirty minutes into the flight, he informed a stewardess that he had a bomb and unless he was given $200,000 in cash, he would blow up the plane. The plane landed in Seattle and Cooper was given a sack containing the money and four parachutes he had demanded in return for the release of the passengers. Then thirty-two minutes after the plane took off, Cooper opened the rear exit door and jumped out. What happened to Cooper still remains a mystery. Three weeks later, a Los Angeles newspaper received a letter supposedly from Cooper that read, "I have only 14 months to live. The hijacking was the fastest and most profitable way to gain a few last grains of peace of mind."

So many like Cooper think that peace is found in what they have. As it has been well stated, money may buy you a bed but not a night's rest. Many millionaires have testified to the emptiness of their soul and the lack of joy that their wealth brought them. Peace of mind is never found in things. It can only be found in a person—the Lord Jesus Christ. C.S. Lewis was correct when he said, "God cannot give us happiness and peace apart from Himself, because it is not there. There is no such thing." The Psalmist declares, "*The Lord will give strength unto his people; the Lord will bless his people with peace.*" Today, rejoice that you have found the source of peace. You may not have $200,000 but then again you don't need money to have peace of mind.

November 25

1 Peter 2:24, "Who his own self bare our sins in his own body on the tree, that we, being dead to sins, should live unto righteousness: by whose stripes ye were healed."

On This Day in 1970, Japanese author of novels, essays, poetry, and traditional plays, Yukio Mishima, publicly committed suicide by disemboweling himself with a sword. A prolific writer educated in Western traditions, Mishima had increasingly become interested in the culture and customs of imperial Japan. An expert in traditional martial arts, Mishima organized the *Tate no Kai* (Shield Society) which attempted to revive the traditional Samurai code of honor. In 1970, he seized a government office urging his followers to reject the new Japanese constitution and rearm the country's military. In an attempt to rouse Japan to its pre-war nationalist ideas, he committed the ritual suicide called *seppuku* (belly-slitting) with a sword.

As believers, we are not called upon to die for the Lord but to live for Him. Our cause is much greater than dying to rally a nation to a former way of life, but to live unto righteousness to tell people about a new way of life. I have heard a few "humble" testimonies where someone spoke of being willing to die for the Lord. The Lord is interested in our living for Him. Throughout Church history there have been many who gave their life for the cause of Christ, but the ultimate price they paid was because of the life they were living and their refusal to deny the name of Jesus Christ. The greatest way to advance the cause of Christ is not by taking your life, but by giving your life to God and living for Him. Today, live "unto righteousness." Live for God and let your life be a testimony that there is a new life that is much, much better than the old.

November 26

Psalm 72:6, "He shall come down like rain upon the mown grass: as showers that water the earth."

ON THIS DAY in 1970, the most rain ever recorded in one minute fell in the Caribbean Islands. A total of 1.5 inches fell on the island of Guadeloupe. For your interest, let me share with you a few other rain records. The fastest foot of rain fell on Holt, Missouri in 1947 in forty-two minutes. The rainiest day on record was in 1952 when more than six feet of rain fell at Cilaos on Reunion Island. Cherrapunji, Assam, India received 189 inches of rain between July 24 and July 8, 1931 for the most rain during a fifteen-day period.

The Psalmist speaks of the Lord coming down as rain upon the mown grass. He was speaking of the refreshing and reviving blessings of God upon His people. We often sing, "Let there be showers of blessings." When it comes to God's blessings, I am interested in record amounts of rain. How about you? God wants to bless His people. He wants to give us more than a few drops here and there. He wants his blessings to come as floods in our life. If you are discouraged, rain from heaven is what you need. Are you tired in the work? A good rain from heaven has many refreshing and reviving qualities about it. Is your soul spiritually dry and barren? The best thing for parched ground is rain from heaven. In case you are interested, the driest place on earth is Arica, Chile in the Atacama Desert. No rain fell there for more than fourteen years. Over a fifty-nine year period, Arica averaged three-hundredths of an inch of rain a year. I hope that does not describe your life. I would rather be the island of Guadeloupe than Arica. Today, pray for rain in your life.

November 27

Proverbs 1:5, "A wise man will hear, and will increase learning; and a man of understanding shall attain unto wise counsels:"

ON THIS DAY in 1779, America's first University was established. The Pennsylvania state government converted the College of Philadelphia, which it considered a Royalist institution, into the University of the State of Pennsylvania. Located in Philadelphia, the college had been founded as a charity school for the children of Philadelphia in 1740. In 1749, Benjamin Franklin proposed that the school be expanded into the "Publick Academy of Philadelphia" as an institute of higher education in both liberal arts and practical skills necessary to make a living. Established as a university in 1779, in 1791, the school became a privately endowed university and known today as the University of Pennsylvania.

Solomon declares that a characteristic of wisdom is a desire to expansion of learning and the increase of knowledge. Of course, his proverb had more in mind than going back to school to get a Master's degree, but an increase in our knowledge of God's Word, ways, and will. As believers, we should always be learning and growing in our understanding. We should never be satisfied with what we know but possess a insatiable thirst to know more. Henry Ford once said, "Anyone who stops learning is old, whether this happens at twenty or at eighty. Anyone who keeps on learning not only remains young but becomes constantly more valuable, regardless of physical capacity." Today, get out "The Book" and become a student of God's Word. Make your spiritual education a lifetime pursuit and never stop learning until its "Graduation Day."

November 28

Ephesians 4:17, "This I say therefore, and testify in the Lord, that ye henceforth walk not as other Gentiles walk, in the vanity of their mind."

ON *THIS* DAY in 1953, Dr. Frank Olson jumped to his death from the tenth floor of the Statler Hotel in Manhattan, New York. His wife later reported that "he was very melancholy and talked about a mistake he had made." It was not until June 1975 that his family learned what the mistake was. Dr. Olson, a biochemist working on top-secret germ warfare at Fort Detrick, Maryland, had taken LSD as part of a $25 million dollar experiment secretly funded by the Central Intelligence Agency (CIA). The program was a series of mind-control experiments at universities, prisons, and hospitals. It was discovered that the program consisted of 150 projects, of which 39 involved human projects.

A very popular book in the early 80's was entitled, "The Battle for the Mind." There is a battle for the mind. Satan knows that if he can control our thought life, he can control our actions. Our actions are often determined by how we think and what we think about. In computer language, "Garbage in, garbage out." Paul speaks of those whose walk was reflective of the way they thought. Satan is in the business of "mind-control." He seeks to get us to fill our mind with the filth and "garbage" of this world in order to control what we do and how we live. I think of Job's words: *"I made a covenant with mine eyes; why then should I think upon a maid*" (Job 31:1)? In simple language, Job was saying that he was in the mind-control business. Today, guard what you see, read, and hear. It is the kind of mind-control that will help you live a godly life.

November 29

Mark 15:1, "And straightway in the morning the chief priests held a consultation with the elders and scribes and the whole council, and bound Jesus, and carried him away, and delivered him to Pilate."

On This Day in 1963, President Lyndon B. Johnson established the Warren Commission. The commission was established one week after President John F. Kennedy was assassinated in Dallas, Texas to investigate the assassination. Headed by Supreme Court Justice Earl Warren, the commission spent ten months gathering evidence and interviewing witnesses to determine whether or not a conspiracy was involved in the murder of the President. When the Warren Commission Report was released, it concluded that there was no conspiracy and that Lee Harvey Oswald had acted alone. The report also concluded that Jack Ruby, who murdered Oswald had had no prior contact with him.

What if a commission had been established to investigate the death of the Lord Jesus? What would their findings have been? There is no question that findings of a conspiracy to put Him to death would have been included in the report for several groups, religious and political, conspired together in His death. Pilate, after the crucifixion, wrote in a letter, "Then the chief priests, moved with envy against Him, seized Him and delivered Him to me, and telling me one lie after another, they said that He was a wizard and did contrary to their law." Was there a conspiracy? Yes, without a doubt, but then we must remember that behind it all was the eternal plan of God that was in action. Today, give thanks that the death of Jesus was more than a conspiracy but a loving Heavenly Father who was providing the way that all men might be saved.

November 30

2 Corinthians 5:2, "For in this we groan, earnestly desiring to be clothed upon with our house which is from heaven:"

ON THIS DAY in 1954, a meteorite struck Elizabeth Hodges. Sleeping on her couch in her Sylacauga, Alabama home, a meteorite crashed through the roof of her house and into her living room, bounced off a radio, and struck her on the hip. The space rock was a sulfide meteorite weighing eight and one-half pounds and measuring seven inches in length. It was the first modern instance of a human being struck by a meteorite, although ancient Chinese records tell of people being injured or killed by falling meteorites. Mrs. Hodges was not permanently hurt but suffered a nasty bruise along her hip and leg.

As believers, there are certain things we want to see come "from heaven", but a meteorite is not one of them. The Apostle Paul speaks of a great longing that is in the heart of the believer for a "house" that is "from heaven." The house he refers to was the believer's new body. Even though our bodies are fearfully and wonderfully made (Psa. 139:14), they bear the scars of the presence of sin in this world. Sickness, disease, pain, and the increasing limitations of old age are all common with the house (body) in which we now live. Yet, one day we will be clothed upon with a new house that will be immune from all we have known in this life. It is a body that will never get sick and in which there are no deformities. Paul describes it as a body "from heaven." It will be a glorified body given to us by God. The older a person gets, the greater the longing for this body from heaven. Today, give thanks that one day we will receive a new body from heaven. That's one thing that will come from heaven that I am excited about.

December 1

Hebrews 11:24, "By faith Moses, when he was come to years, refused to be called the son of Pharaoh's daughter."

On This Day in 1955, Rosa Parks refused to give her seat on a Montgomery, Alabama bus to a white man. In that simple act, Rosa Parks said "no" to racial discrimination and became known as the mother of the civil-rights movement. In Montgomery, blacks formed seventy percent of the bus riders; but they were forced to pay fares at the front of the bus, disembark, and then reboard through the back door to sit in the black section. For Rosa Parks, it had been a long day at the Montgomery department store where she worked in alterations. She was tired and her tolerance for injustice was low. The bus driver noticed a white man standing and ordered all those sitting in Rosa Park's row to vacate their seats in the black sections to make room for the white passengers. Three blacks moved to stand in the back of the bus, but Rosa Parks did not.

As believers, there are times when we must say no. There are certain things we must refuse. Moses made the important choice of refusing to be called the son of Pharaoh's daughter, but instead chose to be identified with the people of God. It was not without a cost. Rosa Park's decision to remain seated led to her arrest. But the cost of saying yes to some things is more costly than saying no. The believer must say no to the pull of this world. We must say no to each temptation of the flesh. We must say no to every offer of the devil. Today, take a stand. Say no to the world, the flesh, and the devil. If you have to say yes to something, say yes to whatever God wants for you.

December 2

Revelation 6:2, "And I saw, and behold a white horse: and he that sat on him had a bow; and a crown was given unto him: and he went forth conquering, and to conquer."

ON THIS DAY in 1804, Napoleon crowned himself emperor of France. In November of 1799, he had ousted the French government through a coup and had himself voted commander-in-chief of the troops in Paris. In August of 1802, the senate had proclaimed Napoleon "Consul for Life" and in so doing, assumed regal powers. In a magnificent ceremony in Notre Dame, Napoleon placed two golden laurel wreaths on his own head and then crowned his wife, Josephene.

Many kings have sat upon earthly thrones and ruled over the kingdoms of this world. Yet the greatest king of them all, the King of kings and Lord of lords, will take His throne and rule over His kingdom. His kingdom shall know no borders and His rule will be universal. This King is the Lord Jesus Christ and when He comes back to this earth, He will take His rightful place as King. Every knee shall bow and every tongue shall confess that He is King of kings and Lord of lords. The first time He came, a crown of thorns was placed on His head in mockery. The next time He comes, He will be wearing His regal crown and He will be acknowledged as King. For believers, it grieves their heart when the name of Christ is blasphemed and treated with scorn and ridicule. Yet, we rejoice that one day He will sit upon His throne and rule in all His splendor, glory, and majesty. Today, rejoice that Jesus has already been crowned King of kings and Lord of lords in your life. Others may crown themselves as king, but we know who really is King.

December 3

Acts 11:29, "Then the disciples, every man according to his ability, determined to send relief unto the brethren which dwelt in Judaea:"

ON THIS DAY in 1931, Alka-Seltzer went on sale for the first time. In the late twenties, the United States experienced a severe flu epidemic that affected almost half the population. On a visit to the editor-in-chief of a local newspaper, Hub Beardsley, the president of Miles Laboratories, noticed that the newspaper staff seemed to be resistant to the flu epidemic. He discovered that they were taking a combination of acetylsalicylic and bicarbonate until their cold symptoms disappeared. Beardsley asked chemist Maurice Treneer to develop an effervescent tablet with acetylsalicylic and sodium bicarbonate as the main ingredients. Alka-Seltzer was born. Today, Alka-Seltzer is sold in more than fifty countries, and millions have joined with "Speedy Relief" in saying, "Plop, plop, fizz, fizz, oh what a relief it is."

The saints at Judea found themselves in need of relief. It was a time of famine, and the believers at Antioch reached out in an expression of care and compassion. They took up money for the believers at Judea, each person giving all they were able to give, to help them financially. When others are in need, believers are to demonstrate love and compassion by reaching out to help and provide "relief." John said, *"But whoso hath this world's good, and seeth his brother have need, and shutteth up his bowels of compassion from him, how dwelleth the love of God in him"* (1 John 3:17). The love of God that has been shed abroad in our hearts (Rom. 5:5) creates within us a love for others, and a love that reaches out when others are in need. Today, be an "Alka-Seltzer" Christian.

December 4

Ezekiel 36:26, "A new heart also will I give you, and a new spirit will I put within you: and I will take away the stony heart out of your flesh, and I will give you an heart of flesh."

ON THIS DAY in 1967, the first human heart transplant was performed. The operation was performed by a team of surgeons led by Dr. Christian Barnard at Groote Schur Hospital in Cape Town, South Africa. The patient was fifty-three year-old Louis Washkansky, who was a grocer. The heart came from a twenty-five year old woman who was killed in a car accident. Washkansky had been extremely ill with heart disease, and the operation was considered his only chance to live. Washkansky would only live for eighteen days, dying from lung complications. Doctors said that the heart continued to beat strongly to the end.

It has been well said that the heart of the problem is the problem of the heart. We all had a serious heart problem. The symptoms of our heart condition varied from person to person. For some, the condition was worse than others, but all had a bad heart. Our heart condition was so serious that it needed more than repair. We had to have a new heart. In order for us to get a new heart someone had to die. In our case, our new heart was not the gift of someone's accident, but was provided through Christ who willingly gave His life that we might have a new heart. Have you had a heart, transplant? Have you received the new heart that is offered to you through the Lord Jesus? The only hope for eternal life is a new heart. Today, rejoice that one day the Great Physician gave you a new heart. I'm sure that you have found it is still beating strong.

December 5

Deuteronomy 31:6, "Be strong and of a good courage, fear not, nor be afraid of them: for the Lord thy God, he it is that doth go with thee; he will not fail thee, nor forsake thee."

On This Day in 1872, the American ship *Mary Celeste* was found abandoned in the Atlantic. On November 7, Captain Benjamin Briggs, his wife and daughter, and an eight-man crew set sail from New York for a routine journey across the Atlantic to Europe. The *Mary Celeste* was spotted by the crew of the *Dei Gratia*, boarded and found completely deserted. The crew had apparently abandoned ship nine days earlier. The lifeboat was gone and the ship had drifted some 700 miles from the last point of entry. Captain Morehouse of the *Die Gratia* could find no apparent reason why the ship had been abandoned. There was plenty of food and water on board—six months supply. The cargo was fully intact, so piracy was ruled out. The final entry in the ship's log detailed a minor course direction: "At eight eastern point bore SSW six miles distant." Captain Briggs, his wife, their daughter, and crew were never to be seen again. Many theories have been put forth to explain what happened, but to this day, the abandonment of the *Mary Celeste* remains a mystery.

As we near the end of another year, we can look back and say, "The Lord was with us each day of the year." As believers, we live with the assurance that the Lord will never abandon us nor forsake us. He has been with us through each day and events of this year and we are promised that in the year to come, we can count on His faithful presence. Today, give thanks that we have a Heavenly Father that is with us and will never leave nor forsake us. He never abandons ship!

December 6

2 Timothy 2:21, "If a man therefore purge himself from these, he shall be a vessel unto honour, sanctified, and meet for the master's use, and prepared unto every good work."

ON THIS DAY in 1648, Thomas Pride carried out what is known as "Pride's Purge." Pride, an English parliamentary solider in the English Civil War (the conflict between King Charles I and a large body of his subjects), expelled 143 members (96 of them Presbyterians) from the English Parliament mostly on the grounds that they were royalist sympathizers. The members of the Parliament who retained their seats were called Rumps. The Rump Parliament, completely under army control, then arranged the trial of Charles I, condemned him and signed his death warrant. The defeat and execution of Charles led to the establishment of a republican commonwealth (a form of government by the common consent of the people).

There are times when purging is healthy and necessary. Paul told Timothy that if he wanted to be a vessel that brought honor to God and usable in the hands of God, there had to be a purging. I have heard it said that because God is hard up for workers, He would use anyone. I agree that God needs workers, but He will not use just anyone. God will not and cannot use a dirty vessel. If we want to be used of God and expect to be used by God, there must be a purging from our life anything that is displeasing to Him. God can use anyone and He wants to use everyone, but we must be clean. Today, search your heart for anything that would keep God from using you. Purge from your life anything you find that displeases God. If you want to be used, it is necessary.

December 7

Ephesians 6:12. "For we wrestle not against flesh and blood, but against principalities, against powers, against the rulers of the darkness of this world, against spiritual wickedness in high places."

ON *THIS* DAY in 1941, Japan attacked and bombed Pearl Harbor. In a surprise attack on the U.S. Pacific fleet anchored at Pearl Harbor on the Hawaiian island of Oahu, 2,433 Americans were killed; eighteen warships and 188 airplanes were destroyed. President Roosevelt denounced the Japanese attack to Congress, declaring it as "a date which will live in infamy," and the U.S. declared war on Japan. On board the *U.S.S. Nevada*, a brass band played the Star Spangled Banner as a Japanese bomber passed overhead and fired a torpedo at the nearby *Arizona*. The torpedo missed, but the bomber sprayed machine-gun fire at the *Nevada's* band and tore up its ensign. A sailor on the *Arizona* said, "This is the best...drill the Army Air Force has ever put on." But it was no drill. It was the real thing.

Paul describes the devil and his demons as a highly organized army arranged in rank and order. He speaks of the believer as in a wrestling match against these principalities and powers. Be it understood that when Paul describes the believer as a wrestler, he was referring to much more than the kind of "wrestling" one may see on TV. Paul was describing an event where the objective was to pin the opponent to the ground and where the penalty for losing was death. You could say that he was speaking of the real thing. No drills, no faking, no putting on a show, but the real thing. As believers, we must realize that we are in a spiritual warfare. Today, realize that you have an enemy that wants to "sink" you. Never forget that when the enemy attacks, it is no drill.

December 8

Romans 3:23, "For all have sinned, and come short of the glory of God."

ON THIS DAY in 1854, Pope Pius IX proclaimed the total sinlessness of the Virgin Mary. In a bull, *Ineffabilis*, it was declared, "From the first moment of her conception, the Blessed Virgin Mary was, by the singular grace and privilege of Almighty God, and in view of the merits of Jesus Christ, Saviour of mankind, kept free from all stains of original sin." The doctrine of the Immaculate Conception had been debated from as early as the 16th century but now was made an official doctrine of the Church at Rome.

The announcement of the angel to Mary was, "*Hail, thou that art highly favoured, the Lord is with thee: blessed art thou among women*" (Luke 1:28). Mary was indeed favored by God and holds a special place among women, to have been chosen to be the one to give birth to the Lord Jesus. Yet, she understood that the child that she was to give birth to was more than her son; He was also her Saviour (Luke 1:47). Mary was aware that she was a sinner in need of a Saviour. The simple truth is that all men and women are sinners in need of a Saviour. Mary understood that even though she had been chosen by God to give birth to His Son, she came short of God's glory like every other human being. There is only one man who ever lived on this earth who was without sin and that was the Lord Jesus. He was the sinless One that came to save sinful ones. Do you remember the day when you saw yourself as a sinner, and you turned to the Lord Jesus and accepted Him as your Saviour? Today, give thanks that God has sent His Son to be the Saviour of all sinners, such as you and me, and yes—even Mary!

December 9

1 Timothy 4:2, "Speaking lies in hypocrisy; having their conscience seared with a hot iron."

On This Day in 1980, John Lennon, a former Beatle, was killed outside his department building in New York City. David Chapman, a twenty-five year old security guard with a history of mental illness, had quit his job in Hawaii, purchased a .38 caliber pistol, and flew to New York. He began staking out the Dakota Department Building where Lennon lived. Chapman first approached Lennon and asked him to sign his latest album, Double Fantasy. Six hours later, as the singer walked back to his department, Chapman called out to the singer. He fell to one knee, held his gun in both hands as he had been taught, and fired five times, striking Lennon in the back four times. He then simply dropped his gun and waited to be arrested. It seems that in his twisted mind, he was acting out a war against "phonies," as waged by a character in J.D. Salinger's *The Catcher in the Rye*.

The Bible speaks of "phonies." These phonies are called hypocrites. A hypocrite is simply one who pretends to be one thing but in reality is something else. The word was often used to speak of an actor on a stage acting out the part of another. Paul speaks to Timothy about believers waging war against hypocrisy in their personal lives. Of course, to wage a war against hypocrisy does not mean that we murder someone. Only a twisted and disturbed mind would even consider such actions. However, as believers we should hate any form of hypocrisy in our life. We want to be the "genuine article" and not just play the part. Today, search your heart for any "phoniness." Ask God to help you to be real. Actors may get an award, but there is no reward for the hypocrite.

December 10

Luke 12:7, "But even the very hairs of your head are all numbered. Fear not therefore: ye are of more value than many sparrows."

ON *THIS* DAY in 1945, Preston Tucker revealed his plans to produce a "car ahead of its time." Commonly known as the *Tucker*, the car was quite impressive for its day. The car featured an all-independent suspension and a rear-mounted flat six engine that gave the car a top speed of 120 mph. It also included unique features such as interchangeable rear and front seats, a "Cyclops eye" in addition to its two standard lights that tracked with the front wheels, and safety features such as a padded dash and crash wells for both driver and passenger to drop in if a crash were to occur. It was indeed a car ahead of its time. However, due to investigations by the Securities and Exchange Commission and the Justice Department, only fifty-one *Tuckers* were built in 1948. Amazingly, forty-eight of them still exist. The projected price of the car was $2,450. Today, a *Tucker* is worth anywhere from $250,000 to $500,000. In March 1996, *Tucker* #1030 sold at an auction for $259,000.

Things have a way over time of increasing in value, especially if they are rare as Preston's *Tucker*. Yet, the believer is of greater value to God than any other car or item. Jesus speaks of the value of the believer. Jesus directs the disciples' attention to the little sparrow and speaks of how not one falls to the ground without the Father's knowledge. Yet, the believer is even more important and of greater value to God. Do you ever feel like you are unimportant? Today, give thanks that you have a Heavenly Father who values you above all that He has created. You are more valuable than a *Tucker*.

December 11

1 John 4:19, "We love him, because he first loved us."

ON THIS DAY in 1936, King Edward VIII announced that he was abdicating his throne. In a moving and dignified radio address from Windsor Castle, Edward told the British people that he had found it impossible to discharge his royal duties "without the help and support of the woman I love." The prospect of his marriage to the twice-divorced American Wallis Simpson of Baltimore had been met with dismay by both Parliament and the Church. Simpson and Edward had met while he was the Prince of Wales. As rumors of their affair snowballed, Edward came under pressure to make a choice – his throne or his love. He chose his love. Albert, the Duke of York was proclaimed King George VI in his brother's place.

The decision of Edward to give up his throne for the woman he loved was a great demonstration of love. Yet, the greatest demonstration of love this world has ever known was when the Lord Jesus, the King of kings, stepped down from His throne in heaven and came to this earth because of His love for you and me. He left the glory place for the gory place. He left the cheers of heaven for the sneers of earth. He left the hallelujahs of heaven for the hisses of earth. Why? Because he loved us! John declares, *"Herein is love, not that we loved God, but that he loved us, and sent his Son to be the propitiation for our sins"* (1 John 4:10). John tells us that our love for Him is inspired by His love for us. When we think of how much He loved and demonstrated His love, how can we not love Him when we realize how much He loved us? Today, spend some time thinking of the Lord's great love for you. The more you think of His love, the more you will love Him. You can't help it.

December 12

1 Corinthians 16:1-2, "Now concerning the collection for the saints, as I have given order to the churches of Galatia, even so do ye. Upon the first day of the week let every one of you lay by him in store, as God hath prospered him, that there be no gatherings when I come."

On This Day in 1955, the Ford Foundation announced that it was giving $500,000,000 to private hospitals, colleges, and medical schools. Since its inception, the Ford Foundation, a national and international foundation, has provided more than $10 billion in grants and loans. These funds are derived from an investment portfolio that began with gifts and bequests of the Ford Motor Company stock by Henry and Edsel Ford. According to its mission statement, the goals of the foundation are to strengthen democratic values, reduce poverty and injustice, promote international cooperation, and advance human achievement. As recently as April 2001, the foundation gave a $50 million endowment grant to Harvard University's John F. Kennedy School of Government, the largest single donation ever made by the Ford Foundation.

One of the greatest lessons the believer can ever learn is the joy of giving. The Bible has much to say about our giving. Paul, writing to the church at Corinth, gave them specific instructions about when to give, where to give, why to give, and even what to give. Unfortunately, some believers have never learned the joy of giving. When it comes to giving, some will stop at nothing. Have you learned the joy and blessing of giving? Today, make giving a priority in your life as a believer. After all, this is the season of giving.

December 13

Isaiah 44:3, "For I will pour water upon him that is thirsty, and floods upon the dry ground: I will pour my spirit upon thy seed, and my blessing upon thine offspring."

On This Day in 1915, Charles Mallory Hatfield promised the San Diego, California City Council that he could fill the Morena Reservoir to overflowing. The reservoir had been built to meet the water needs of the growing population but had never been more than half full, and at the time, the thirteen billion gallon reservoir was down to less than five billion gallons due to lack of rain. Hatfield, who called himself a "moisture accelerator," told the city council that he would fill the reservoir for $10,000. Using secret chemicals that were dissipated into the atmosphere, Hatfield went to work immediately. Over the next two weeks, there were only a few showers but by the end of January, more than forty inches of rain had fallen. The result of so much rain in such a short time left San Diego completely flooded, washing out 110 of its 112 bridges, as well as rail service, leaving the city isolated for over two weeks.

It is not unusual for Christians to experience those dry times in their life. All seems barren and the soul is like the parched ground. Is the reservoir getting low in your life? God has promised rain for the thirsty soul. It may get dry at times, but heavenly floods always follow the dry seasons. Hatfield went to the grave with the secret of the chemicals that he used, but the believer knows the source of the rain. Today, consider that those dark clouds in your life may be bringing the rain you are so thirsty for. You may be about to experience a flood.

December 14

Psalm 116:1, "I love the Lord, because he hath heard my voice and my supplications."

On This Day in 1970, former Beatle, George Harrison, received a gold record for his hit song "My Sweet Lord." Always regarded as the quiet one of the Beatles, he was the first to make his mark after the Beatles split. Maybe you are familiar with Harrison's hit song, but if not, here are a few of the lyrics:

My sweet Lord, (hallelujah)
Hm, my lord (hallelujah)
Hm, my Lord (hallelujah)
I really want to see you
Really want to see you
Really, want to see you Lord…

Sounds good, you say. Someone might be asking what was George Harrison doing writing a gospel song? Maybe a few more lines from the song will answer your question:

My, my, my lord (hare Krishna)
My sweet Lord (Krishna Krishna)

Harrison wasn't writing about the Lord Jesus but a Hindu lord. As believers, the Lord we love is not some Consciousness of Eastern philosophy but a living Lord. He is indeed Lord and the more you know Him, the more you join with the Psalmist in saying, "I love the Lord," and the more you love Him, the more you want to see Him. Today, take time to tell the Lord, the real and only Lord, that you love Him.

December 15

1 Peter 3:15, "But sanctify the Lord God in your hearts: and be ready always to give an answer to every man that asketh you a reason of the hope that is in you with meekness and fear:"

ON THIS DAY in 1979, Chris Haney and Scott Abbot invented the game "Trivial Pursuit®." With newspaper backgrounds, Haney, a photo editor and Abott, a sportswriter, while playing a game of Scrabble, "conceived the idea of a game dealing with current events and asking questions that dealt with the five W's—Who, What When, Where, and Why. They called it "Trivia Pursuit" but Chris' wife called it "Trivial Pursuit®," thus its name. They borrowed $40,000 to manufacture the game, first producing 1,100 sets that were sold for $15. However, by late 1983, three and one-half million games had been sold and sales rose to twenty million in 1984. Retail sales have now exceeded one billion dollars, and people play Trivial Pursuit® in eighteen different languages and in many different versions.

Have you ever played Trivial Pursuit®? How did you do? Peter talks about being able to give an answer to questions asked by those who question us about our faith. If someone were to ask you how to be saved, would you be able to answer him or her? If someone asked you why they needed to be saved or why salvation can only be found in the Lord Jesus, would you be prepared to give an answer? As believers, we are to be ready (prepared) to give such answers. Today, remember we are not dealing with trivia but eternal truths. It is important that we be able to answer those who ask us about our faith in Christ.

December 16

Psalm 126:6, "He that goeth forth and weepeth, bearing precious seed, shall doubtless come again with rejoicing, bringing his sheaves with him."

ON THIS DAY in 1773, Colonial patriots dumped hundreds of cases of tea into the Boston Harbor. In what is known as the Boston Tea Party, a thousand patriots brandishing axes and whooping like Indians, their faces disguised with bronze paint, ran from the Old South Meeting House and boarded three British ships. None of the crews were harmed but in a matter of minutes, the *Dartmouth*, the *Eleanor* and the *Beaver* had been stripped of their cargo of tea which it was poured into the harbor. As the sea level fell, tea piled upon the beaches "like haystacks." John Adams said of the event, "The people should never rise without doing something to be remembered, something notable and striking. This destruction of the tea is so bold, so daring, so firm, intrepid and inflexible, it must have important consequences."

I think of a sign that I have seen on several occasions in churches:"Enter to worship, leave to service." When God's people leave church says they should involve themselves in a cause that is notable and will have important consequences. As the Psalmist says, we should "go forth" and bear "precious seed." Being a Christian is more than just attending church on Sunday. It also includes being a witness for Christ the other six days of the week. There is nothing more notable or that will have greater consequences than telling others about Jesus Christ and leading someone to Him. Do you want to do something for which you will be remembered? Today, tell someone about Jesus. The one you lead to Christ will never forget you!

December 17

2 Peter 3:7, "But the heavens and the earth, which are now, by the same word are kept in store, reserved unto fire against the day of judgment and perdition of ungodly men."

ON THIS DAY in 1919, Albert Porta's prediction of a major disaster to strike the earth passed without occurring. Porta, a seismographer and meteorologist living in San Francisco, had successfully predicted several earthquakes. When he made his prediction, the world took notice. He predicted the conjunction of six planets, which would result in a magnetic current that would pierce the sun causing great explosions of flaming gas that would eventually engulf the earth. His prediction caused widespread alarm and as December 17th approached, suicides and hysteria were reported throughout the world. The fatal day arrived. The planets did align but the world catastrophe, he predicted never came to pass.

The Bible tells us how one day, the earth will experience a destructive catastrophe. This earth is reserved and destined for destruction. It will be the ultimate act of God's judgment on this earth. Yet the believer does not have to live in fear of that day for when it occurs, all believers will be with the Lord. It is possible that the Lord could return before this year comes to an end. If so, a new life and a new home await us. Today, give thanks that when this world is destroyed, you will be living in a new heaven and earth—one that is eternal.

December 18

Titus 1:10, "For there are many unruly and vain talkers and deceivers, specially they of the circumcision:"

ON THIS DAY in 1656, M Jacquin first manufactured artificial pearls. Real pearls are formed when a foreign substance, such as a grain of sand or parasite, enters the body of oysters or other shell-forming mollusks. The oyster secrets thin sheets of nacre which cover the invading substance and continue to build circular layers of nacre until the foreign substance is enclosed in a shell, forming the pearl. A real pearl is one of the most valuable gems, and large, perfectly shaped pearls rank in value with the most costly stones. Artificial pearls, sometimes called imitation pearls, are often made out of glass and covered with a substance known as pearl essence. Jacquin's first artificial pearls were made of gypsum pellets covered with fish scales.

Paul warns of those who were not the real thing. They talk like the real thing but their walk gives them away. I think of something that Mahatma Gandhi once said to a group of Christian ministers. They asked Mahatma about conversion. He replied, "I believe in Christian conversion if it is genuine. On the other hand, there is nothing worse than being something on the outside that you are not on the inside. If a man has found God through Jesus Christ, then he must show the world he is a follower of Jesus or else be a living lie!" Although not a Christian, Ghandi was right. Nothing hinders the work of God more than someone who professes to be a Christian, yet their walk does not match their talk. Today, let what people see on the outside be a reflection of what you have on the inside. Be a real pearl and not an artificial one.

December 19

Hebrews 9:28, "So Christ was once offered to bear the sins of many; and unto them that look for him shall he appear the second time without sin unto salvation."

ON THIS DAY in 1980, the World Health Organization (WHO) announced that smallpox had been eradicated at last. Smallpox had been one of the world's most feared diseases. It killed hundreds of millions of people and scarred and blinded millions more. In 1796, Edward Jenner, an English physician, developed the first vaccine. When WHO, an agency of the United Nations, began a program to get rid of smallpox completely, more than thirty countries was infected by disease. In a statement signed by the twenty member Global Commission for the Certification of Smallpox eradication, it was declared that the scourge of human mankind had finally been halted. The last person to catch the disease naturally was a three-year old Indian girl, Rahima Banu, in 1975. The last person to die from smallpox was Janet Parker, a laboratory worker at Birmingham University in 1978.

The first time the Lord Jesus came, He came to save us from the penalty of sin. Through the person of the Holy Spirit, He is presently working to save the believer from the power of sin. When He comes the second time, He will remove the believer from the very presence of sin. I wish we could say that sin has been and could be eradicated in the life of the believer. Yet, every honest believer knows that we cannot at the present claim that sin has been halted. Yet, we look forward to that day when we will sin no more. Today, as you confess your sins to God, give thanks that one day you will be able to say that sin has been eradicated. Until then, let's try to live as sinless as possible.

December 20

Romans 5:10, "For if, when we were enemies, we were reconciled to God by the death of his Son, much more, being reconciled, we shall be saved by his life."

ON THIS DAY in 1803, the largest land sale in history was made. In what is known as the "Louisiana Purchase," the United States acquired from France 828,000 square miles, the whole of the Mississippi Valley to the Rocky Mountains. The price was $15 million dollars. Napoleon had wanted to sell the former Spanish territory, after having abandoned his ambition of establishing a colonial empire in the West Indies and North America. President Jefferson sent a special envoy to begin negotiations. The former border of the United States was the Mississippi River, but with the sale, the United States literally doubled in size overnight.

Salvation is one of the greatest things that can happen to a person. To be saved is to be reconciled to God. To be reconciled is to be brought into a relationship with God that formerly did not exist. In the past we were separated from God, but now, through the death of the Lord Jesus, we have been brought into fellowship with God. But salvation is just the beginning. It is the starting gate, not the stopping point. Paul declares that there is "much more." If I may put it this way, there is much more land to be acquired. By the death of the Lord Jesus, we are reconciled to God. By the life of the Lord Jesus, there is much more to be experienced and enjoyed. There are many wonderful blessings that God has for the believer, a heavenly home being one of them. Today, ask God to give you "much more" of the Christian life. Let God expand your borders, and always be growing and appropriating all that you have in Christ.

December 21

Romans 6:19, "I speak after the manner of men because of the infirmity of your flesh: for as ye have yielded your members servants to uncleanness and to iniquity unto iniquity; even so now yield your members servants to righteousness unto holiness."

On This Day in 1620, the *Mayflower* and its 102 passengers (36 of whom were English Separatists or Pilgrims as they were later called) landed at Plymouth Rock, Massachusetts. An inscription on the Plymouth Rock monument reads: "This spot marks the final resting place of the Pilgrims of the Mayflower. In weariness and hunger and cold, fighting the wilderness and burying their dead in common graves that the Indians should not know how many had perished, they here laid the foundations of a state in which all men for countless ages should have liberty to worship God in their own way. All you who pass by and see this stone remember, and dedicate yourselves anew to the resolution that you will not rest until this lofty ideal shall have been realized throughout the earth."

As we close out an old year and near the new, this would be a good time to dedicate ourselves anew to God, His work, and will for our lives. There are many things to inspire us to yield our lives to God. God's faithfulness in the past and all the blessings we have received and enjoyed from the hand of God should cause us in gratitude to dedicate ourselves anew. As the pilgrims began a new life in the new world with a great cause and goal, the year before us awaits with many opportunities to serve God. These opportunities should bring us before God with a fresh commitment and yielding of our lives to the Lord. Today, dedicate yourself anew to God.

December 22

Psalm 118:8, "It is better to trust in the Lord than to put confidence in man."

ON THIS DAY in 1912, Charles Darwin announced the discovery of two skulls that were hailed as the missing evolutionary link between ape and man. The two skulls, along with a canine tooth were estimated to be up to a million years old. For the next decade, scientists heralded the finding of *Eoanthrapus dawsoni* (the scientific name given to the remains) as confirmation of Darwin's theory of evolution. However, during the 1920's and 1930's, the authenticity of the remains began to be questioned. By the 1940's, the remains were considered to be a mixture of ape and human fossils. In 1953, at an international congress of paleontologist, the Piltdown Man (what the fossils had come to be called) was declared a fraud. Using microscopic tests, scientists had discovered that the teeth had been doctored, and the skull and jaw fragments were no more than 600 years old and had been treated with chemicals to make them look older.

Darwin and others have put forth their theories about man and creation, but when it is all said and done, what God says still stands the test of time. Man is very smart and his skills and knowledge are continually increasing, but what God says can always be trusted. If God says He created man, then you can believe He created man. Anything God says is reliable and when it is all said and done, what He said remains as truth. The Piltdowns of this world will come and go, but God's Word will always stand. We can always trust the Lord and hold His Word as true. Today, trust in the Lord. Man is not always right, but the Lord is never wrong.

December 23

Luke 12:40, "Be ye therefore ready also: for the Son of man cometh at an hour when ye think not."

On This Day in 1823, an anonymous poem appeared in the *Troy Sentinel* entitled "A Visit from St. Nicolas." The poem has become known as "Twas the Night Before Christmas." It was later discovered that the poem was written by a professor of Oriental and Greek Literature at the Episcopal General Seminary in New York City by the name of Clement Clark Moore, who had written the poem in 1822 as a Christmas present to his children.

Today, I want to share with you a portion of another version of the poem and let it speak for itself:

Twas the night before Jesus came and all through the house,
Not a creature was praying, not one in the house.
Their Bibles were lain on a shelf without care,
In hopes that Jesus would not come there.
Their children were dressing to crawl into bed,
Not once ever kneeling or bowing the head.
And Mom in her rocker with baby on the lap,
Was watching the Late Show while I took a nap.
When out of the East there arose such a clatter,
I sprang to my feet to see what was the matter.
Away to the window I flew like a flash,
Tore open the shutters and threw up the sash.
When what to my wondering eyes should appear,
But angels proclaiming that Jesus was here.
(Author Unknown)

Be ye ready, for we know not what hour the Lord will return.

December 24

Psalm 32:8, "I will instruct thee and teach thee in the way which thou shalt go: I will guide thee with mine eye."

ON THIS DAY in 1945, Flight 19 set out from its base never to return. Flight 19, consisting of five Torpedo Bombers and their crews, joined about 1,000 airmen, sailors and passengers in over 100 different aircrafts and ships that are alleged to have disappeared in the Bermuda Triangle. The expanse of sea between Bermuda, Puerto Rico, and Miami, known as the Bermuda Triangle, is surrounded with lore of instruments failing, compasses swinging wildly, and mysterious disappearances. After Flight 19 had successfully completed a U.S. Navy training exercise around the Bimini Islands, it was due to return to its base in Ft. Lauderdale, Florida. It never returned. What happened? It is largely suspected that due to faulty equipment and darkening skies, they lost their direction, running out of fuel and crashing into the sea. The final transmission from Flight 19 called for the planes to close into a tight formation and to prepare to ditch into the sea together.

The Lord is the believer's compass and guide. What a comfort to know that our Lord knows each path we take. His eye watches over us and guides us daily. There are times when we do not know the correct path to take but when we look to the Lord, we will find guidance. How long will the Lord guide us? The Psalmist says in Psalm 48:14, *"For this God is our God for ever and ever: he will be our guide even unto death."* Today, rejoice that you have a Divine compass to guide you, one that not even the Bermuda Triangle can affect.

December 25

Matthew 1:21, "And she shall bring forth a son, and thou shalt call his name Jesus: for he shall save his people from their sins."

On This Day in 1946, William Claude Dukenfield, better known as W.C. Fields, died. Born in Philadelphia, he began earning a living as a juggler at the age of fifteen. He went on to become a famous magician and vaudeville entertainer and even performed for King Edward VII at Buckingham Palace. He perfected two roles in his career: that of a small time gambler and con man and the bumbling henpecked husband. He died on Christmas, a day he always claimed to hate.

I do not know the reason why W.C. Fields hated Christmas, but as a believer, Christmas is a day that is loved and cherished. The believer's love for Christmas is not in the gifts and festivities that are so often associated with Christmas. It is not even in the time spent with families and friends. What makes Christmas so special to the believer is that it is the one day on our calendar that reminds us that Jesus Christ came to this earth and was born of a virgin to save us from our sins. Christmas is a special day for the believer because it is the day commemorating God's great love demonstrated in the giving of His Son. Christmas is special because it reminds us that we have a Saviour. It is true that the real meaning of Christmas is often lost in our day, but for the believer, it is a day greatly loved. Today, as you open your gifts, give special thanks for the greatest gift ever given to man—the Lord Jesus Christ. Oh yes, don't forget to give Jesus a gift. After all, it is His birthday. Your worship would be a good gift.

December 26

Luke 2:11, "For unto you is born this day in the city of David a Saviour, which is Christ the Lord."

ON THIS DAY in 1776, General George Washington, under the cover of darkness, crossed the Delaware River. With 2,400 men in small boats, Washington crossed the icy river for a surprise attack on Hessian mercenary troops under the command of Johann Rall. Rall had dismissed intelligence reports that the Americans might attack. "Let them come," he said. "We will go at them with bayonets." But before his men could fix their bayonets, they were overwhelmed and a hundred Hessians, including their commander, were killed and 900 taken prisoner. They were taken by surprise as they slept off the Christmas festivities. Johann Rall, the Hessian commander sound asleep in his tent, was dead drunk.

Today, there are many who are "getting over Christmas" after partying and attending festivities that completely left the Lord out of the day that commemorates His birth. To many, Christmas is nothing more than another holiday to party and "have a good time." The real meaning of Christmas is missed or ignored. As for believers, the day after Christmas our hearts are still filled with praise that God gave His Son and that a Saviour was born. The believer realizes that Christmas is more than gifts under the tree, but the celebration of the greatest gift ever given. It is more than a party or festivity that leaves our head aching the next morning. It is a wonderful event that leaves our soul overwhelmed with God's love and goodness. Today, the day after Christmas, give thanks that one day the real meaning of Christmas was made real in your heart. It totally changes how you celebrate Christmas.

December 27

Genesis 1:1, "In the beginning God created the heaven and the earth."

ON THIS DAY in 1968, the *Apollo* 8 returned to earth after a historic six-day journey. The *Apollo* 8 was the first manned mission to the moon. Astronauts Frank Borman, James Lovell, Jr., and William Anders became the first human to view the earth in its entirety and see the dark side of the moon. On Christmas Eve, the astronauts entered into orbit around the moon and as they did so, they did a live television broadcast in which they showed pictures of the Earth and Moon. The three astronauts ended the broadcast by taking turns reading from Genesis chapter one. Anders said, "For all the people on Earth, the crew of the *Apollo* 8 has a message we would like to send to you." Anders then read Genesis 1:1-4, Lovell read Genesis 1:1-8, and Borman read Genesis 1:9-10 and then added, "And from the crew of *Apollo* 8, we close with good night, good luck, a Merry Christmas, and God bless you—all of you on the good Earth."

During this time of the year, we are reminded that the Creator of heaven and earth sent us a wonderful message in His Son. That message was that, "*God so loved the world that He gave His only begotten Son that whosoever believeth in Him should not perish but have everlasting life*" (John 3:16). God's work as creator is a testimony of His power. His work as Saviour is a testimony of His love. The sight that the astronauts saw from lunar orbit left them in awe at the majesty of God's creation, yet the thought of His coming leaves us in greater awe. Today, worship the One who not only created this world but loved us as well. It is a Merry Christmas for God has blessed us all.

December 28

Acts 15:39, "And the contention was so sharp between them, that they departed asunder one from the other: and so Barnabas took Mark, and sailed unto Cyprus;"

ON *THIS* DAY in 1832, John C. Calhoun resigned as vice-president of the United States. Born near Abbeville, South Carolina, he was first elected vice-president under John Quincy Adams in 1824 and then reelected vice-president under Andrew Jackson in 1828. Under Jackson, he found himself isolated from national affairs, and he had political differences with Jackson. This led him to take the South Carolina senate seat left vacate after the resignation of Senator Robert Y. Hayne. He was elected to the seat on December 12, and on the 28th, he resigned from his office, citing his difference with Jackson. He became the first vice-president in U.S. history to resign from his office.

It may surprise you to know that some of the Bible characters we admire so much in the Bible, at times had their differences. As Paul and Barnabas prepared for another missionary journey, they discussed who would go with them. Barnabas recommended young Mark. Immediately Paul cast a nay vote, citing Mark's leaving them on a previous trip. Yet Barnabas was determined to take him, but Paul refused to give in. The end result was that the great missionary team was divided and the two went their separate ways. We don't always see eye to eye with one another, but there is one thing we must always keep before us and that is we have a great work to do and must not let anything hinder us from doing that work. Today, realize that our differences are not as important as doing God's will. There is no place to resign or divide. I'm sure Paul and Barnabas would say "Amen!" Stay in "office" and keep working.

December 29

Ephesians 4:15, "But speaking the truth in love, may grow up into him in all things, which is the head, even Christ:"

ON THIS DAY in 1924, J.M. Barrie's tale *Peter Pan* was released on film for the first time. Barrie's best known play, *Peter Pan* was first presented in 1904. It was adapted as a play with music in 1950 and a feature length animated cartoon in 1952. Barrie retold the play in narrative form as "Peter and Wendy" in 1911. Because Barrie wanted his creation to benefit children, he donated his rights to *Peter Pan* to a London children's hospital. It is the story of a boy, Peter Pan; Wendy, who was his "mother wannabe;" the pirate Captain Hook; and fairy Tinkerbell. Peter Pan was a boy who refused to grow up and created his own world of Indians, pirates, and fairies.

Would you not agree with me that there are a few "Peter Pan's" in the family of God? Paul's first letter to the Corinthians is a good example of believers who remained as "babes" and were not growing spiritually. We are at a time when we are often reflecting and looking back over the past year. A good question we all ought to ask is whether or not we have grown spiritually? Paul's prayer for the believers at Ephesus was that they *"may grow up unto Him in all things."* As believers, we should constantly be growing in our Christian life. We "oooh" and "aaah" over the newborn baby but in time, if there is no growth, our delight turns to concern. The lack of spiritual growth in our life should cause great concern in our life. Today, ask God to let the coming year be one of spiritual growth. Don't be a *Peter Pan* and refuse to grow.

December 30

John 18:37, "Pilate therefore said unto him, Art thou a king then? Jesus answered, Thou sayest that I am a king. To this end was I born, and for this cause came I into the world, that I should bear witness unto the truth. Every one that is of the truth heareth my voice."

ON *THIS* DAY in 1903, less than a month after it opened, the Iroquois Theater caught fire, claiming 588 lives. Supposedly fire-proof, a standing room only crowd gathered for a holiday matinee of the popular musical "Mr. Blue Beard." At 3:35 p.m., a hot light caught a velvet curtain on fire and panic set in. Trampled bodies were piled ten high in the stairwell area. where exits from the balcony met the exit from the main floor. Others died as they jumped from the balcony and windows. The first to jump died as they hit the main floor or hard pavement.

An interesting story related to the Iroquois tragedy involved the nephew of a Dr. Gonzales, a Chicago pastor. Earlier that day, as he was preparing his sermons, his nephew approached him and asked what his sermon was about. He quoted John 18:37 and said that his subject was, "To This End was I Born." His nephew then asked, "Do you know why I was born?" The preacher replied that he did not know but God would show him. The young nephew left and started walking down the street and came upon the theater fire. He immediately began to assist people across a ladder, which was placed across a street from a building to the theater. He had helped several people when the ladder gave way and he fell to the pavement below. He said to his uncle just before he died, "Now I know why I was born. I was born to help save these people." Today, realize that you have a purpose in life. As a New Year comes upon us, seek God's will and purpose for your life.

December 31

2 Timothy 4:11, "Only Luke is with me. Take Mark, and bring him with thee: for he is profitable to me for the ministry."

ON THIS DAY in 1793, Thomas Jefferson resigned as secretary of state. The author of the Declaration of Independence announced that he was retiring to his Virginia farm despite pleas by many leaders. He had been disillusioned by Congress's refusal to impeach Alexander Hamilton, his archenemy, for financial impropriety. The two men had been adversaries since the framing of the Constitution. Hamilton had advocated a strong central government while Jefferson preferred to see greater power in the states. Jefferson confided to his friend James Madison that "the motion of my blood no longer keeps time with the tumult of the world."

For some reason, young John Mark turned back during one of Paul's missionary journeys. Maybe the hardness of the journey, the constant threat of persecution, or just being homesick was at the root of his departure. It was not without the displeasure of Paul. Jefferson, although he called it quits, would not remain in retirement but returned to public life and would later become president of the United States. At some point, Mark returned to God's work and Paul asked for Mark and declared that he was a profitable part of his ministry. There are times when the "motion of our blood" loses that zeal and fire for the work of God. We lose heart and find ourselves ready to call it quits. When this happens, we don't need to retire but be refired. Today, as we close out another year, ask God to put a fire in your soul for His work and a motion in your blood that keeps time with the need of this world. We are too near the crown to lay down the cross.

Subject Index

Abbott, Jim: . . . . April 8
AIDS: . . . . .Mar 30
Air Disasters
KLM Flight 4805 and Pan Am
Flight 736: . . . . .Mar 27
Alaska: . . . . .Jan 3
Alcatraz: . . . . .Aug 11
Aldrin, Edwin: . . . . .July 20
Alka-Seltzer: . . . . .Dec 3
American Red Cross: . . . . . . .May 21
Amistad: . . . . .Aug 26
Apollo 8: . . . . Dec 27
Arc, Joan of: . . . . April 19
Armstrong, Neil: . . . . .July 20
Aspirin, Bayer: . . . . .Aug 10
"Axis Sally": . . . . .Sept 10

Baby "M": . . . . .Mar 31
Bakker, Jim: . . . . .Mar 19
Bar Code: . . . . .Oct 7
Barbie Doll: . . . . .Mar 9
Barnard, Christiaan: . . . . .Dec 4
Barton, Clara: . . . . .May 21
Baseball Hall of Fame: . . . . . . .Jan 29
Bedell, Grace: . . . . .Oct 15
Begin, Prime Minister: . . . . . .Sept 18
Bell, Alexander Graham: . . . . .Mar 7
Belushi, John: . . . . .Mar 5
Bennard, George: . . . . .Feb 4
Berlin Wall: . . . . .Aug 13
Bermuda Triangle: . . . . .Dec 24
Berry, Marcellus F: . . . . .July 7
Bible: .Oct 4
Big Ben: . . . . .May 31
Blackwell, Elizabeth: . . . . .Jan 23
Blessitt, Arthur: . . . . .Oct 5
Bliss, Henry M: . . . . .Sept 13
Blue Jeans: . . . . .May 20
Bonaparte, Napoleon: . . . . . . .May 5,
. . . . .June 18,
. . . . .Dec 2, 20

Booth, William: . . . . .July 5
Boston Tea Party: . . . . .Dec 16
Bremer, Arthur: . . . . .Aug 4
Brooklyn Bridge: . . . . .Jan 2
Buddy: . . . . .April 25
Buchanan, James: . . . . .Aug 16
Buford, Col. Guion S: . . . . . .Aug 30
Bundy, Ted: . . . . .Feb 15
Bush, George: . . . . .Mar 22, 28

Calculator: . . . . .April 15
Calendar: . . . . .Feb 24
Calhoun, John C: . . . . .Dec 28
Camp Sumter: . . . . Feb 27
Cardiff Giant: . . . . .Feb 2
Carnegie, Andrew: . . . . .Mar 12
Carnegie Hero Fund: . . . . . . .Mar 12
Carrier, W.H.: . . . . .April 28
"Casey at the Bat": . . . . .June 3
Carter, Howard: . . . . .Nov 4
Cavell, Edith: . . . . .Oct 12
Challenger: . . . . .Jan 28
Chapman, David: . . . . .Dec 9
Chernobyl: . . . . .April 26
"Chicago Eight": . . . . .Sept 24
Christ of the Andes: . . . . . . .Mar 13
Clay, Cassius: . . . . .Jan 12
Clay, Henry: . . . . .Feb 7
Cleopatra's Needle: . . . . .Sept 12
Cloning: . . . . .Feb 23
Coca-Cola: . . . . .May 8
Cody, William F (Buffalo Bill): Jan 10
Cooke, Janet: . . . . .Sept 28
Columbine High School: . . .April 20
Columbus, Christopher: . . . .April 17
. . . . .Aug 3
Concorde: . . . . .Jan 9
Constitution, U.S.(Ship): . . . Aug 20
Cooper, D.B: . . . . .Nov 24
Cornwall, Charles: . . . . .Oct 19
Corrigan, Douglas: . . . . .July 17

Coverdale, Miles: . . . . .Oct 4
Cracker Jacks: . . . . .Feb 19
Crippen, David: . . . . .July 31
Cronkite, Walter: . . . . .Mar 6
Crosby, Bing: . . . . .May 29
Cullinan Diamond: . . . . .Jan 26
Custer, George Armstrong: . .June 25

Dare, Virginia: . . . . .Aug 18
Darkness: . . . . .May 19
Darwin, Charles: . . . . .Oct 2, Dec 22
Davis, Jacob: . . . . .May 20
Death:
    By execution: . . . . .Feb 8
    Of John Belushi: . . . . . . .Mar 5
Declaration of Independence: . .July 8
Dempsey, Tom: . . . . .Nov 8
Dillinger, John: . . . . .Mar 3
Dionne Quintuplets: . . . . . . .May 28
Dolly: . . . . .Feb 23
Douglass, Andrew Ellicott: . .Nov 12
Dreyfus, Alfred: . . . . .July 21
Dueling: . . . . .Nov 10
Dugas, Gaeton: . . . . .Mar 30

Earp, Wyatt: . . . . .Oct 26
Earthquake
    San Francisco: . . . . . . .April 18
Eastman, George: . . . . .April 6
Ederle, Gertrude: . . . . .Aug 6
Edison, Thomas A: . . . . Feb 11
    . . . . .Oct 21
Edsel: .Sept 4
Edward VIII, King: . . . . .Dec 11
Edy's Ice Cream: . . . . .Nov 6
Eisenhower Tunnel: . . . . .Mar 8
Elephant: . . . . .Sept 23
Elsener, Karl: . . . . .June 12
Emma, Queen: . . . . .Aug 8
Empire State Building: . . . . . . .May 1
Esperanto: . . . . .July 26
E.T. (Extra-Terrestrial): . . . . . June 11
Etch A Sketch: . . . . .July 12
Eustis, Dorothy: . . . . .April 25

Fantus, Bernard: . . . . .Mar 15
Father's Day: . . . . .June 19
Fawkes, Guy: . . . . .Nov 5
FBI.
    Ten Most Wanted: . . . . .Mar 14
Fagan, Michael: . . . . .July 9
Ferdinand, Archduke Franz: .June 28
Ferris Wheel: . . . . .June 21
Fields, W.C.: . . . . .Dec 25
Fires
    Gillingham, Kent, England
    Irpquois Theater: . . . . . .Dec 30
    Rome: . . . . .July 18
    Triangle Shirtwaist Company:
    . . . . .Mar 25
First
    Academy Awards: . . . . . May 15
    Automobile fatality: . . .Sept 13
    Child born in America: .Aug 18
    Communications between cities:
    . . . . .May 24
    Ferris Wheel: . . . . .June 21
    Hospital: . . . . .May 11
    Insurance policy: . . . . . .May 23
    Living creature to orbit the earth:
    . . . . .Nov 3
    Oil wells in U.S. to yield oil: . .
    . . . . .Aug 28
    Queen to visit U.S.: . . . .Aug 8
    Separation of Siamese twins: . .
    . . . . .Sept 17
    Solo flight around the world: . .
    . . . . .July 22
    State to outlaw dueling: Nov 10
    Submarine voyage across the
        North Pole: . . . . .Aug 27
    University in America: .Nov 27
    Woman to fly a plane: . .Sept 2
    Woman to swim the English
        Channel: . . . . .Aug 6
First-Fifth Norfolks: . . . . .Aug 12
Fleming, Alexander: . . . . . . .Sept 30
Flight 19: . . . . .Dec 24
Flying Saucers: . . . . .June 24
Food rationed: . . . . .May 4
Ford Foundation: . . . . .Dec 12
Ford, Gerald: . . . . .Sept 22
Forsyth, William: . . . . .Sept 8
Foster, Stephen: . . . . .Jan 13
Frank, Morris: . . . . .April 25

Franklin, Benjamin: . . . . .May 11
. . . . .June 15
. . . . .Nov 27
Fujita, Nobuo: . . . . .Sept 9

Garland, Judy: . . . . .June 22
Gehrig, Lou: . . . . .April 2
. . . . .July 4
Germany: . . . . .Oct 3
. . . . .Nov 11
Ghandi, Mahatma: . . . . .Jan 20
Gibbon, Edward: . . . . .Feb 17
Golden Gate Bridge: . . . . .Feb 26
Grant, Ulysses S: . . . . .Feb 16
Gravelot, Jean Francios: . . . . .Aug 14
Great Emigration: . . . . .May 22
Great Train Robbery: . . . . . .April 16
Great Society: . . . . .Jan 4
Greyfriars Bobby: . . . . .Feb 28
Greyfriars Kirk: . . . . .Feb 28
Griswold, Roger: . . . . .Jan 30
Gunpowder Plot: . . . . .Nov 5

Hall, Aspah: . . . . .Aug 7
Hamilton, Patrick: . . . . .Feb 29
Handel, George Frederick: . . .Sept 14
Handler, Ruth: . . . . .Mar 9
Harding, Tonya: . . . . .June 30
Harrington, Judge: . . . . .Mar 2
Harrison, George: . . . . Dec 14
Harrison, John: . . . . .Nov 6
Harrison, William Henry: .April 4, 11
Hatfield, Charles Mallory: . . .Dec 13
Hatfield's & McCoy's: . . . . . .Mar 21
Hawthorne, Nathaniel: . . . . .Mar 16
Hearing aid: . . . . .Nov 15
Heart
Artificial heart: . . . . .Jan 31
Pacemaker: . . . . .Oct 29
Transplant: . . . . .Dec 4
Hemingway, Ernest: . . . . .July 2
Henry, Patrick: . . . . .Mar 23
Hickok, "Wild Bill": . . . . .Aug 2
Hillary, Edmund: . . . . .June 2
Hindenburg: . . . . .May 6
Hitler, Adolf: . . . . .Sept 1
Hodges, Elizabeth: . . . . .Nov 30

Hoffman, Felix: . . . . .Aug 10
Holloway, Wanda: . . . . .Sept 3
Hong Kong: . . . . June 9
Hoover, Herbert: . . . . .May 1
Houston, Sam: . . . . .April 21
Hurricanes: . . . . .May 12

Income Tax: . . . . .Feb 25
Israel: . . . . .May 14

Jackson, Reggie: . . . . .May 13
Jackson, Thomas (Stonewall):
. . . . .May 2, 10
James, Jesse: . . . . .Feb 13
Jefferson, Thomas: . . . . . .Dec 20, 31
Jews: .Sept 6
Johnson, Andrew: . . . . .May 16
Johnson, Ben: . . . . .Jan 11
Johnson, Lyndon B.: . .Jan 4, Nov 29
Jones, Jim: . . . . .Nov 18
Judson, Whitcomb L: . . . . . . .Aug 29

Klondike Gold Rush: . . . . . . .Aug 17
Kodak Camera: . . . . .April 6
Know-Nothing Party: . . . . . . .Feb 18
Kunst, David: . . . . .Oct 5
Labor Day: . . . . .Sept 5
Landers, Ann: . . . . .Oct 16
Lee, Robert E: . . . . .April 9
Lennon, John
Death: . . . . Dec 9
Nutopia: . . . . .April 1
Lim, Poon: . . . . .April 5
Lincoln, Abraham: . . . . .Oct 15
. . . . .Nov 19
Lincoln Memorial: . . . . .Feb 12
Livingstone, David: . . . . .Nov 13
London Bridge: . . . . .Oct 10
Lone Ranger, The: . . . . .Sept 15
Louisiana Purchase: . . . . .Dec 20
Los Angeles riots: . . . . .April 29
Ludwig, Karl: . . . . .Oct 8
Lund, Mary: . . . . .Jan 31
Luther, Martin: . . . . .Oct 31
Lyon, Matthew: . . . . Jan 30

Macarthur, Gen. Douglass: . . .Mar 11

Manson, Charles: . . . . .Jan 25
Maravich, Peter: . . . . .Feb 10
Mary Celeste: . . . . .Dec 5
Mason-Dixon Line: . . . . .Oct 18
Mayflower: . . . . .Dec 21
McCarthy, Joseph Raymond: . . Feb 9
McCorvey, Norma: . . . . .Jan 22
McEnroe, John: . . . . .Jan 21
McGuire, Major Thomas: . . . . .Jan 7
Memorial Day: . . . . .May 30
Menegele, Josef: . . . . .June 6
Meriweather, Charles A: . . . . Nov 22
"Messiah," The: . . . . .Sept 14
Meteorite: . . . . .Nov 30
Michelangelo: . . . . .Nov 1
Mishima, Yukio: . . . . .Nov 25
Mitchell, Jackie: . . . . .April 2
Model A, Ford: . . . . .July 23
Monopoly: . . . . .eb 6
Monroe, Marilyn: . . . . .Aug 5
Morgan, Garrett A: . . . . .Nov 20
Morse, Samuel: . . . . .May 24
Mother's Day: . . . . .May 9
Mount St. Helens: . . . . .May 18
Movietone News: . . . . .May 25
Mullikin, Hans: . . . . .Nov 23

Nation, Carrie: . . . . .June 7
Nautilus, The: . . . . .Aug 27
New York Stock Exchange: . .May 17
. . . . .Oct 24
Niagara Falls
Daredevils: . . . . .Aug 14
. . . . Sept 8
Stopped flowing: . . . . . .Mar 29
Nixon, Richard: . . . . .July 24
. . . . Aug 4, 9
. . . . Oct 20,
. . . . .Nov 17, Nov 21
Nolde, William B: . . . . Feb 5
Nuremberg Trials: . . . . .Oct 1

Officer's Knife: . . . . .June 12
O'Hanlon, Virginia: . . . . .Sept 21
O.K. Corral: . . . . .Oct 26
Oklahoma Land Race: . . . . .April 22
Olson, Frank: . . . . .Nov 28
Oil: . . . . .Aug 28
Osgood, Samuel: . . . . .Feb 20
Owens, Jesse: . . . . .Mar 28
Owens, Robert: . . . . .May 26

Parks, Rosa: . . . . .Dec 1
Pasteur, Louis: . . . . .July 6
Pearl: May 7, ...Dec 18
Pearl Harbor: . . . . .Jan 16
. . . . .Dec 7
Pentagon: . . . . .Jan 15
Peter Pan: . . . . .Dec 29
Piccard, Auguste: . . . . .May 27
Pied Piper: . . . . .June 26
Pietri, Dorado: . . . . .July 30
Pledge of Allegiance: . . . . . . .June 14
Pony Express: . . . . .April 13
Popeye: . . . . .Mar 26
Porta, Albert: . . . . .Dec 17
Post, Wiley H: . . . . .July 22
Presley, Elvis: . . . . .Mar 24
. . . . .Aug 23
Pride, Thomas: . . . . .Dec 6
Prince Charles: . . . . .July 29
Prison Population: . . . . .Oct 27
Purple Heart, The: . . . . .Feb 22

Quiz Show Scandal: . . . . .Oct 17

Rain: . . . . .Nov 26
Randolph, Martha: . . . . .Jan 17
Reagan, Ronald: . . . . .May 3
Regan, Donald: . . . . .May 3
Reese, Miller: . . . . .Nov 15
Richard III, King: . . . . .Aug 22
Rim, Lee Jang: . . . . .Oct 28
RMS Queen Elizabeth: . . . . .Sept 27
Roe V. Wade: . . . . .Jan 22
. . . . .Oct 11
Roosevelt, Frankin D: . . . . . . .Mar 4
. . . . .June 16
. . . . .Nov 14
Roosevelt, Theodore: . . . . . . .Mar 17
. . . . .Oct 14
Rose, Peter: . . . . .July 27
Rosetta Stone: . . . . .July 19

Ruth, Babe: . . . . .April 2

Sadat, President: . . . . .Sept 18
Salisbury Cathedral: . . . . . . .Sept 20
Scopes Monkey Trial: . . . . . . .July 10
Scott, Blanche: . . . . .Sept 2
Senning, Ake: . . . . .Oct 29
Shackleton, Sir Ernest: . . . . . . .Jan 5
Sheppard, Sam: . . . . .Nov 16
Shiloh Baptist Church: . . . . .Sept 19
Siamese twins: . . . . .Sept 17
Silver, Bernard: . . . . .Oct 7
Simpson, Wallis: . . . . .Dec 11
Sipple, Oliver W: . . . . .Sept 22
Six Day War: . . . . .June 5
Slave trade: . . . . .Mar 2
Smallpox: . . . . .Dec 19
Smith, Susan: . . . . .Oct 25
Smithson, James: . . . . .June 27
Smithsonian Institute: . . . . . . June 27
SOS: . . . . .June 10
Space Shuttle
    Columbia: . . . . .April 12
Spencer, Lady Diana: . . . . . . .July 29
. . . . .Aug 31
Spock, Benjamin: . . . . .July 14
Spurgeon, Charles: . . . . .Jan 6
St. Bartholomew's Day: . . . . .Aug 24
St. Valentines Day Massacre: .Feb 14
Stanley, Henry Morton: . . . . .Nov 13
Statue of Liberty: . . . . .June 17
Stowe, Harriet Beecher: . . . . .Mar 20
Strauss, Levi: . . . . .May 20
Superman: . . . . .June 1
Supreme Being and Nature, The: . . .
. . . . .June 8

Telephone: . . . . .Mar 7
Test Tube baby: . . . . .July 25
Thorpe, Jim: . . . . .Jan 18
. . . . .Oct 20
"Three Servicemen" statute: . .Nov 9
Tiananmen Square: . . . . .June 4
Titanic: . . . . .April 10
Tokyo Rose: . . . . .Jan 19
Tornado
    Tri-State Tornado: . . . . .Mar 18
Tour de France: . . . . .July 1
Triangle Shirtwaist Company: Mar 25
Trivial Pursuit: . . . . .Dec 15
Truman, Harry: . . . . .Nov 2
Tucker, Karla Faye: . . . . .Feb 3
Tucker, Preston: . . . . .Dec 10
Turner, Ted: . . . . .Oct 9
"Twas the Night Before Christmas":
. . . . .Dec 23
Tylenol: . . . . .Sept 29
Tyler, John: April 4, Sept 11

U.N. General Assembly: . . . . .Oct 23
Uncle Sam: . . . . .Sept 7
U.S. Amendment
    14th Amendment: . . . . .July 28
    26th Amendment: . . . . .Mar 10
U.S. Census: . . . . .Mar 1
U.S. Library of Congress: . . .April 24
U.S. Flag: . . . . .Aug 21
U.S. Postal Service: . . . . .Feb 20
U.S. Seal: . . . . .June 20
U.S. Social Security: . . . . . .April 27
U.S. Supreme Court: . . . . .Feb 1
    Decisions: . . . . .Jan 22
    . . . . .April 3
    . . . . .June 13, 29
    . . . . .July 24
    . . . . .Oct 11

Victoria, Queen: . . . . .Aug 16
Viking 1: . . . . .Aug 20
Vincennes, U.S.: . . . . .July 3
Virgin Mary: . . . . .Dec 8

Wadlow, Robert: . . . . .July 15
Walker, Viola: . . . . .July 16
Wallace, George: . . . . .Jan 14
. . . . .Aug 4
Warren Commission: . . . . . . .Nov 29
Washington, Booker T: . . . . .April 7
Washington, George: . . . . . .April 30
. . . . .Sept 26
. . . . .Oct 13
. . . . .Dec 26
Washington Monument: . . . . .Feb 21
Watergate: . . . . .Nov 21

Webster, Noah: ....April 14
Welles, Orson: ....Oct 30
Wellington, Duke of: ....June 18
"White Christmas": ....May 29
White House: ....Jan 17
.......................Aug 25
.......................Oct 13
Whitman, Joseph: ....Aug 1
Williams, Hank: ....Jan 1
Wilson, Sam: ....Sept 7
Wilson, Woodrow: ....Jan 8
.......................May 9
Woodland, Joseph: ....Oct 7
Woodstock: ....Aug 15
Wycliffe, John: ....Oct 4

Xerox: ....Oct 22
Xiuquan, Hong: ....Sept 25

Yokoi, Shoichi: ....Jan 24

Zamenhof, L.L: ....July 26
Zipper: ....Aug 29

Scripture Index

Genesis
1:1 .... Dec 27
1:27 .... July 10
2:7 .... July 25
13:8 .... Oct 26
26:18 .... Mar 29
35:7 .... Sept 20
50:17 .... Sept 9

Exodus
3:11 .... May 16
4:10 .... April 8
13:3 .... Aug 11
20:12 .... May 9
21:6 .... Aug 26

Leviticus
23:22 .... May 23

Numbers
23:10 .... Aug 23
32:7 .... Sept 10
32:23 .... Feb 15

Deuteronomy
6:7 .... Sept 3
6:12 .... Feb 27
31:6 .... Dec 5

Joshua
10:14 .... June 5
10:26 .... Sept 23
21:45 .... June 3
23:14 .... Feb 2
24:15 .... Mar 10

Judges
8:23 .... June 9

Ruth
2:12 .... June 14

1 Samuel
12:24 .... May 24
16:7 .... Oct 8
17:4 .... July 15
20:3 .... Aug 2

2 Samuel
12:14 .... Mar 19

1 Kings
19:4 .... Aug 5
19:16 .... April 4

2 Chronicles
7:14 .... April 9

Nehemiah
4:8 .... Aug 21
6:3 .... Feb 21
9:17 .... Jan 19

Job
10:1 .... June 22
22:27 .... Aug 16
26:7 .... Feb 23
33:4 .... Oct 11
33:9 .... July 21
38:25 .... June 15

Psalms
1:1-2 .... Oct 18
16:7 .... May 3
18:30 .... June 12
19:1 .... Aug 20
19:10 .... Aug 17
23:4 .... Mar 5
27:1 .... Mar 4
27:13 .... Aug 3
31:15 .... Feb 24
32:8 .... Dec 24
33:12 .... June 8

33:18 . . . . June 20
34:17 . . . . April 28
37:23 . . . . Sept 13
37:25 . . . . Sept 11
37:35 . . . . Nov 24
40:8 . . . . Jan 2
41:9 . . . . Nov 14
44:18 . . . . Oct 21
50:6 . . . . Feb 1
56:3 . . . . June 16
58:11 . . . . Mar 28
62:8 . . . . July 9
62:10 . . . . Oct 24
72:6 . . . . Nov 26
73:24 . . . . Oct 16
85:8 . . . . June 25
89:15 . . . . Jan 1
92:10 . . . . May 5
94:1 . . . . June 28
103:2 . . . . Jan 6
103:19 . . . . May 27
107:30 . . . . Sept 8
109:22 . . . . Feb 22
116:1 . . . . Dec 14
118:8 . . . . Dec 22
119:103 . . . . Nov 6
119:161 . . . . July 18
121:1-2 . . . . June 10
122:6 . . . . Sept 6
124:4 . . . . Aug 27
126:6 . . . . Dec 16
129:8 . . . . April 3
133:1 . . . . Oct 3
144:15 . . . . July 2
145:4 . . . . May 25
147:3 . . . . Aug 10

Proverbs
1:5 . . . . Nov 27
4:23 . . . . Jan 28, Oct 29
8:8 . . . . Nov 21
10:1 . . . . Feb 13
10:7 . . . . Nov 9
12:5 . . . . Feb 7
13:4 . . . . Aug 6
14:9 . . . . April 16, Nov 22
14:34 . . . . Feb 17
15:18 . . . . Sept 24
16:32 . . . . April 29
18:8 . . . . Feb 9
20:9 . . . . Sept 26
22:6 . . . . July 14
24:16 . . . . Feb 6
24:28 . . . . Sept 28
25:25 . . . . Feb 20
27:1 . . . . April 10
28:13 . . . . Nov 17
30:5 . . . . April 14

Ecclesiastes
4:11 . . . . Oct 23
5:4-5 . . . . June 26
12:14 . . . . Feb 18

Isaiah
1:16 . . . . June 7
37:16 . . . . April 23
40:11 . . . . Aug 14
40:31 . . . . Sept 2
44:3 . . . . Dec 13

Ezekiel
18:31 . . . . Jan 31
22:30 . . . . Mar 14
36:26 . . . . Dec 4

Jeremiah
30:3 . . . . May 14
32:17 . . . . June 1
45:5 . . . . Aug 4

Daniel
3:25 . . . . Jan 5
6:4 . . . . July 3
12:3 . . . . Feb 12

Amos
4:11 . . . . Mar 25

Nahum
1:9 . . . . Oct 25

Zecharíah
4:10 .... May 17
7:11 .... Nov 15

Malachi
4:2 .... Jan 23

Matthew
1:21 .... Dec 25
5:24 .... Nov 10
6:33 .... Oct 30
7:15 .... Nov 18
7:22 .... Sept 12
13:46 .... May 7
14:25 .... April 5
16:18 .... May 1
17:16 .... July 6
20:6 .... Mar 23
22:10 .... July 29
22:21 .... Feb 25
24:24 .... Jan 25
24:40 .... Aug 12
24:42 .... Jan 16
27:51 .... April 18

Mark
4:37 .... Mar 18
5:20 .... May 11
9:23 .... Nov 8
11:2-3 .... Sept 27
11:26 .... .Oct 12
12:37 .... July 23
15:1 .... Nov 29
16:6 .... June 18
16:15 .... Mar 6

Luke
2:11 .... .Dec 26
4:4 .... Oct 4
8:18 .... .Mar 27
12:7 .... .Dec 10
12:40 .... Dec 23
12:43 .... May 19
17:32 .... June 27
24:1 .... Aug 31
24:2-3 .... .Jan 10
24:23 .... June 6

John
1:45 .... Jan 26
1:14 .... Jan 20
1:42 .... April 7
1:45 .... Sept 30
3:3 .... Jan 17
4:14 .... May 8
4:35 .... Oct 27
8:36 .... Jan 27, Mar 2
10:10 .... Aug 1
12:32 .... April 2
13:35 .... Oct 7
14:2 .... Oct 13
14:3 .... Mar 11
14:27 .... Jan 8
15:13 .... April 26
16:13 .... April 25
18:36 .... June 11
18:37 .... .Dec 30
19:17-18 .... Feb 8
19:30 .... Jan 24
20:7 .... .Nov 4
21:25 .... April 24

Acts
1:14 .... April 17
4:12 .... Oct 9
4:36 .... Aug 7
11:26 .... Mar 9
11:29 .... Dec 3
12:5 .... Mar 3
15:39 .... Dec 28
17:6 .... Oct 19
27:14 .... May 12

Romans
1:16 .... .Oct 2
3:19 .... Nov 16
3:25 .... .Oct 31
3:35 .... .Mar 15
5:8 .... .April 22
3:9 .... .June 21
3:23 .... Dec 8
5:10 .... .Dec 20

6:13 .... Feb 16
6:19 .... Dec 21
6:23 .... Feb 3
8:16 .... Mar 31
8:28 .... Mar 7
8:39 .... May 28
10:13 .... Jan 14
12:5 .... Nov 3
15:20 .... June 2, July 5

1 Corinthians
1:10 .... Sept 19
1:18 .... Feb 4
3:3 .... Jan 30
3:9 .... June 21
3:14 .... Aug 25
3:15 .... Feb 29
4:2 .... Feb 28
8:6 .... Sept 25
9:24 .... Feb 19
9:27 .... July 27
12:18 .... July 7
12:21-22 .... Feb 10
12:25 .... May 21
14:19 .... Nov 19
15:3-4 .... April 13
15:10 .... Oct 15
15:26 .... Feb 5
15:34 .... July 11
15:42 .... July 22
15:57 .... Nov 2
16:1-2 .... Dec 12
16:13 .... April 20

2 Corinthians
4:4 .... Oct 6
4:8-9 .... Oct 14
5:2 .... April 1, Nov 30
5:8 .... May 10
5:17 .... Jan 22
9:11 .... July 4
9:15 .... June 17
10:3 .... Nov 11
11:14 .... Feb 14

Galatians
5:1 .... June 4
5:7 .... Jan 13
6:2 .... Aug 29
6:9 .... Jan 18
6:10 .... Aug 30

Ephesians
2:3 .... Sept 15
2:8 .... April 6
2:14 .... Mar 13
2:18 .... Aug 13
4:15 .... Dec 29
4:17 .... Nov 28
4:27 .... July 8
4:31 .... Jan 21
5:6 .... July 17
5:18 .... Aug 28
5:30 .... Sept 17
6:2-3 .... June 19
6:11 .... Jan 7
6:12 .... Dec 7
6:16 .... Aug 19

Philippians
1:3 .... May 30
2:9 .... Oct 20
3:20 .... May 26
4:21 .... April 19

Colossians
1:12 .... July 28
1:20 .... Feb 26
1:28 .... Sept 29
2:14 .... July 12
3:9 .... Feb 11
3:10 .... Sept 7
3:15 .... Nov 20
3:24 .... May 15

1 Thessalonians
1:10 .... July 16
4:16 .... Oct 28
4:17 .... Jan 9
5:3 .... Sept 18
5:12 .... Sept 5

1 Timothy
3:16 .... Aug 18
4:2 .... Dec 9

2 Timothy
1:12 .... April 27
2:3 .... Jan 12
2:4 .... Mar 24
2:8 .... April 21
2:19 .... Mar 1
2:21 .... Dec 6
4:10 .... Sept 4
4:11 .... Dec 31

Titus
1:10 .... Dec 18
2:7 .... April 30
2:10 .... Oct 10
3:2 .... Mar 17

Hebrews
4:13 .... July 24
9:28 .... Dec 19
10:22 .... July 31
11:8 .... May 22
11:13 .... Jan 29
11:24 .... Dec 1
11:36-37 .... Aug 24
12:1 .... July 30
12:15 .... Mar 30

James
1:2 .... May 6
2:25 .... May 13
3:16 .... Mar 21
5:7 .... Nov 1
5:11 .... July 1
5:20 .... Sept 22

1 Peter
1:25 .... Mar 20
2:2 .... Mar 22
2:7 .... May 2
2:21 .... Oct 22
2:24 .... Nov 25
3:15 .... Dec 15
4:6 .... July 13
4:12-12 .... Jan 3
5:5 .... May 20
5:8 .... Sept 1

2 Peter
1:3 .... May 4
1:5 .... April 15
2:9 .... Oct 1
3:3-4 .... May 18
3:7 .... Dec 17

1 John
1:9 .... Mar 16
2:1 .... June 13
2:6 .... Oct 5
2:14 .... Mar 26
2:27 .... July 19
2:28 .... Aug 9
4:1 .... Oct 17
4:19 .... Dec 11
5:11 .... Nov 13
5:16 .... June 29

2 John
1:8 .... June 30

Revelation
1:3 .... May 31
1:18 .... Sept 21
2:5 .... Nov 23
4:1 .... April 12
4:2 .... July 20
5:9 .... Nov 5
5:11 .... Aug 15
6:2 .... Dec 2
6:13 .... Nov 12
19:1 .... June 24
19:6 .... July 26, Sept 14
19:12 .... Aug 22
19:16 .... Aug 8
21:1 .... Jan 4, May 29
21:10 .... Mar 8
22:12 .... Mar 12
22:16 .... Jan 15
22:17 .... April 11